T5-ARF-583

About the Fraser Institute

The **Fraser Institute** is an independent Canadian economic and social research and educational organization. It has as its objective the redirection of public attention to the role of competitive markets in providing for the well-being of Canadians. Where markets work, the Institute's interest lies in trying to discover prospects for improvement. Where markets do not work, its interest lies in finding the reasons. Where competitive markets have been replaced by government control, the interest of the Institute lies in documenting objectively the nature of the improvement or deterioration resulting from government intervention.

The **Fraser Institute** is a national, federally-chartered, non-profit organization financed by the sale of its publications and the tax-deductible contributions of its members, foundations, and other supporters; it receives no government funding.

Ordering publications

To order additional copies of this book, any of our other publications, or a catalogue of the Institute's publications, please contact the book-sales coordinator: via our **toll-free order line: 1.800.665.3558, ext. 580;** via telephone: 604.688.0221, ext. 580; via fax: 604.688.8539; via e-mail: sales@fraserinstitute.ca.

Media

For media information, please contact Suzanne Walters, Director of Communications: via telephone: 604.714.4582; via e-mail: suzannew@fraserinstitute.ca

Website

To learn more about the Institute and to read our publications on line, please visit our web site at www.fraserinstitute.ca.

Membership

For information about membership in The Fraser Institute, please contact the Development Department: The Fraser Institute, 4th Floor, 1770 Burrard Street, Vancouver, BC, V6J 3G7; or via telephone: 604.688.0221 ext. 586; via fax: 604.688.8539; via e-mail: membership@fraserinstitute.ca.

In **Calgary**, please contact us via telephone: 403.216.7175; via fax 403.234.9010; via e-mail: barrym@fraserinstitute.ca.

In **Toronto**, please contact us via telephone: 416.363.6575; via fax: 416.934.1639.

Publication

Editing and design by Kristin McCahon
Cover design by Brian Creswick @ GoggleBox.

Fixing Canadian Democracy

Fixing Canadian Democracy

Edited by Gordon Gibson

The Fraser Institute
Vancouver, Calgary, Toronto
Canada

Printed and bound in Canada.

Canadian Cataloguing in Publication Data

Main entry under title:

Fixing Canadian Democracy / edited by GordonGibson

> Papers from a conference held in Vancouver, Nov. 22, 2001
> Includes bibliographical references.
> ISBN 0-88975-201-X

  1. Representative government and representation—Canada—Congresses. 2. Democracy—Canada—Congresses. 3. Canada—Politics and government—1993- —Congresses. I. Gibson, Gordon, 1937–II. Fraser Institute (Vancouver, B.C.)

JL167.F59 2003   328.71'07456   C2003-910751-5

Table of Contents

Acknowledgements

I want to especially thank the John and Lottie Hecht Foundation for their initial suggestions, and they and our other sponsors for their indispensable financial assistance, and Fraser Institute Executive Director Michael Walker for his unflagging support of the conference, which formed the core of this book.

Our speakers and conference participants gave generously of their time, ideas, and experience. We were extremely fortunate to gather such an outstanding pool of talent, each in his or her own way very much devoted to improving our democracy.

Thanks are due as well to then Fraser Institute Director of Events and Conferences Lorena Baran for looking after the logistics, Events Assistant Adele Waters for help keeping track of all the submitted papers, and especially to Publications Director Kristin McCahon for pulling together a sometimes disorderly record of proceedings into the coherent whole that follows.

—GFG

About the authors

Barry Cooper, Professor of Political Science, University of Calgary

Barry Cooper, a fourth generation Albertan, was educated at Shawnigan Lake School, the University of British Columbia, and Duke University, where he received a PhD in 1969. He taught at several universities in eastern Canada before moving to the University of Calgary in 1981. He has published over 20 books and numerous articles in political science and public policy. He is a Senior Fellow at The Fraser Institute and a Fellow of the Royal Society of Canada. His weekly column with David Bercuson in the *Calgary Herald* is reprinted in the *Saskatoon Leader Post*, the *Regina Star-Phoenix*, and other newspapers in the Southam chain. His articles have also appeared in the *Globe and Mail* and the *National Post*. Professor Cooper has been a guest on many radio and television programs across the country and has appeared as an expert witness before the House of Commons and in several Charter-based court cases.

Peter C. Dobell, CM, Founding Director, Canadian Parliamentary Centre

Peter Dobell was born in Montreal in 1927. He joined the Department of External Affairs in 1952 and served in Ottawa, Czechoslovakia (1954-1957), and in the Canadian Mission to the United Nations (1960- 1965). He resigned in 1968 in order to set up, in Ottawa, the Parliamentary Centre, an NGO dedicated to strengthening the role of Parliament. Mr. Dobell is the author of many studies and books including: *Canada's Search for New Roles*; *Canada in World Affairs* 1971-73; *Parliament and the Control of Public Expenditure* commissioned by the Royal Commission on Financial Management and Accountability; *Comments on Parliamentary Reform* prepared for the Royal Commission on the Economic

Union and Development Prospects for Canada; and *Anger at the System,* assisted by Byron Berry. He also assisted in forming the Institute for Research on Public Policy (IRPP) in 1971 and serves on the institute's Board. Mr. Dobell is a Member of the Trilateral Commission and a Member of the Order of Canada.

David Elton, Vice Chair, Canada West Foundation
David Elton is a professor emeritus of the University of Lethbridge, where he was a faculty member for 27 years. From 1980 to 1997, he served as President of Canada West Foundation, which is a Calgary-based public policy think tank. He continues to serve on the Boards of a number of national research and public policy oriented organizations, and is now president of the Max Bell Foundation.

Gordon F. Gibson, Senior Fellow, The Fraser Institute
Gordon Gibson was born in Vancouver in 1937. He attended the University of British Columbia (BA Honours Mathematics and Physics, 1959) and Harvard Business School (MBA—Distinction, 1961) and subsequently did research in political science at the London School of Economics. He has been involved in a number of businesses including prefabricated buildings, hotel and real estate development, and has served on the boards of several public companies. He has served as Assistant to the Minister of Northern Affairs (1963-68), Executive and later Special Assistant to the Prime Minister (1968-72), and ran in three federal elections.

He has been active in both business and public affairs in Western Canada, including 12 years on the Canada West Council. Over the years he has been a regular columnist with, successively, *The Financial Post, The Vancouver Sun,* and *The Globe and Mail* and *The National Post.* He joined The Fraser Institute in 1993 as Senior Fellow in Canadian Studies, specializing in the research on federalism, and has published several books and papers with the Institute. Mr. Gibson has produced a major public discussion document of British Columbia's position on the restructuring of federalism and other issues, commissioned by the province of British Columbia and released in the summer of 1997. Most recently he was commissioned by British Columbia's government to develop guidelines for the creation of a Citizens' Assembly on Electoral Reform.

Herbert G. Grubel, David Somerville Chair in Canadian Fiscal Studies, The Fraser Institute

Herbert G. Grubel is Professor of Economics (Emeritus) at Simon Fraser University and a Senior Fellow at The Fraser Institute. He has a BA from Rutgers University and a PhD in economics from Yale University (1963). He has taught full-time at Stanford University, the University of Chicago, and the University of Pennsylvania. He has held temporary appointments at universities in Berlin, Singapore, Cape Town, Nairobi, Oxford, and Canberra. Herbert Grubel was an elected member of the Parliament of Canada from 1993 to 1997 and served as the Finance Critic in his party's shadow cabinet. He has published many books and articles on economics and finance.

Gary Lauk, Former BC Minister of Economics and Mines and Petroleum Resources

Born in Vancouver in 1940, Gary Lauk was educated in public and parochial schools before graduating from UBC law school in 1966. He practiced criminal law until he was elected in 1972 as an NDP member of the BC legislature. He was appointed to the cabinet in 1973 as Minister of Economics and Mines and Petroleum Resources. Lauk was re-elected in 1975,1979, and 1983, whereupon he stepped down to let the new leader of the NDP, Mike Harcourt, enter the legislature. Since that time he has practiced as a personal injury lawyer in Vancouver. He is currently on the board of the Trial Lawyers of BC, is a governor of the Trial Lawyers of America, and serves on the board of Corpus Christi College at UBC.

Nick Loenen, Fair Voting BC

Nick Loenen is a former Richmond City Councillor (1983-87), and former Member of the British Columbian Legislature (1986-91). He obtained his MA in political science from UBC in 1995. His book, *Citizenship and Democracy: A Case for Proportional Representation* was published by Dundurn Press in 1997. He is a member of the Canadian Study of Parliament Group, and travelled to Gabon, Africa, as one of four Canadians to observe and monitor the elections there on December 6, 1998. Nick chaired the Reform Party of Canada's Task Force on Electoral Reform in 1997. He is co-founder of Fair Voting BC, a citizens organization dedicated to changing the way British Columbians elect their MLAs. He serves on the national board of the Canadian Taxpayers Federation.

Rafe Mair is a former lawyer and cabinet minister, and is now a broadcaster and public affairs writer. During his public career, Mair was the British Columbia minister responsible for constitutional affairs leading up to the patriation of the Canadian Constitution, and through 1980 attended all the critical meetings either as Premier Bill Bennett's representative or adviser. He has unique training and insight into political and constitutional matters, having travelled extensively researching these matters. Included in this research were trips to Germany to evaluate their bicameral federal system, Switzerland to learn about their federation with its theme of participatory democracy, and the United States, courtesy of the State Department, for an in-depth study of the inter-relationship of the White House and Congress as well as relations between state governments and Washington.

Andrew Petter, QC, Dean of Law, University of Victoria
Andrew J. Petter, QC, was called to the Bar of Saskatchewan in 1983. Prior to joining the law faculty at the University of Victoria in 1986, he taught at Osgoode Hall Law School in Toronto, and practiced law with the government of Saskatchewan. From 1991 to 2001, he served as a Member of the Legislative Assembly of British Columbia and held numerous cabinet portfolios, including Attorney General. His major fields of interest are constitutional law, legal and political theory, and legislative and regulatory processes. He has written extensively on these topics and has contributed chapters to several works on constitutional law. He is currently Dean of Law at the University of Victoria.

The Honourable P. Geoffrey Plant, MLA (Richmond Steveston) British Columbia Liberal Party, Attorney General and Minister Responsible for Treaty Negotiations, Province of BC
Hon. Geoffrey Plant attended Harvard (AB 1978), Southampton University (LLB1980), Dalhousie University (LLB 1981) and Cambridge University (LLM 1989). Mr. Plant was called to the Bar of British Columbia in 1982. From 1982 to 1996 he was a litigation lawyer at Russell & DuMoulin in Vancouver, BC, with an

emphasis on aboriginal rights. He has also lectured and written extensively on aboriginal and education law. He served as counsel in several landmark cases including *Delgamuukw vs. The Queen*, *Martin vs. The Queen* (the Meares Island case) and *R. vs. Alphonse and Dick*.

The Honourable John Reid, Information Commissioner for Canada

John Reid was born in 1937 in Fort Frances, Ontario. He received a BA in 1959 and an MA (History) in 1961 from the University of Manitoba.

In 1963 Mr. Reid became the Special Assistant to the Minister of Mines and Technical Affairs. In 1965 he was elected to the House of Commons as the youngest person elected in that Parliament, where he served from 1965 to 1984, through six elections. Among other duties, Mr. Reid served as Parliamentary Secretary to the President of the Privy Council (1972 to 1975), in which capacity he was charged with improving the flow of requested information to MPs. This led him to join forces with Ged Baldwin, M.P., to work for a general right of access to government-held records for all Canadians. Out of their efforts came a report on information and privacy in the Scandinavian countries, a series of committee hearings, the first Access to Information Bill introduced by Walter Baker in 1979, culminating in the current *Access to Information Act*, introduced by Francis Fox in 1983.

In 1984, he started John Reid Consulting, a public policy and government affairs consulting business. Mr. Reid was the President of the Canadian Nuclear Association in Toronto from 1990 to 1995. In 1996, he represented Canada as a senior member of the Organization for Security and Cooperation Europe (OSCE) Mission to Bosnia and Herzegovina, and was a member of the Provisional Election Commission with responsibility for the writing of an Election Act and its implementation. In 1997, he joined the United Nations Transitional Administration in Eastern Slovenia (Southern Croatia), where he was Political Advisor to the Chief Electoral Officer. On July 1, 1998, Mr. Reid began his seven-year term as Canada's Information Commissioner.

Scott Reid, Member of Parliament, Lanark/Carleton

Scott Reid was born in 1964 in Hull, Quebec. He received his BA in political science (1985) and his MA in history (1989) from Carleton University in Ottawa. Since aquiring his degrees he has been an Assistant Editor for *Liberty Magazine*, a senior researcher for the Reform Party of Canada, a Visiting Scholar at the Centre for Canadian Studies, University of Western Sydney, Australia, as well as an author, editor and journalist in Ottawa. Among his many publications are, in 1998, the chapter "The Quebec Question: Debt Division and the Rule of Law" in William Gairdner, ed., *After Liberalism* (Toronto: Stoddart). He has also written *Lament for a Nation: The Life and Death of Canada's Bilingual Dream* (1993) and *Canada Remapped: How the Partition of Quebec will Reshape the Nation* (1992), as well as numerous articles in the *National Post*. Currently, Mr. Reid sits on the Board of Directors of Giant Tiger Stores Ltd., Ottawa, as well as a serving as a contributing editor for *Liberty Magazine*. He has several works in progress about the state of the nation.

Casey Vander Ploeg, Senior Policy Analyst, Canada West Foundation

Casey Vander Ploeg is a Senior Policy Analyst at the Canada West Foundation. Currently, he is working on the Foundation's Urban Finance Initiative. He has a BA in political science from the University of Lethbridge, and worked as a journalist before joining the Canada West Foundation in 1991. During his tenure at the Foundation, he has authored or co-authored over 50 research reports and programs on a diverse range of topics including government finances, consultative practices, Senate reform, constitutional renewal, national unity, and immigration policy.

Jack Weisgerber, Former BC Minister of Aboriginal Affairs

First elected to the BC legislature in 1986 as MLA for Peace River South, Jack served in government as the Minister of State for the Northeast and Nechako, Minister of Energy, Mines and Petroleum Resources, and British Columbia's first Minister of Native Affairs. Re-elected in 1991, Jack was elected Leader of Reform BC. Re-elected again in 1996, he sat as an Independent MLA until retiring from politics in 2001. During this time, Jack was a vocal advocate for parliamentary reform. In 2000, he commissioned a study of reforms in other parliamentary jurisdictions entitled *Towards Greater Efficacy for the Private Member* available at http://www.pris.bc.ca/mla-prs/parliamentary_reform_report.htm.

Ted White, Member of Parliament, North Vancouver
Although Ted spent the early part of his life in New Zealand, he and his wife Sue immigrated to Canada in 1979 and have lived in North Vancouver for 22 years. Ted played an active role in the development of the Reform Party. He submitted amendments to the party constitution that were passed at the Saskatoon, Winnipeg, and Vancouver National Assemblies and has served as a Director of the Riding Association in North Vancouver.

Ted was elected as the MP for North Vancouver in 1993 and was re-elected with increased majorities in 1997 and 2000. His main goals are to work for reform of the political system to permit truly free and representative votes in the House of Commons, and to legislate for Canadians the right to citizens' initiatives, referendum, and recall. He is a member of the Standing Joint Committee for the Scrutiny of Regulations.

Introduction

The genesis of this book was a Fraser Institute conference on democratic reform in November 2001. This, in turn, was inspired by the evident openness of the new government of British Columbia (elected in May of 2001) to consider these topics. Indeed, one of the first measures of that government was to pass legislation providing for fixed-term elections (with exceptions in case of defeat on a confidence motion). Further promises included a Citizens' Assembly on Electoral Reform, now constituted, and less clear commitments to parliamentary reform.

In this climate it seemed to us that the timing was right for a new focus on democratic reform, building on the BC example. While the central government was resisting any reform in its procedures and institutions, other provincial forces—all parties in Quebec, the Liberal Party of Ontario and the PEI legislature—were actively considering some changes of this sort. There is good reason for hope that progress in one part of Canada on this or that reform may prove contagious to the benefit of the overall system.

Accordingly, the conference was convened with the crucial assistance of a generous grant from the Hecht Foundation. It brought together a remarkable group of presenters and discussants before a knowledgeable audience including many practitioners—MPs, MLAs, and municipal councillors. The updated record of that meeting is the main body of this book, with two significant additions. The first chapter is an overview of the entire field of democratic reform in Canada, as written by the undersigned as editor and conference convenor. It first appeared as a series of articles in *Fraser Forum* over the period October 2001 to October 2002. A final appendix is a particular proposal for major BC reform as put forward early in 2001 by former MLAs (two of them former Ministers) Gary Lauk (NDP), Nick Loenen (Social Credit), Rafe Mair (Social Credit), and myself (Liberal).

In between these bookends lie papers from experts across the country, along with questions and comments from those assembled.

The first session dealt with "Selecting Representatives"—the business of electoral reform. Nick Loenen, BC's foremost campaigner on this topic presented, with former NDP Finance Minister (and now Dean of Law at the University of Victoria) Andrew Petter as discussant. Both present much practical wisdom.

The next topic is "Empowering representatives"—the business of parliamentary reform. Peter Dobell, founder of the Canadian Parliamentary Centre and dean of Canadian students of this topic, presented the main paper, with comments from Ted White, MP (Alliance), Jack Weisgerber, long serving and much respected MLA who concluded his political career as leader of the BC Reform Party, and the above mentioned Gary Lauk, former NDP minister, as discussants. (A reform-minded Liberal MP had agreed to take part but had to withdraw at the last moment because of parliamentary commitments.) They recommend various changes with a common theme: there are no constitutional barriers to parliamentary reform. All that is required is the will to do it.

The section following is "Powers Reserved to the People"—direct democracy, in other words. Prof. Barry Cooper of the University of Calgary discusses the interaction of direct democracy and the parliamentary system, and Scott Reid, MP (Alliance) gives a scholarly critique and lessons from Canadian history.

The next chapter is devoted to the luncheon speech by and following questions for Hon. Geoff Plant, Attorney General of BC and Minister Responsible for Democratic Reform. Mr. Plant sets out the goals of his government in the area, some of which have been achieved by the publication date of this book.

Following Mr. Plant's speech is a chapter on subject matter too little considered in this context, i.e., "Constitutional Constraints." Federal Information Commissioner Hon. John Reid sets out some of the challenges and hopes of his office. A paper by Fraser Institute Senior Fellow Herbert Grubel considers the potential advantages of adding constraints, such as private property, to the Charter, and networks of international agreements in the fields of trade and currency as a check on governments.

The final segment is "Getting There." Many would-be reformers focus only on where they would like to end up without considering the practicality of how to make that happen. David Elton, Vice-Chairman of the Canada West Foundation and Casey Vander Ploeg, also of Canada West Foundation, give an overview of how progress has been made in other parts of the world and the possible application in Canada of the new technique of "deliberative democracy" to this field.

To end the book, as noted above, the paper of the Ad Hoc Committee for a Provincial Constitution is appended to illustrate what full-blown reform might deliver for a province like British Columbia.

A note on style: the proceedings have been lightly edited to remove many of the pleasantries and banter so central to a conference, but not so to a book. Some anachronisms have been tidied up and some subsequent events accounted for. While every effort has been made to seek the advice of participants on the text, errors of course remain the responsibility of the editor.

It remains but to thank all of the contributors and wish the reader a rewarding passage through what follows.

—G.F.G.

Overview

CHAPTER 1
The Fundamentals of Democratic Reform

Gordon Gibson

Why worry about such an esoteric subject as democratic reform? After all, Canada is reasonably free and prosperous. Surely we should concern ourselves with more urgent things, such as health care, or the value of the dollar, or threats to national unity. Well, it turns out that we might be far better off in all of these areas if our democratic system worked better.

Canada could be, in fact *should be,* the most harmonious and prosperous land in the world. We are not, by a considerable way. Our living standard is much lower than in the US, or in many other, smaller, countries. The public is broadly cynical and apathetic with respect to our political process. We have major regional alienation, of which the Quebec sovereigntist movement has the highest profile but is certainly not the only example.

At the federal level, we have what is effectively a one-party government. This party (and the previous Conservative government in its day) is driven by perverse incentives that make political sense, but are in other ways injurious. These include, as examples, the payoff for votes bought in the Atlantic region with economically damaging subsidies, and an immigration policy designed not for the advantage of Canada, but instead chiefly with Vancouver's—and especially Toronto's—ethnic voting patterns in mind.

Essentially, all central government postures, from foreign and defence policy, through banking legislation, issues of our relationship with the United States, health policy, and to environmental issues, stem not from open and informed public debate, but rather from the behind-closed-doors accommodation of a governing elite to polling data. There is nothing wrong with a government seeking to react to public attitudes. There is much wrong with failing to inform those attitudes in the first place.

And though it may seem a hopelessly naïve view, surely government should be about something more than being re-elected, important as that is.

The state of our democratic debate is such that tough-minded and realistic discussion in some areas is simply not allowed. Such debate raises difficult and inconvenient issues. The most enduring example is the ridiculous idea that health care ought to be provided only by public employees. A recent example (as expressed by our government) is that it is in some way illegitimate for the United States to want to develop missile protection against rogue states. This latter absurdity has been decisively banished by tragedy, but the former—inefficiently supplied health care—is daily inflicting a less dramatic tragedy of its own kind.

In short, our system is not working as well as it should.

Three levels of democracy

Canadian democracy can be much improved. My own analysis recognizes three "levels" of democracy. The first is one in which the voters get to choose the people who, in turn, decide who is the all-powerful boss. That person effectively runs the government as they see fit for the next four or so years, more or less as an elected dictatorship.

Is this an over-statement? Hardly. The prime minister unilaterally and with no check appoints the heads of all government departments and all deputy heads, and they do what they are told. He or she appoints all senators, and more importantly, all of the judges of the Supreme Court, which says what is legal in this country, and adjudicates disputes with the provinces (who have no say in the tribunal).

The prime minister must sign all significant legislation for it to have any chance of passage in the House of Commons. He or she (through agents) manages the business of the House, and allocates time, permission for foreign travel, and even office space.

The prime minister, with no hindrance, appoints the heads of the Bank of Canada, the CBC, the CRTC, the ethics commissioner (who reports to him!), all ambassadors, the head of the national police, the chief of staff of the military, and dozens of other significant jobs. He or she must approve of all tax and expenditure decisions. While in theory Parliament has the power to control some of this, it never does. "Four-year elected dictator" is an accurate description, except in rare periods of minority government.

This, where voters get to elect the members wo elect the boss who then runs things totally until the next election, is the first level of democracy and the most primitive one. There Canada is firmly stuck, the most embarrassing system (for true democrats) in the developed western world.

The second level of democracy again sees the people elect the representatives (as in Canada) but those representatives then go on to make the laws and budgets acting independently of, or at least not fully controlled by, the executive branch. The fullest development of this second level is probably to be found in the United States, which for many Canadians, unhappily, is all the proof necessary that the system must be unsuitable for us.

Canadians should look instead at quieter examples, such as Switzerland, where few people even know the president's name. (The job is rotated among members of a seven-person council of ministers, itself made up of members of several political parties.)

This "second level" is a reasonable aspiration for Canadians. It would be characterized by an increase in the influence of elected representatives upon legislation and government oversight. After all, if my representative, the individual MP—the only person I get to vote for—is not important because the prime minister makes all the decisions, that means that I and my vote are not important either.

The third level of democracy is what we often call direct democracy, in which the voters themselves make the detailed decisions. Without further elaboration here (to be found later in this chapter) my view is that this third level, while essential, has a quite restricted applicability to our governance needs. But it can provide a "safety valve."

Before proceeding further to an analysis of democratic reforms, it is important to suggest a couple of limits. First, government is not and should not be the main thing in our lives. Indeed, in many areas, the real need is not for more government, however democratic, but rather for much less.

Reform is tough

Second, one must caution that the task of reformers is tougher than usually admitted.

Two watchwords are appropriate for those who would change the system. They are "humility" and "restraint."

On restraint, the point is this. Our system has many problems, but at least it stumbles on from day to day. Change for its own sake in such a complex area should be avoided. Not only are the consequences of potential error rather high, but even more certainly, change in the fundamental rules that govern the relationships of citizens are bound to be disruptive, carry frictional costs, and take a lot of getting used to.

On humility: the American biologist, Garrett Hardin, coined the phrase (speaking of complex systems) that, "You can't do just one thing." What he meant was that any change you make will inevitably work through the system to make other changes. For example, in our field of democratic reform, you can't just change the electoral system. At a very minimum, changing the electoral system will affect how Parliament works, the relationship between the executive and the legislative branches, the kinds of laws that get passed, and the relationship between the federal and provincial governments and the regions of the country. Yet advocates of electoral reform are almost invariably silent on these downstream effects.

In any constitutional area, one of the most powerful rules at work is the Law of Unintended Consequences. Things may not work out as planned. Our most famous historical example is the "confederation" set up by Sir John A. Macdonald. Sir John A. didn't really want even a *federation*, much less a looser *confederation*. An admirer of Britain, and deeply troubled by the horrible experience of the just-ended US Civil War, what he really wanted was a unitary state. Never mind, he would accept the Quebec and Maritime realities and leave the provinces room for matters of a strictly local nature, but only that—or so he thought.

But no one had ever before married a federal system and the British parliamentary system. This latter system tends to centralize power, above all in the executive branch. However, Sir John A. created not one, but (at the time) *five* executive branches, of which only one was the central government resident in Ottawa. The provincial executives quickly took like ducks to water to the centralization of their own power, and in the process challenged that of Ottawa. The aggressive provincial administrations of Oliver Mowat in Ontario and Honoré Mercier in Quebec, along with the sympathetic ear of the highest court for Canada at the time (the Privy Council in London) quickly turned Sir John's plan on its head. Decentralization became the rule until the economic and military disasters of the Great Depression and the Second World War. Recentralization flowed from those experiences; decentralization is again the tide of today, not just in Canada, but around the world.

As a more recent, simpler example, many Canadian political parties thought they were bringing democracy to their own operations by adopting a "universal ballot" to choose their leaders, whereby every party member, of whatever duration, of whatever provenance, had one vote to cast. This was in marked distinction to previous practice where either the full-time professionals (the caucus) or the engaged, long-time militants (as elected convention delegates) chose the leader.

No one thought at the time that the net result of this might be to create a new kind of leader who, with impunity, could ignore his or her caucus and the senior members of the party by claiming that he had a "mandate from the grassroots," absolute and inviolate (meaning, in effect, that he could do whatever he wanted). The universal ballot system, therefore, turned out to be the opposite (or, at the very best, a retrogression) of democracy.

But if humility and restraint are essential, there is a second great force lurking in the constitutional thicket which any successful reform must overcome, and that is the Law of Equal and Opposite Reaction. While reformers may see great virtue in democratic reform, those benefiting from the current system—those I call the "gatekeepers to reform" because they have the power to say *yea* or *nay*—think that system is just fine. For a prime minister, any system that elected and then thrust him or her to an all-powerful top role is something that works pretty well. All of those who owe their influence, station, and jobs to the current system will normally support that system, fearful that more talented or vengeful successors might turf them out.

The gatekeepers may bend with the wind—may appoint an "Ethics Commissioner" without independence as a current example—with no intention of supporting any real change.

One may sum things up thus for the would-be reformer: change is very hard to make stick, and very unpredictable in its effect if you do. That is no reason not to try reform, but it is deep reason to do it thoughtfully and sincerely.

Democracy versus freedom

To expand on the earlier statement that we don't need more government, however excellent, one should note that "democracy" is not equal to "freedom." Through the careless linguistics of a generation of politicians and commentators, most people talk as if the two were synonymous. This is not true. Democracy is not the same as freedom. Indeed, democracy sometimes is the *enemy* of freedom.

One characterization of democracy is "government with the consent of the governed." For some of the governed some of the time, that is true. That is the fairer face. The darker face of democracy lies in this fact: democracy can equally be described as the institutionalized oppression of minorities by the majority. Indeed, given that most governments in Canada are elected with a good deal less that 50 percent of those voting, let alone the total vote, it can even be the oppression of the majority by a minority! And since the rules of Parliament allow for an elected dictatorship between elections, that governing "minority" may be not much larger than the prime minister's office establishment.

So democracy is only, as Churchill famously put it, the least bad system of any that have been tried.

Happily there is a better way of making most of the decisions in a free society. We have two ways of making decisions in Canada. One does not involve democracy at all. It is the free market, where decisions are made in their millions on a daily, precise, context-specific basis by the voluntary interaction of individuals with each other and with private sector organizations on a voluntary basis.

Thanks to the work of economists and philosophers over the years, we know quite a lot about free markets, and what makes them work well or badly. We know that competition is good, as is maximum information for the consumer (transparency), accountability (standards, liability, contract, and the rule of law), and clear incentives. Full, true, and plain disclosure is the general rule, whether what is being marketed is a stepladder or stock in a company.

The essence of a free market is that it is voluntary. Every transaction is mutually agreed upon. Of course, there is not complete freedom. One needs to buy food; that is not a choice. But at least one can seek the best buy through comparing the corner store,

Safeway, Costco or the local farmers' market. There is a choice of supplier, and that keeps everyone reasonably honest.

However, many decisions are not made in the free market, but rather in the *political* market. That is where governance and democracy come in. The political market is where others make decisions for us, whether we agree or not. This is not a voluntary market; quite the contrary. It is based on coercion. The consumer has no choice as to what he will pay (i.e., taxes) and no choice as to what he will buy (i.e., the expenditures of government departments).

Many of the choices forced upon consumers by governments are not even easy to measure, not being denominated in dollars. I refer to the immense world of government regulation, which tells you what you can and cannot do in myriad ways. (Why can't you legally pick up an American satellite signal for television entertainment, even if you pay for it? Why can't you buy a can of soup with the information in only one language? Well, you can't, that's all. Don't ask.)

The political, coercive market is unavoidable in some areas. We need a justice system, for example. Some things seem best done by government for practical reasons, such as the provision of national security, or a municipal road system. Other things, though probably fewer than usually believed, are arguably more efficiently done by government. Many scholars believe there is an "optimal size" for government, though there is much debate as to what this might be. It certainly varies with the size and technological sophistication of a society, as well as such things as general education of the public, especially literacy.

The political market is much less "efficient" than the free market, in terms of giving citizens something close to their preferred resource allocation and the "biggest bang for the buck." This is to be expected for the following reasons:

• The political market is not competitive. It is a monopoly, and moreover, an inescapable monopoly. You not only have only a sole supplier at its fixed price, but you are forced to buy (through taxation).

- The political market is not transparent. Any stockbroker who signed a prospectus requiring "full, true, and plain disclosure" based on the standards of an election platform or even routine government policy statements would be in jail for providing insufficient or deliberately misleading information. This is considered clever in the political market, rather than illegal.
- The political market is not accountable, except in the grossest sense at election time. The consumer has no way to say, "I'll take this defence policy, but not that one." Or, "You screwed up on providing hip replacements; I'm going down the road."
- The political market is chock-full of perverse incentives. In the free market, people are dealing with their own assets and liabilities, and treat them with respect. In the political market, politicians are dealing with other people's money and power, and so don't treat them with as much respect. Public resources are routinely deployed in a quest for votes (the currency of democracy) rather than in a quest for efficiency, or even equity.

Given the above, it is not surprising that the output of the political market is not very satisfactory to most people. However, it is commonly believed that there is no alternative, which leads to the despair of, "What can you do?" which, in turn, leads to apathy.

That is where size of government comes in. I recall as a young politician some 25 or so years ago being on a platform with Bob Stanfield, the great and wise leader of the Progressive Conservatives who was never able to out-politic the faster and flashier Pierre Trudeau. We were at the University of Victoria, and the subject was parliamentary reform. All of us, save Mr. Stanfield, were full of the latest, brightest, and best ideas on parliamentary reform. (I do not wish to disparage the importance of such ideas.)

But the former premier and federal Tory leader had another point to make. The best and fastest way to parliamentary reform, he said, was for Parliament to do less. What he meant by that was that Parliament should restrict itself to doing the things it really needed to do. It would then have more time and resources to do those things better, and would leave the rest to the private sector.

To conclude to this stage, the first major step in democratic reform is pretty clear. It is this: Minimize the size of the governmental/coercive sector to whatever is "optimal"—which in this author's view is considerably smaller than at present, but that is a respectable debate. After that debate is concluded, we will surely be left with a continuing wide area of government control. Further guiding principles are needed.

Greatest among these is the design principle of *subsidiarity* and the distribution and division of governmental powers among various power centres. In due course, we will come to the main preoccupation of most reformers, which is the question of checks and balances *within* power centres, but there is an intermediate step.

Dividing power

As with the first principle of keeping government activity overall as small as possible, this second principle of dividing power immensely simplifies the control of government by building in limits and competition, and minimizing the size of mistake any single power centre can make.

"Subsidiarity" is a word much used by the architects of the European Union, though curiously the principle is often violated there. Subsidiarity is the concept that decisions should be taken by the smallest decision-making authority with the information, resources, and enforcement ability to take them. A basic rule of subsidiarity is that the onus of proof is on those who would move any given power "upstairs."

The more familiar concepts of "decentralization" and "federalism" are encompassed by the idea, but subsidiarity is a broader way of thinking about things. "Decentralization" is a one-way street of downward devolution, but sometimes centralization instead may be the right way to go. (It is ridiculous, for example, that our federal government does not have the required power to enforce interprovincial free trade in Canada.)

"Federalism," as we use the word, is restricted to the division of power between federal and provincial orders of government, but in fact other actors—towns and cities, or regional districts, or even international agencies—may be the better decision makers in particular areas.

Subsidiarity is an idea that is philosophically harmonious with liberty and freedom, unlike, for example, the legal foundation of Canadian authority, which is that sovereignty resides in the Crown or the state. Subsidiarity, properly understood, sees the individual as the sovereign, as the fundamental decision-making unit, with all "higher" authorities drawing their legitimacy only from upward delegation.

Thus, the fundamental unit is the citizen. He or she may delegate powers upward to the family, the community, the city, the regional district, the province, the central government, NAFTA, the WTO or even the United Nations, but the legitimacy that underpins those powers is always on sufferance, with the ultimate sovereigns—individual citizens—always free to withdraw powers, or change the levels or executives exercising them.

Of course, this is theory. In practice, power, once ceded, is extremely difficult to retrieve, and power centres, once created, invariably act to extend their powers and the domain in which they may be exercised. In practice, individuals have almost no chance of changing things, except by one of two devices.

One is the ability to act in common with other like-minded individuals. The other is to balance the great forces in play so that the individual may play off one force against another, whether by "voice"—direct influence—or "exit"—the ability to go somewhere else more congenial.

Thus, a major consideration in the actual design of subsidiarity systems is to enhance the opportunity of individual power whereby people can act in common with each other, or use the balance of power, or, *in extremis,* simply "vote with their feet." In practical terms, that means a bias in favour of smaller decision-making units, for one has much more clout with City Hall, say, than with Ottawa. One also has a better chance of acting with "like-minded people" in a smaller jurisdiction, where one can actually know and communicate with a significant fraction of the citizenry. Thus, one might often decide that while a concentration and centralization of power might be more "efficient" in other ways, citizen control considerations over-rule such arguments in favour of a smaller, less "efficient" local rule.

In practical terms, that also means a proliferation of units of the same hierarchical level—lots of cities rather than "megacities," lots of provinces rather than a few large provinces, so that mobility, or the "exit" option, has real meaning.

But to demonstrate again that things are never simple, a regime of too many, too small provinces inevitably escalates the power of the central authority. The United States central government has no giants (in relative terms) such as Ontario and Quebec to deal with, and thus Washington, DC finds centralization to be an easier thing than does Ottawa, notwithstanding the fact that the Canadian constitution was explicitly designed to be centralist, and the American version to be decentralist. Through an irony of history, the framers of the US version could not have guessed that the electorate would force a constitutional amendment removing the power to appoint senators from state governments (and thus significantly weakening the control of the states over Washington), nor did Sir John A. and his colleagues foresee that the growth in party discipline in the provinces, and the rulings of the British Privy Council (Canada's highest court until 1950) would give premiers considerably more power.

But the complexity does not detract from the overall lesson: division of power enhances freedoms.

The other matter to be addressed in designing subsidiarity systems is that of inherent economies of scale versus the locus of knowledge. Readers may be familiar with the Hayekian thesis that knowledge is essentially local and distributed, which is why the voluntary market is more efficient than a centrally-planned system. On the other hand, large governments are likely to be much more efficient at extractive things like collecting taxes, and scalar things like buying national defense. Worldwide organizations (or binding treaties) are likely to be best at restraining individual governments from interfering with global rights like the freedom to trade.

Detailed considerations for the division of power are beyond the scope of this chapter, though, for Canadian purposes, I have addressed them in The Fraser Institute book, *Thirty Million Musketeers*.

As important as power distribution are issues of communication and coordination among governing agencies, and issues of accountability and transparency vis f vis the citizenry. The coordination issue is the essence of the study of intergovernmental relations, and beyond the scope of this book, though also addressed in *Thirty Million Musketeers*. Accountability and transparency, on the other hand, are fundamental to democratic reform and will be addressed later in this essay and in particular later in this book in the section entitled "Constitutional Constraints."

For current purposes, the message is this: subsidiarity is one of the most powerful organizing concepts for those concerned with maximal freedom and efficiency at any given level of governmental activity, and thus one of the matters always to be kept in mind when considering proposals for democratic reform.

To summarize: the best way to control governments is to keep them small, to have them active only in areas where such activity is a demonstrable net benefit. This quest is for the *optimal size* of government. The next best means of control is to *diffuse and decentralize* power among different governments and levels of government according to the principles of subsidiarity. But once one has defined the total optimal role of government, and diffused and decentralized as much as makes sense, the challenge remains of mandating, controlling, constraining, and overseeing those governmental entities that pass the above tests.

Types of democracy

For this task, the Western world has a settled consensus that the proper means is democracy—government "of the people, by the people, for the people," as Lincoln said. Democracy is often defined as government with the consent of the governed, though in truth, the support is usually better described as sufferance rather than consent. (No one much likes government, except those activists who see it as an instrument for shaping the world as their superior wisdom suggests.)

In its rawest form, democracy means that the majority prevails on any given topic. It is a measure of the problems inherent in the democratic idea that this raw form does not exist anywhere. As an ethical matter, such democracy would routinely trample minorities. As a practical matter, the majority desires of any polity tend to be in perpetual conflict—full and free health care coupled with low taxes, for example. So a great many devices have been invented to refine the basic concept.

First of all, modern democracies are constitutional democracies. That is, they are ultimately governed by a set of rules to which every person and every government body is subservient. (Not all of these rules must be written, but they must all be clearly understood and followed.) Constitutional provisions such as the Charter of Rights and Freedoms explicitly set out protections for minorities—even minorities of one, such as accused criminals.

Moreover, all successful modern democracies are subject to the rule of law, not just of the constitution, but of general law in force from time to time. Agreement on these two things is absolutely fundamental to the implied social contract underlying democratic societies, and to the order and predictability that are pre-conditions of modern life and economies. That is why even absolute monarchs of the past saw it to be in their own interest to subject themselves, gradually, to the rule of law. It makes for a far more prosperous society.

Beyond these fundamentals the paths of societies vary. The first branch point is how much decision making is done by way of direct democracy, and how much by way of representative democracy.

Direct democracy describes the procedure whereby citizens choose policies jointly and directly through voting in a referendum or other means of expressing preferences. Direct democracy has many tools, but the hallmark is direct action by each citizen, unmediated by any representative. What can certainly be said about direct democracy at this point is that it is essential for some things (electing representatives, for example, is the most common act of direct democracy), desirable in others (approval of constitutional amendments, for example) and a useful safety valve within limits in other areas.

It can also be said with certainty that even though it is technically possible today (with remote electronic balloting and so on) to try to decide all questions of governance by direct democracy, this would be utterly impractical. The inconsistency of majority wishes and the tyranny of the majority alluded to above are only two of the reasons. The tolerance of citizens would certainly not extend to such a huge call on their time. The Swiss practice where citizens can vote in a couple of dozen referendums per year may be near the upper limit of direct democracy usage, and democracy in that country is still overwhelmingly representative, not direct.

But if, as a practical matter, direct democracy is little used and even little discussed in the Canadian context, it has a small but essential place in our system. Beyond the election of representatives directly, the direct approval of constitutional amendments is required by law in BC and Alberta, and by quite strong precedent elsewhere. The nation-wide vote on the Charlottetown Accord (which of course rejected that constitutional plan notwithstanding its support by the federal government, every provincial government, most local governments, and essentially the entire "establishment" of the country from business through unions, churches, and the media) has probably set a pattern which governments will be unable to ignore in the future.[1]

Less established in Canada, but equally essential, is the "safety valve" aspect. This does not include referendums proposed by

---

[1]   It is interesting that those who claim that "third-party" election expenditure must be restricted on the grounds that money can buy votes ignore the fact that virtually *all* of the advertising money was on the side that lost the vote on the Accord.

governments, though these have their useful place. Rather, the "safety valve" consists of machinery that can be activated by an outraged public against government action or refusal to act. The two main instruments here are the "initiative" and the "recall." The initiative allows a group of citizens of a stipulated minimum size to force a vote on any given proposition of public policy. The recall provides for a vote than can potentially prematurely end the term of the local representative.

While Canadians are familiar with these instruments, largely through reading about their frequent usage in many of the American states, both of these measures are in fact available in British Columbia. They were instituted by the NDP government of Mike Harcourt in reluctant recognition of an overwhelming vote in favour of such machinery in a referendum proposed by the losing Social Credit government in 1991. The Socreds lost the election to the NDP, but their referendum on instituting the initiative and recall was so popular—over 80 percent in each case—that the result could not be ignored.

The NDP government hated the idea, but managed to live with it by bringing in the machinery in formal terms, but effectively making it impossible to use. To effect a recall of an elected member, one must obtain the signatures of 40 percent of the total voters list at the time of the previous election, *even if that list was flawed by containing deceased people and the like*—and notwithstanding that the recall cannot be triggered for a minimum period of 18 months, by which time many voters have moved elsewhere.

The initiative can only be activated when 10 percent of the people on the voters list sign a petition in *every* single constituency.

Even against the much disliked (as they came to be) NDP, the recall was never successfully employed against the government that instituted it, though its probable success against a Liberal MLA who had written phony letters to the editor of a local newspaper did cause him to resign. In 2003 a recall petition came close to being successful against a member of the Liberal government caucus, but its use remains controversial as many argue that the action was in fact targeted against the *government as a whole* rather than the hapless incumbent of that constituency.

The initiative option has never come remotely close to being implemented. British Columbia's new Liberal government was elected on a platform that specifically promised easier activation of these two tools, but we have not yet had any specifics.

In the opinion of this writer, each of these safety valves should be available to discipline governments or representatives that get too far out of line or fail for too long to address problems, but the machinery should be difficult to use, though not effectively impossible as is at present the case with the current BC initiative legislation. In addition, legislation passed as a result of an initiative directive from the voters would, of course, need protection from immediate repeal by a hostile legislature, but should also contain mandatory "sunset" provisions for review. Direct democracy after all is not the voice of God, but merely a mass opinion on one issue at one point in time.

Our society is unused to the tools of direct democracy, and given the awesome power of these tools and the ample possibilities for their misuse, the implementation of them should be undertaken cautiously. But the process should begin. Governments need checks and balances. Direct democracy provides some options, but the energy of most reformers turns to the far more commonly-used tools of *representative* (i.e. indirect) democracy.

Representative democracy

Government in Canada, taken collectively, is immense. In 2003, its spending will still total some 37.1 percent of GDP. In addition, laws and regulations have enormous monetary and non-monetary impacts on our everyday lives.

The point for the moment is not whether this situation is right or wrong, but rather that government is awesomely important to us. Why, then, do most of us pay so little attention to the makeup of government, seeing it more as a plague sent for us to endure rather than as an instrument for us to use and control?

The problem lies with our main control mechanism, which is representative democracy. Almost all government decisions are made by our representatives, and, as argued earlier, necessarily so. Our representatives are paid to spend their time gathering information and making decisions on our behalf. Ideally (and this seems obvious but is seldom said) we would like our representatives to make the same decisions in any given case as we ourselves would, were we there and similarly well informed.

That means that representatives should be, well, *representative* of the whole community, which is a tall order given the diversity of our land. Ideally, therefore, if 10 percent of the population prefer the colour black, 17 percent prefer green, and so on, our legislatures should reflect those preference proportions.

But that is not enough. Our representatives should also have similar incentives to the rest of us. If some of us worry in a very personal way about rising unemployment, or inadequate pensions, or inferior schools, or neighbourhood crime, or high taxes, so, ideally, should they. Customarily, of course, our representatives do everything they can to insulate themselves from the harsher incentives of life.

Our system, in fact, tends to fail these tests of representativeness and incentives in six ways.

1. *artificial majority* As Nick Loenen sets out in chapter 2 of this book, "A Case for Changing the Voting System," our current electoral system (so-called "first-past-the-post," or more technically, "single member plurality") makes certain that much of the electorate is not represented in the legislature in any way at all, because only the votes for the winner count, and the winner in our system often takes as little as 40 percent of the vote—sometimes even less.

2. Entire regions may be very incompletely represented. Only half of Ontarians voted for the Liberals in the last federal

election, but (with three exceptions out of 103 seats) only Liberals were elected in that province. In the West, the Canadian Alliance benefited from the same phenomenon, if less dramatically.

3. Once a legislature is elected, only those on the government side have any power. All constituencies foolish or ornery enough to support an opposition candidate are frozen out.

4. Even among the government members, only a few get close to real power, which is to say, into the Cabinet.

5. The way Cabinet government works in our system, only the first minister and a very few close advisors wield all real power—and most of those advisors are not even elected! In other words, our real government is by a minority of a minority of a minority.

6. In the matter of incentives and as alluded to above, elected people's incentives quickly become very different from those of the people they represent. The money the representatives are spending is other people's money, not their own. Their chief incentive is to obtain good media and get re-elected, not to ensure good government.[2] Fortunately, there is some correlation between good media, getting re-elected, and good government. However, it is rather weak, and is made even more so by lack of information and government secrecy, the latter being a nigh universal problem in our system.

Indeed, when matters are put so baldly, it is a wonder that our governance is even as marginally adequate as it is at present. That it is not worse is a tribute to the many fine elected men and women who really do want to make the world a better place in spite of the perverse system, and, to some extent depending upon the jurisdiction, a tribute as well to a reasonably professional civil service.

2　This discordance in incentives is at the heart of public choice theory. A good primer is to be found in Mitchell and Simmons, *Beyond Politics*.

From this viewpoint, the requirements for reform are pretty simple. First, the electoral system should be modified to make the legislature more reflective of the community as a whole. Thereafter, the rules of the legislature should be changed to ensure that each representative has a real voice. Finally, the incentive package should be changed to ensure a greater concordance between the rulers and the ruled.[3]

Electoral reform

The first of these tasks, electoral reform, has been the subject of an enormous amount of study over the years, and a great deal of experimentation around the world. There is no single "right" system, for communities and countries differ greatly in their circumstances.

Our Canadian system, for example, is well suited for a primitive society that is advanced enough for minimal democracy but still needs a "strong man" form of government. We no longer fit that profile.

Appropriate electoral systems will vary according to the relative homogeneity of a society, both locally and across its regions. The best choice will also depend upon not only the education and sophistication of the electorate, but also on the quality of communication links. Most importantly, the rules of election and the rules of the ensuing government structure are very inter-related. Parliamentary democracies, where the executive branch requires continuous parliamentary support, will have different electoral considerations than republican systems enjoying a separation of powers.

With all of these caveats, it is my opinion—and, I believe, a generally shared one—that our system needs to be changed to deliver more "representativeness," or "proportionality," as it is often called.

---

3   Note that this is in reference to *legislators*. Judges are in quite a different situation. They are interpreters, not makers of the law—or at least, that is what they should be—and therefore they need a degree of isolation from ordinary incentives. This is why they have well-paid jobs for life, and are expected to refrain from most ordinary partisan and business activities.

This does *not* necessarily mean what is usually referred to as "proportional representation," or "PR." As Nick Loenen points out later in this book, there is a whole family of systems that deliver more or less proportionality, giving greater or less voter control over exactly which personalities are to rule them. These systems also offer greater or less direct geographical (i.e., constituency) representation, as opposed to, say, a nation-wide "list" system.

There are literally dozens of variations. Faced with this complex and important challenge, the government of British Columbia has just adopted a promising approach to the question of electoral reform. There is to be a Citizen's Assembly on Electoral Reform charged with not just studying the various options in light of the needs of British Columbia, but then recommending appropriate change, if any. In line with the logic that an electoral system is the proper concern of the citizenry, not the government, the recommendations are then to be put to the people in a referendum, and subsequently implemented if approved.

Thus, there are grounds for believing that the electoral system, at least, is on its way to reform in British Columbia—a reform that may spread to other parts of the country.

However, another, private electoral system also cries out for attention, namely, the internal democracy of political parties in choosing leaders and candidates.

Political parties

We now turn briefly from the constitutional and public dimensions of democratic reform to an examination of the political parties in the system. While of immense importance, they are but lightly governed by the law. Their checks and balances exist largely in their own, private rules.

The important question for our purposes is the internal governance system of the party. Why should this be a public concern? After all, these are private organizations in competition with others of their kind, and we might expect that those with the most successful governance mechanisms would be those that endure.

The reality is that competition is very imperfect among parties (for various reasons of linguistic and regional redoubts, voter inertia, media imperfections, vote splitting, bundling of unrelated policies, and so on) and such competition as there is comes only at roughly four-year electoral intervals. Obviously, such imperfect competition allows party organizations with their hands firmly on the levers of power to do an enormous amount of harm in one or two mandates.

In between elections, and with our current parliamentary system, the only realistic checks on majority governments (with the exception of the tools of direct democracy plus whatever embarrassment can be caused by the media) are their own memberships and political professionals.

While political parties are private organizations, they have an enormous effect on the public interest. In addition, directly (at election time) and indirectly (through unusually large tax credits and funding used for political purposes by politicians in office), the public pays most of the operating cost of these "private organizations."[4]

That does not mean that the public, acting through the government, should control internal party governance. While an argument can be made for very sweeping conditions of disclosure, regulation beyond that should not be taken too far. Since governments invariably act in their own interest, much government control over private political parties would quickly come to work to the advantage of the government party of the day, thereby further reducing political competition. But outsiders certainly have a legitimate interest in how parties operate, and what follow are

---

4   Hence the current debate on controlling party finances, not only at election time, but also in respect of internal party affairs. It is this author's view that transparency and disclosure are the main requirements here. Other matters—special interest voting blocs, for example—have far more influence on politicians than monetary contributions.

some benchmarks for deciding which parties have internal processes worthy of support.

The first issue is *membership*, which is to parties as citizenship is to nation states. It is absolutely fundamental. Most parties impose trivial conditions of membership. Pay a few dollars, wait a few days, and all the privileges are yours. Even Canadian citizenship or voting age is not normally required in order to join a party. Little specific knowledge or commitment to principle is normally necessary.

By contrast, Canada says a voting citizen must either be born a Canadian and have attained the age of 18 years, or be a landed immigrant (and thus subject to security checks) and resident for at least three years, with the ability to answer some minimal skill-testing questions and a willingness to swear allegiance. Compare the far more stringent requirements for citizenship in Canada with the fact that party members, especially (for now) members of the Liberal Party of Canada, have far, far more influence over who will be the next prime minister than ordinary Canadian citizens who don't get to vote for the Liberal leader.

In assessing parties, outsiders would do well to note how greatly or how little the parties themselves value membership, in terms of ease of acquisition. It is an observed fact that where adhesion to full membership is quick and easy, "instant" party members often decide who is to be the next candidate in a riding, or who is to be leader (or prime minister, in the case of the government party). The qualities required to organize thousands of "instant" members do not necessarily relate to the qualities required to be a good leader. (Indeed, they may be the opposite.)

It is a curious fact that people who are long-time, hard-working party members have recently been prepared to give total newcomers the deciding role in the most important decisions a party can make, namely, who is to be candidate and leader. Contemporary debates indicate this could be changing. However, "party bosses" (and there most certainly are such in every party) value the "instant membership" because as professionals inside the party, they can use that system expertly to trump the wishes of ordinary members, should that be expedient. In addition, many believe that large membership campaigns give evidence of party strength and vitality.

Another curious error of some parties is the modern trend toward "one member, one vote," or the "universal ballot" in the selection of leaders. On the face of it, this sounds very democratic. Indeed, it *is* very democratic, if you adopt the American system of primaries where every single citizen has such an opportunity. But as practiced in Canada with controlled membership dominated by "instant" members, this is an invitation to party takeover by special interest groups. For example, people implacably opposed to abortion constitute, by most surveys, around 20 percent of the electorate. This fraction is not enough to win general elections, but *easily* enough to capture any political party with a universal ballot and "instant" membership.

By the same token, the universal ballot allows "swamping" by regions. In the Canadian Alliance, for example, the vast majority of members are in the West, and they elect the leader. But this system is not how votes are counted in a general election.

The question is, should parties count their own votes in a different way than does the legislative system they are attempting to capture? The federal Tories perhaps have a better system in assigning an equal weight to each riding in a leadership contest, irrespective of the number of Progressive Conservative members therein. Since the chief electoral officer weights general votes that way, so perhaps should parties intent upon forming government, unless they can achieve their ends without caring about one or more regions.

The third consideration is party control, if any, of its elected politicians and, above all, the leader. Remember that ordinary voters have essentially no control over politicians between elections. If there is to be any mid-term steering, it can only come from the parties. In fact, there is little party control either. In Canada, parties have almost no influence over their politicians between elections.

To examine first the case of the ordinary member—MP, MLA, or even Cabinet minister—he or she is normally quite independent of the wishes of party members between elections. This lack of accountability is not necessarily a bad thing. Politicians are elected to serve *all* of their constituents, not simply party members. Indeed, special attention to party members (policy or patronage favours) is rightly criticized. The wise politician will keep an ear close to the ground on party sentiment, but in practice, he or she has a very wide latitude of conduct.

Controlling party leaders

But if it is a good idea that ordinary members are, in practice, relatively independent of their electors *pro tem*, what about leaders? Ordinary members are subject to a degree of discipline by their colleagues (who can outweigh or out-argue them in caucus), and total control by the leaders, but in the Canadian system the leaders themselves are virtually out of the control of *anyone*. This applies in particular to a sitting prime minister with the immense patronage and other powers at his or her disposal, but it is also true most of the time for opposition leaders.

An attempt to depose a sitting leader is considered very serious in Canada, and the rule is, if the challengers don't successfully kill the leader (politically) they will surely be destroyed themselves. This tradition has recently been buttressed by the mode of electing leaders. Unlike members, only a leader can claim election *by all of the party*. And if, as is increasingly the case, that election has come about by the so-called "universal ballot" (one member, one vote, as discussed above), the leader is doubly impregnable. Who else has such a mandate?

So, effectively, there are no party controls on leaders, except *in extremis*. That is how, in an avowedly "parliamentary system," the prime minister can and increasingly does act with the imperial authority of an American president, but without that office's checks and balances. This leads to the oft-cited situation of a "four-year elected dictatorship."

There is no lack of theoretical ways to constrain party leaders. In some countries, the caucus elects ministers; it only falls to the PM to assign their jobs. This establishes a collection of true peers.

In other countries, the caucus can and does bring down a prime minister when it chooses. The action of the British Tories *vis a vis* Margaret Thatcher is the most recent but by no means the only example of this. The Canadian Alliance convention came within a few votes of the required two-thirds majority of adopting this system recently.

In Canada, there have been proposals in the Liberal Party (by the 1985 Reform Commission) for a "National Council of Presidents" which would meet at regular intervals to consider the works of the prime minister. While normally supportive, such a council could greatly embarrass the leader with a vote of no confidence in this or that policy, or even express no confidence in the leader. The Liberals declined to adopt the reform, which could literally have changed the course of history. The Tories have a national council of all riding presidents and central officers, which must meet annually. The federal NDP and the Parti Quebecois have machinery similar to this, and it is notable that these mechanisms have very seldom led to public embarrassment. The very existence of the power causes any sensible leader to take more account of party views.

As in all human systems, checks and balances are a very good idea. They are minimal in the most important and successful of our Canadian political parties. Something may be learned from this. The most successful parties in our system have, in effect, been paramilitary organizations, the federal Liberal party above all. This is so because absolutely rigid discipline is more perfectly adapted to survive in the perverse incentives of our political system than is a loose debating society of mixed erudition and wisdom. This brings us to the central issue of parliamentary reform—i.e., changing that system.

Changing the system

Legislatures have as their main purposes, first, the setting of broad policy (through the imposition of laws, taxes and expenditures) and, second, the oversight of government in its execution of those purposes. Our Canadian legislatures achieve the first, but largely fail in the second function.

In a democracy, legislatures are also to be representative of the governed. They may be wise or not, and consistent or not, depending on the general wishes of the voters, but they must at least be representative. Canadian legislatures often fail this test[5] because one person, the first minister, normally dominates them.[6]

As well, in a *parliamentary* democracy, legislatures are expected to furnish the senior personnel of government. This function is nominally discharged—ministerial posts are invariably filled and salaries drawn—but many of the personnel are clearly inadequate by any private-sector standard. A strong public service and a few talented elected people can generally make the system work. But, as representative institutions, our legislatures are very imperfect.

In a complex modern society where big government significantly affects the lives of ordinary citizens, this matters. And, naturally, the bigger the government, the more it matters. Surveys in 2002 showed very clearly that most (70 percent) think there is corruption in federal and provincial governments (Léger Marketing, April 2002).

Regional alienation is endemic at the federal level. Waste and inefficiency are widely assumed as the natural order of things governmental. There is a lack of trust and so little apparent representativeness to the system that most citizens assume there is little they can do about any given issue. Consequently, they opt out. Thus, we see a decline in voting participation (now below 60 percent at the federal level, and falling)[7] and a rise in what the pub-

---

5   This comment does not apply to municipal councils and the like.

6   They may also fail the test because of the manner of selection of representatives, see the section in this chapter on electoral reform.

lic-choice theorists call "rational ignorance"—the chilling view that it is not logical to waste one's time on that which one can do nothing about.

In addition, the perceived nature of our legislatures as they currently exist discourages people of talent from offering their services. The extremely adversarial nature of the system (not only between political parties but with the media as well), the almost total lack of influence unless one is a first minister or senior advisor, and the relatively low compensation outweigh the opportunity for public service and ego gratification that are the principal rewards.

So, the system does not work well. Our society is in tolerable shape in spite of our legislatures, rather than because of them. Thus, the constant call for parliamentary reform.

That there has been no significant reform for over a century (indeed, by many measures matters have deteriorated as governments have grown and first ministers have concentrated power) gives ample testimony to the difficulty of the task, even though, as we shall see, parliamentary reform is in theory one of the easier democratic reforms to enact.

The direction for useful parliamentary reform can be gleaned from a consideration of three of the above words: "representative," "oversight," and "adversarial."

"Representative"

A main reason why Parliament is not representative today is because our MP or MLA, the only person we can directly influence, normally has virtually no power. As noted earlier, we remain at the primitive, democratic stage one, wherein the only important purpose of members is to be counted to determine who shall

---

7 Our Canadian calculations of voter participation would be much lower if we used the American method of percentage of eligible voters, rather than names on the Voters' List. In BC, for example, there are 3.1 million "eligibles" but only 2.2 million on the Voters' List.

be the first minister, which worthy (with senior advisors) thereafter makes all important decisions until the next election.

Government members may be afforded influence over marginalia; opposition members may wield some influence through the power to embarrass, but their combined effects are trivial. Count the column inches devoted to the policy views of backbencher Member X. The answer is almost always "zero." Must it be so? Count the column inches devoted to the views of Congressman X in the US. The answer is "many." The press has it right. The answer to the problem of "representativeness" is simple: it is the empowerment of the ordinary member.

The technical means of achieving this empowerment include, above all, a reduction in the disciplinary carrots and sticks available to the first minister, which range from appointments (to Cabinet and elsewhere, such as committee assignments) to such minor but personally important things as foreign travel or desirable office space. Finding the best balance is a matter for much thought. For example, as mentioned previously, in some countries the government caucus chooses the Cabinet, leaving the first minister only the assignment of tasks. Members, not the first minister, should undoubtedly choose committee chairmen; this change has finally been forced, at least on paper, in Ottawa. It remains to be seen how it actually works.

Of first importance in achieving repesentativeness is a severe narrowing of the doctrine of "confidence"[8] so that members are genuinely free to vote as they wish on many more measures than they now can. In addition, the iron grip of the government on the management of House business, and especially the work of committees, needs much loosening, with the power shifted to ordinary members.

---

8   "Confidence" as it is understood in Canada, is the draconian notion that the first minister may, or even must call an election, in response to any defeat of his legislative or budgetary initiatives. This notion is the ultimate disciplinary tool over caucus members who fundamentally despise elections.

That said, a sense of balance must be retained. We must guard against the creation of 301 (or however many, in the provinces) political entrepreneurs, trading favours and log-rolling for pet projects, trashing the treasury, and over-regulating the country in the process. The idea behind reform is certainly not to create bigger government. That would fly in the face of the fundamental proposal at the beginning of this paper that the best and easiest democratic reform is indeed *smaller* government.

From that point of view, a major virtue of the present system is that of overall *responsibility*. A government still must bear the responsibility for that overall direction, which implies the tools to do that job. For example, a relaxation of the rule that ordinary members cannot propose expenditures (only the Crown has this prerogative) would lead to disaster, unless at a minimum the same measure raised taxes or reduced other expenditures to compensate. So, the lesson here is that the balance of power must be changed to increase representativeness, but it must be done with caution.

"Oversight"

No such restraint is required in reforms connected with the words "oversight" and "adversarial."

"Oversight" is the monitoring function of elected representatives *vis-à-vis* the work of government. Tax monies are to be voted for such and such. What exactly is the plan? How will results be measured? Who is responsible? And, after the fact, did it work as planned?

Most citizens believe that between Parliament and the auditor general such oversight is routine and effective. It is not. Committees lack staff resources, continuity of membership, and expertise to do their jobs at the political level. Even when they try to do their jobs, they are often ignored.[9] The reports of the auditor general are embarrassing, nothing more. No one is fired, basic policies are seldom changed, no consequences need flow.

Committees do not cut the budgets of under-performing departments or programs and, in the intensely partisan atmosphere of the legislature, the main object of a committee's majority is to protect the government, not the public. It is as simple as that, and that is what needs to be changed. Permanent and wide mandates for committees, expert research staff, control by the committee of work plans and choice of chair, and the development of an actual practice of amending legislation and cutting budgets would make an enormous change in the culture of government, much for the better.

And, of course, fundamental to oversight is access to information. The pervasive practice of secrecy by the Canadian government is its best weapon in the control of debate. Policies are always presented as the only logical thing to do; alternatives that may have been debated internally are suppressed. Results, when reported, are almost invariably selected to put the best face on things. Yet a huge amount of information exists within government that would be a great help in assessing the formulation and execution of policy. We shall return to this subject of information later, but for now it suffices to note that committees already have in theory and in law all of the powers required to extract most of the information they need from government if they could ever give up their assumed role as defenders of the government instead of the taxpayer.

"Adversarial"

Finally, there is the word "adversarial." Outside of politics and the courtroom—two famously unproductive venues—our whole society is built on the cooperation of voluntary transactions. This cooperative mode includes the idea of competition, but we try to set the rules so that the competition benefits markets rather than rigging them.

---

9   The Scrutiny of Regulations Committee has for six years found that the Aboriginal Fishing Strategy regulations are unlawful (see Stanbury, 2003). The courts will have to sort it out. In a proper system, the committee would simply have cut the program pending government repair of the defects.

In Canadian legislatures, the opposite applies. Governments, of course, are based on coercion rather than voluntary transactions. But worse, legislatures in the Westminster system are based on destructive competition. To be able to achieve anything, one must be in government and preserve that position at all costs; to gain government, one must destroy the one currently in place. In a vicious cycle, this forces our representatives constantly to choose sides, to contest rather than cooperate, and to distort and misrepresent issues to the public in the pursuit of advantage. That is the system and the lion is not about to lie down with the lamb. However, there are some things that can be done to mitigate these facts.

Some of the above recommendations that would allow representatives to act as free men and women and wield real power in many situations would inevitably cause the gradual formation of associations and coalitions across parties in various policy areas. But the main driver of the adversarial system is the rule of "winner takes all." Where there is no second prize, the competition is single-minded and ugly, and the public is forgotten. A key parliamentary reform is the development of "second prizes." These already exist in minor ways: the opposition is entitled to set the subject for debate on a few selected days and parties are entitled to designate their own committee members.

There should be much more, however. For example, the official opposition party normally has received the support of at least one-third of Canadians, and together, the opposition parties generally have over half of the vote. Why should not the leader of the opposition have the right of appointment of some small fraction of the members of various boards and commissions, as is the practice for the minority party in the United States? Quite apart from anything else, nothing readies a group for government like genuine experience and responsibility beforehand. Why should not certain non-partisan (or so one would hope) committees of Cabinet, like those responsible for CSIS and the RCMP, or national defence, include an opposition member, subject to standard confidentiality rules?

Clearly, in today's political climate, such things are unthinkable. Given the current immense concentration of power in the first minister, this will change only as a result of a great leader or, more likely, the gradual reforms insisted upon by empowered ordinary members over time.

In the end, parliamentary reform is the simplest thing in the world. All of the power to achieve it lies within Parliament; it need only decide. Party discipline, and voluntary servitude for too little compensation preclude that. Until parliamentarians are truly free to represent those who elect them—who would rather have cooperation and oversight and representativeness rather than contestation and secrecy and one-man rule—significant reform is unlikely and our best hope lies with constraints on government, to which we now turn.

Constraints on government

This chapter ends as it began in referring again to the basic underpinning of democracy, namely, the sovereignty of the individual as the ultimate authority. Government's job is to blend the individual sovereignty of thousands or millions of people with the common good where—and only where—there is an argument that coercive transactions inflicted by a government monopoly can do a superior job to voluntary transactions through the free market.[10]

Reference to the guiding star of individual sovereignty brings by necessary implication the doctrine of subsidiarity mentioned earlier as a spur to decentralization. It leads by necessary implication to the above-noted principle of minimizing coercive transactions, i.e., optimal government size.

---

10   This is not the place to debate the size of such a "natural government sector," but some free market economists have suggested in the area of 20 percent of the economy. The subject is very murky, because of the impact of regulations, which do not show up as a fraction of GDP, and transfer payments, which cannot be considered as GDP-neutral because of incentive effects. And, of course, when one (properly) insists that there are important values not captured at all by economic measures, another complexity is added.

But once we have agreed on some size of government, large or small, what then? That has been the main focus of this paper, as it has addressed such issues as electoral reform, parliamentary reform, internal party governance, and so on.

In considering all of these areas for potential democratic reform we have looked at many solutions that could make things better, if still far from perfect. In addition, though, we have noted that those in power under existing rules will always resist changing those rules that act to their advantage.

Recognizing these inherent difficulties with governance leads one to consider enhancing constitutional constraints, that is, those rules that governments must follow in exercising their power, whether they like it or not.

The most fundamental constitutional constraint of all is the oldest, namely, the rule of law. Centuries ago rulers, even despotic rulers, noted that order and predictability, including predictability of the rulers, made for better outcomes. While surely not always observed even in our own times, and even in western societies, the idea of the rule of law is now settled wisdom. What remains is fine tuning, but that is very important, as people who bought early television sets will recall.

Constitutional constraints amount to elaborations of the laws that rule governments. These laws are required because the normal incentive of governments is to maximize their power and to minimize their vulnerability. In fact, the interests of the citizen argue for exactly the reverse, which will never happen without rules to that effect.

The most fundamental check on government springs from citizen knowledge. We must know what governments are doing, and why. We must know this in a timely way. Then, as soon as possible after the deeds are done, we need measurement of the results. No board of directors of even something so relatively unimportant as a medium-sized corporation would settle for anything less. Why should we not demand the same—and more—of governments?

Governments hate this idea. Accounting for their efforts increases their vulnerability. If people know what they are up to before it is done, they may try to stop it. If people know the alternatives available, they may rationally want to go in another direction. If people have the measurement of the results, the results may be seen to be very inadequate.

Secrecy is the shield against all of this, and Cabinet government—the Canadian standard, aside from the far more trusted municipal sector—is founded upon secrecy.

So after the rule of law, which we have, the next absolute essential is a default right to all government information in a timely fashion, except that which can be reasonably be held back on the basis of privacy or security—and even those areas should be subject to inspection by judges or information commissioners to check the propriety of the classification.

We should work towards Freedom of Information laws that provide nothing less. Existing laws are but beginnings.

To practitioners this may seem an impossible dream, for the following reason. Our system of governance is highly adversarial. It is the opposition's job to destroy the government. The opposition (much aided by the media) loves to characterize indecision as weakness, even though decision may not be timely, and to characterize genuine policy debate as evidence of internal splits, even though significant policy debate is really a sign a government is doing its job. For most practitioners, honesty and free information are, in fact, one-way tickets to political oblivion. One must manipulate the facts and data, and conceal or "spin" less than perfect outcomes in the interests of survival. Besides, without secrecy, how could one ever talk frankly?

This view is so deeply embedded that progress will be slow. At the federal and provincial levels of government openness as a policy has never really been tried.[11] One day we will see a government

---

11   The current Klein government in Alberta has probably gone farthest in this direction and has an unusual degree of public support as a result.

somewhere that reaches the reasonable conclusion that if it takes the public into its confidence, the public might, in turn, be more supportive of policies as they emerge, and more tolerant of problems as they arise. Most people are pretty reasonable about such things. A clever government that followed such a policy—and that listened carefully to and shared power with the opposition—might well endure far longer than the two or three terms we are used to.

One thing is certain: almost all current secrecy is not required in the public interest. Most people who have sat in Cabinet rooms will admit this. For several years as an assistant to a federal Cabinet minister, and then later to Prime Minister Trudeau, a part of my job was to review all Cabinet documents for their political implications. I can say with certainty that based upon that sample, 95 percent of all Cabinet documents could be published, and far from damaging the public interest, the publication of them would hugely enhance the public dialogue. Governments are treasure houses of policy information and arguments that you and I are not to know.

We need to keep up the pressure on our representatives. Since most representatives don't mind the idea of forcing others to be open as long as it doesn't involve them, some momentum, some further progress, can be achieved gradually, as indeed FIPA (the Freedom of Information and Privacy Association of BC) has demonstrated in a nigh-two decade successful lobbying effort in this province.

Beyond freedom of information, a number of constitutional constraints have proven wildly popular with citizens. I refer to those human and political rights embedded in the Charter of Rights and Freedoms. The Charter has its critics, largely because of judicial activism in the playpen of deliberate ambiguities left in the law by politicians unable to agree on such things as minority rights. In addition, so-called "positive" or "collective" rights can provide an opening for even greater judicial activity, and must be approached with great caution. But the idea of a law that no government can override is very popular.[12]

---

12   The public opposition to the "notwithstanding" clause is an example of this—even though in my opinion this clause was a wise addition as a little-used safety valve.

As noted by my colleague Herb Grubel in his paper later in this book, a most important omission from the Charter is any reference to property rights. Such rights were included in early drafts by Prime Minister Trudeau,[13] but were removed at the insistence of the NDP government of Saskatchewan (certainly acting in concert with the views of the national party), as the price of assent to the overall deal. A property rights clause would, of course, inhibit many of the confiscatory policies of activist governments.

But as has so clearly been demonstrated, not only by free market writers but by the whole experience of the twentieth century and the failure of fascism and communism, property rights are indeed the bulwark of freedom, quite apart from their demonstrated economic and environmental benefits.

Is there any chance of getting a property rights clause? It used to be thought that amending the constitution (of which the Charter is a part) was so difficult as to effectively be impossible. This view has been importantly modified by the decision of the Supreme Court of Canada in *Re Quebec Secession* (1998) wherein a unanimous bench held (at paragraph 69) that: "The Constitution Act, 1982 gives expression to this principle, by conferring a right to initiate constitutional change on each participant in Confederation. In our view, the existence of this right imposes a corresponding duty on the participants in Confederation to engage in constitutional discussions in order to acknowledge and address democratic expressions of a desire for change in other provinces."

In other words, if we can get just one province (Alberta might be a candidate) to officially support the addition of property rights to the Charter, the others must discuss the idea in good faith. This being the kind of idea that gradually accretes support and seldom loses it, a critical mass will build. (It would, of course, be useful to

---

13   Interestingly, Trudeau also proposed a direct democracy referendum method for amending the constitution, which almost all provincial governments shot down in horror. The idea that the constitution belongs to the people is not congenial to many in power.

get some sort of a commitment from federal leadership candidates as the various parties go through this cyclical exercise.)

There are other devices at a sub-constitutional level that can have an important constraining effect. The independence of the Bank of Canada is a little appreciated example of this. The protection of the currency against inflation and against would-be spendthrift and inflationary governments is one of the rocks of our society.

If we could add to that anti-inflationary bulwark a constraint against the depreciation of our currency internationally, the foundation for economic security and prosperity would be much enhanced. The idea of a North American currency union speaks directly to this issue of constraints on governments, for as members of the European Union have agreed, and found to be the case in practice, a common currency is a major discipline on spendthrifts. Just as provincial governments are subject to financial disciplines, so it would be useful for Ottawa to be so constrained to a greater degree than at present.[14]

Along the same line, federal balanced budget legislation would be a good addition to the experiments in this area by several provinces. While it is true that one Parliament cannot bind its successors by such a law, the very existence of the law acts as a tripwire, bringing at least some embarrassment down upon a future government that crosses the line.

Another way of imposing useful constraints on legislatures is adhesion to international treaties, particularly those that relate to trade and capital flows. NAFTA and the WTO are useful in this regard, as is our membership in such bodies as the OECD in terms of international statistics and comparisons.[15]

Finally in this brief survey, one should note the concept of supermajorities. This idea says that some things are so important that the usual standard of 50 percent plus one of those voting is an inadequate hurdle. For example, many argued that 50 percent

---

14   There are, of course, many other arguments for a currency union than this constitutional one.

plus one could not properly validate Quebec's secession. In many countries, constitutions can only be amended by supermajorities of 60 percent, or even two-thirds of those voting. Other schemes call for 50 percent plus one of the entire voters' list.

Whatever the arithmetic, the idea is that important change should require a greater consensus. A balanced budget law, for example, could be given greater stability by inclusion in the list of items requiring a supermajority for change. Use of the "notwithstanding clause" might usefully be constrained in the same way—which, curiously, would probably make its use more legitimate. Standing orders, which are the rules of legislatures designed *inter alia* to protect the rights of the opposition, should certainly require supermajorities for change. The same might be said of electoral law, or expropriation legislation. Other examples will occur to readers. The idea is not to make government impossible, but to ensure that serious measures ("serious" in the sense that they are about the rules of the game) can only be changed by way of serious support.

Is all of this because government simply cannot be trusted? Not at all. The whole idea is to ensure that governments *can* be trusted, because we have built in enough checks and balances that we can be pretty sure the system will work.

There is no doubt that good people can make just about any system work, but there is also no doubt that bad systems attract bad people, who then get about their business. It is typical even of good people in government, people who want to make the world a better place, that they will invariably see government as the

---

15   Big government activists have quite a different agenda in respect of international treaties. They decry those treaties, such as NAFTA, that limit government action at home. They press for those international treaties such as the International Criminal Court, even though there is no international political system to guide such a body, because it would expand the power of government generally. The Kyoto Accord is an interesting mixture of motives. While on the one hand it constrains local governments to meet certain targets, on the other hand it vastly increases their powers to interfere in the lives of citizens.

answer to every problem. It is not. That wisdom ought to be chiseled in stone above the entrance to Parliament.

References cited

Mitchell, William and Randy Simmons (1994). *Beyond Politics*. Boulder, Colorado: The Independent Institute.

Stanbury, W.T. (2003). *Accountability for Subordinate Legislation: The Case of the Aboriginal Communal Fishing Licences Regulations*. Fraser Institute Digital Publication (May). Vancouver: The Fraser Institute.

Selecting Representatives

Introduction

Most of the work of democratic government is done by a bureaucracy, the detailed activities of which lie beyond the scope of this book. But the bureaucracy itself is directed, in theory at least, by our elected representatives. Exactly how these representatives are selected is thus clearly a matter of great importance, and the subject of this section.

CHAPTER 2
A Case for Changing the Voting System and a Consideration of Alternative Systems

Nick Loenen

In his book *Leviathan,* Thomas Hobbes (1588-1679) depicted government as a sea-monster—huge, ominous, and destructive: the greatest force imaginable. *Leviathan* is a picture of the nearly limitless, coercive powers of government: powers that need to be controlled and channelled to serve the public good.

Some may think that whatever ailed British Columbia's provincial governance was corrected in the most recent election, making further reforms unnecessary. Even if such an optimistic view of the last election were justified, it misses the point. Controls and safeguards on the powers of government are needed not when the system performs well, but when it doesn't.

My assignment is to make a case for changing our province's voting system to one that is more proportional and to briefly discuss possible alternative voting systems.

Making the voting system more proportional has many potential benefits, among which are:

* less party discipline
* a parliamentary check on the powers of the executive

- a legislative role for MLAs
- a closer link between MLAs and their voters
- fewer wild swings in public policy
- public policy driven by the long-term public interest, rather than short-term partisan interests
- fewer wasted votes
- an end to vote splitting
- better representation for all people especially those beyond Hope[16]
- votes of more equal value
- a political culture that is less adversarial and less polarized
- a significantly higher voter turnout
- greater gender equity, if the voters are so minded.

The voting system we have had since 1871, with the exception of the 1952 and 1953 elections, is usually referred to as first-past-the-post (FPTP). It works reasonably well where the electorate is nearly homogeneous, such as in Alberta, or where there is a two-party system, such as in the US.

However, FPTP is unsuitable where the electorate is polarized between two strong factions as in Quebec, Northern Ireland, and British Columbia, or where the political interests are many and diverse, as is the case in Switzerland, Israel, Belgium, South Africa, India, Canada, and, again, British Columbia. Where there is political diversity beyond two parties, FPTP breaks down.

Fairness

For example, in the 1993 federal election, the long-held NDP riding of New Westminster went to the Reform Party. Not only that, but it went from Dawn Black, a member of the left wing of her party, to Paul Forseth, a right winger within his party. What caused such an extreme shift? Was all of New Westminster smitten by a political conversion? Hardly. Paul Forseth won on less

---

16   Hope is a community in British Columbia that demarks the end of the populous Lower Mainland and the beginning of the province's Interior.

than 30 percent of the vote. Seventy percent did not want that candidate, that party, that political platform. Yet that is what they got. In what sense can Paul Forseth and Reform be said to represent the people of New Westminster?

Pundits will tell us that people get the government they deserve. Under FPTP that is simply false. Typically, in BC and federally, over half, and often as many as two-thirds of the candidates, are elected on less than a majority of the votes cast. FPTP distorts voters' intentions and the results are not what people want or deserve.

Sometimes pundits suggest that distortions at the local riding level are balanced by the overall election results. From this view, the losing voters in New Westminster could take comfort because their party was probably over compensated in some other ridings. In total, we're told, it all balances out. Not true.

Consider how many votes it takes for each party to get one seat. In the 1993 federal election, and in the 2001 BC provincial election, votes per seat by party are as follows:

1993 Federal	Votes per seat
Progressive Conservative	1,093,211
NDP	104,397
Bloc	34,185
Liberal	31,730
2001 Provincial	Votes per seat
NDP	171,443
BC Liberal	11,894
Reform	49,216

Clearly, distortions at the local riding level do not even out. In the 1993 election, a Liberal vote was 34 times more powerful, than a Conservative vote. In the 2001 election, a BC Liberal vote was $14\frac{1}{2}$ times more effective than a vote for the NDP. As a result, the makeup of Parliament or the legislature is not an accurate reflection of political interests as they exist among the people. Provincially, for 10 years BC had a majority government supported by only 40 percent of the voters. After the recent election, the other extreme is the case: 40 percent of the voters are virtually without representation. Forty percent should not ever be in total control nor completely excluded. Neither situation is healthy.

But there is more. Not only are votes for some parties far more effective than votes for other parties, but votes in one region are more effective than votes in another region. For example, federally, one Liberal vote in Ontario is worth as much as three Liberal votes in the West. Provincially, in 1996, the Liberals took all five Okanagan ridings with 42 percent of the vote. In Burnaby, the Liberals also received 42 percent of the vote, but not one of the three ridings. In that election, a Liberal vote in Burnaby was not equal to a Liberal vote in the Okanagan.

There are many such examples, and all such inequalities cast doubt on how representative our governments are, and whether such governments can rule impartially. Might it not be supposed that federal government decisions are, on occasion, influenced by the political reality that a Liberal vote in Ontario is worth three times a Liberal vote in the West?

FPTP is a crude instrument for determining people's political preferences and translating those preferences into seats. In addition to producing votes of different values, under FPTP the majority of votes are wasted in that such votes have no effect on the outcome. Typically, between 50 and 53 percent of all votes cast do not contribute to the election results. In the example above, the 70 percent who did not vote Reform had no impact on the election. They could have stayed home and not voted for all the difference their vote made. That is increasingly the case. Under FPTP, that 70 percent could not combine their losing remnants with similar losing remnants in adjoining ridings, as would be possible under other voting systems. Those voters, by failing to support the winning candidate, wasted their vote. Wasted votes are votes that do not count toward the election of any candidate or party.

In a more robust democracy, all, or nearly all votes, contribute to the makeup of the legislature. As a result, in those systems every significant political interest is represented in numbers commensurate with its level of popular support. That on election night the majority of those British Columbians who bother to vote cannot point to anyone they helped to elect violates every and all democratic sentiments. It need not be so, and in most democracies worldwide, it is not so.

The first argument against FPTP is a cluster of reasons dealing with fairness. Is it fair that the vote of some citizens has a different value than the vote of other citizens? Is it fair that votes in some regions have a higher value than votes in other regions? Is it fair that the majority of votes have no value at all in forming the legislature? Is it fair that the value of votes for some parties is different from the value of votes for other parties?

There are those who accept such shortcomings because our system usually produces governments by parties that would win in one-on-one contests against all other parties. There are notable exceptions. Among them are the NDP administrations in BC, the Parti Quebecois administrations in Quebec, and the Bob Rae administration in Ontario. But if none of the above has convinced you to consider changes to the voting system, perhaps the following will. In addition to fairness in representation, there is a second set of reasons for reviewing our voting system, reasons surrounding questions of accountability in government. For me, those reasons clinch the argument for change.

Parliamentary accountability

Like Parliament, provincial legislatures are dysfunctional. They are unable to perform their most important function, which is to hold the executive accountable, to place a check on executive power. Margaret Thatcher lost 22 bills on the floor of the House of Commons. Their loss did not bring the government down, nor did it cause an election. It simply meant that the minister responsible had to redraw the legislation. This is unthinkable in the Canadian context. Our legislatures are chronically compliant. Every bill, every revenue measure, every budget is approved. All decisions of importance are made outside of the legislature, mostly in the premier's office by non-elected political appointees. We call our laws acts of the legislature. They should more appropriately be stamped "Made in the Premier's Office."

MLAs are industrious, hard working, and public spirited, but have no legislative function. They sacrifice family and forego personal satisfactions to better serve their community and constituents, but they are not law-makers. They are ombudsmen for constituents, but have no role in developing public policies. They will lobby for their communities, but can't call the government to account. Professor Franks in his definitive study, *The Parliament of Canada* (1987, pp. 97, 162, 204, 214, 219), reaches the astounding conclusion that no group is more systematically excluded from the development of public policy than are MPs. The same holds for MLAs. They are called "legislators," but they have no legislative function. A cursory comparison with those serving in the US congress shows how profoundly impoverished is the legislative role of our representatives. In Britain, MPs have fewer resources than our MPs, but they do have more legislative power. Increasingly, voters in Canada know that their representative has little clout, becomes party property the day after the election, and will do as he or she is told. And voters don't like it.

Not only have MLAs been emasculated, but increasingly large chunks of government operations are placed beyond the scrutiny of the legislature by means of Crown corporations. Such corporations are not accountable to the legislature, they can borrow money without it showing up as a provincial deficit, and they are used as a political tool by the party in power. Former BC Premier Glen Clark created an additional four Crown corporations in 1994 alone.

Respected long-time political observer Jeffrey Simpson's recent book is entitled *The Friendly Dictatorship*. The title refers to the office of Canada's prime minister. The excessive concentration of power at the top, and corresponding lack of political power among the people's representatives in the legislature is our biggest democratic deficit. It imperils responsible government.

To their credit, BC's Liberal Party has introduced a fixed election date and a fixed legislative calendar. Both measures do place some limitation on the powers of the executive, and restricts the opportunity for partisan politics to shape the public agenda. It is a significant step in the right direction.

The BC Liberals have also promised free votes, and claim that free votes, together with a fixed election date, give MLAs all the independence they need to check the powers of the executive. That remains to be seen. For free votes to be a reality will require far more than a declaration that it be so, particularly when all incentives in the system run in a contrary direction. Free votes will have become a reality when, on occasion, government bills are defeated on the floor of the legislature. Until then, skepticism is justified.

In the British parliamentary system where there is no separation of executive and legislative powers, the only parliamentary check on the powers of the executive is on the floor of the legislature. In fact, the primary job of the legislature is to place a check on the executive. That is the theory. In practice, in Canada, such a check is non-existent. Responsible government in the British tradition requires that MLAs have a measure of independence from party control; that they lack in this country.

John Stuart Mill predicted as early as the 1850s that mass, extra-parliamentary parties would rob MPs of their independence, and that without such independence, parliament in the Westminster model cannot place an effective check on the powers of the executive. He was overjoyed when he learned of Thomas Hare's invention—a new voting system, the Single Transferable Vote (STV). For Mill, STV offered MPs the potential for a measure of independence from party control.

Sir Sandford Fleming, of Greenwich time fame, made the same argument in an address entitled, "On the Rectification of Parliament" which he gave in Toronto in 1894. He, too, thought that FPTP was the primary reason why the powers of the prime minister were growing at the expense of Parliament, and he, too, looked to STV for a solution.

How does the dysfunction of the legislature and the resulting lack of accountability in government relate to FPTP? FPTP translates a minority of the vote into a majority of the seats. For example, the 1996 BC election produced a majority government on just 39 percent of the vote; the 1997 federal election resulted in a majority government on 38 percent of the vote. In nearly all elections, majorities are manufactured. In countries with more proportional voting systems, majorities must be earned. FPTP translates 40 percent of the votes into 100 percent of government power. In Canada, it is this feature, more than any other, that fuels the concentration of power at the top.

The essence of democracy is that power is dispersed and diffused. Voting systems that translate 40 percent of the vote into 40 percent of the powers of government lead to the politics of inclusion, partnership, negotiation, and coalition building. Just as in the US congressional system no legislative measure can be adopted without extensive negotiation and coalition building, likewise a more proportional voting system would give our legislature a similar and significant legislative function. No single party could control the legislature, no one leader would control the Standing and Special committees. Power would be shared and diffused.

In addition, within the family of more proportional voting systems, it is possible to adopt or design a voting system that gives MLAs a measure of independence from party control, if the voters are so minded. The British parliamentary system demands that MLAs have some independence in order to hold government accountable. Voters want MLAs to be more responsive to them. We need a voting system that permits MLAs such independence of judgement—and greater loyalty to their constituents—if they are so minded.

Parliamentary reform can largely be accomplished through electoral reform. The need for parliamentary reform, which is the need for greater parliamentary accountability together with the need for greater fairness in our voting system, are compelling arguments in favour of considering changes to our voting system.

If we could start all over and devise a new voting system, would we select one that wastes most votes, nearly always gives government to a minority, and results in an adversarial, inefficient system of government where all decisions of importance are made outside the legislature? Would we choose a system that occasionally is so perverse as to award government to a party less popular than the opposition party, as was the case in 1996? Not likely: it would offend our sense of democracy.

Toward solutions

Unlike 10 years ago, I seldom speak about proportional representation now. Most Canadians think proportional representation refers to the list-PR systems common in Europe. Proportional representation does not refer to any particular voting system. It is the principle that unites a family of voting systems. The principle is that a party's seat-share should equal that party's vote-share. There are many ways to approximate the principle. No system attains complete proportionality with mathematical exactness; it is, therefore, best to speak of systems of greater or lesser proportionality.

Also, voting systems do not come ready-made, off the shelf. British Columbia's unique geography, political culture, and history require a made-in-BC solution. To find a voting system that is best for BC requires a process of public consultation and discussion. The current BC Liberal government has promised such a process.

We British Columbians need to agree on what we expect from our voting system, and then design one to meet those objectives. We suggest the following objectives:

- *Broad proportionality.* A party's power should reflect more closely that party's popular support, but stop short of pure proportional representation
- *Meaningful choice.* Voting should not be constrained by vote splitting or fear of wasting one's vote
- *Stable government.* No "Italian pizza" parliaments

- *Significant local representation.* Voters should have a local MLA
- *Less party discipline.* To check the powers of the executive requires a measure of independence for MLAs.

Assuming British Columbians can find substantial agreement on these objectives, what system will approximate them most nearly? The following are three alternative systems.

List-PR

In its simplest form, each party under list-PR presents a list of candidates to the electorate, voters vote for a party, and parties receive seats in proportion to their share of the vote nation-wide, or within districts. Winning candidates are taken from the list.

Closed list-PR is a form of list-PR in which electors are restricted to voting for a party only, and cannot express a preference for any candidate within the party list. Open list-PR permits electors to choose one candidate, or rank candidates in order of preference, or, as is the case in the Swiss system, to rank candidates from across different party lists. South Africa uses a closed list-PR system, while many European countries use an open list-PR.

Mixed Member Proportional (MMP)

Under MMP systems, which have been used in Germany since 1949 and more recently in New Zealand, Scotland, and Wales, 50 or 60 percent of all seats are filled by FPTP, while the remaining are filled by Closed List-PR. The list-PR seats are assigned to parties to compensate for any disproportionality produced by the FPTP results.

Single Transferable Vote (STV)

STV is a preferential system used in multi-seat districts. Electors rank candidates either within a particular party's list, or, if they so choose, across party lists. To be elected, a candidate must surpass a specified quota of votes. Voters' preferences are reallocated to other continuing candidates when an unsuccessful candidate is excluded, or if an elected candidate has a surplus (for a sample STV ballot, see the appendix).

STV is used in Ireland, Northern Ireland, Australia (Senate), Tasmania (at the state level), Malta, and was used in Winnipeg, Edmonton, and Calgary both for the provincial and municipal elections from the early 1920s to the mid-1950s.

Meeting the objectives

Proportionality

Both list-PR and MMP usually yield near proportional results. STV is generally less proportional, but far more proportional than FPTP. Proportionality depends on thresholds and the number of seats per district. Any voting system demands tradeoffs. For example, greater proportionality usually means less local representation. Such tradeoffs and the degree of proportionality can be adjusted through thresholds and district size. For STV, the minimum number of seats per district is three, while five seats per district yields substantially proportional results. The more seats per district, the greater the proportionality.

Choice

Closed list-PR and MMP offer the least choice to the electors. STV offers the most choice to electors. STV uses preference voting. Preference voting compares to X-balloting as the dimmer switch compares to the on/off light switch. Like the dimmer switch, preference voting allows for a range of options. Expressing a preference for a particular candidate, party, platform, or local issue, does not compel the voter to reject outright all other options. Under X-balloting, voters have only one option, and they cannot express whether their support for that one option is strong, weak, or in-between. Instead of outright approval or rejection, preference voting is like asking voters to register their likes and dislikes on a scale of one to ten. Preference voting registers the degree of support present among all voters for candidates, parties, and issues with exceptional precision. As a result, political convictions and citizens' opinions matter; most can be registered, not in a unrealistic, forced, black-and-white fashion, but with great nuance. Citizen participation becomes more meaningful and significant. Not only do most votes count, but the influence of those votes on public policy is immediate. Preference voting is a mechanism to more nearly attain government "of the people, by the people."

STV is more market-driven than most systems. If, for example in a five-seat district, some political interest shared by 20 percent of the local voters goes unrepresented, some party or candidate will seek election to meet that need and get elected. Unlike the alternatives, STV does permit independents to get elected.

(Note that although no country uses open list-PR with MMP, there is no reason why they can't. Open list-MMP would give greater choice to voters, yet not as much as STV does.)

Stable government

List-PR and MMP can lead to a proliferation of parties and a resulting "pizza legislature" more easily than STV. The reason STV is less prone to do so is twofold. First, STV is less proportional and hence it still somewhat over rewards the larger parties and penalizes the smaller ones (albeit less so than FPTP). Second, under STV, candidates enjoy a measure of independence from party control, if they are so minded. In response, parties permit a greater segment of the political spectrum to co-exist within their walls. This lessens the need for party proliferation.

Local representation

Usually, closed list-PR offers the least local representation, STV the greatest, and MMP somewhere in between.

Less party discipline

Closed list-PR and MMP offer the least prospect for less party discipline; STV the greatest. As noted, STV allows greater opportunity for independent candidates to be elected, if the voters so desire. But most importantly, under STV, all voters, not just paid up party members, participate in the nomination process. STV has a built-in primary. Voters rank candidates within a particular party and, if they so choose, also between parties. Under STV there are no safe seats. In the 1977 Irish election, running mates of their own party ousted 13 of the 33 incumbents who were defeated. To obtain a party's nomination is important, but what happens on election day is far more important. STV links MLAs closer to the voters they represent than to their party. STV gives MLAs a measure of independence and places voters in the driver's seat.

If the objectives listed above are shared by British Columbians, there can be no doubt that STV would be the voting system of choice. STV is particularly promising for restoring a measure of power and independence to the legislature; it is sufficient to place a check on the powers of the executive.

Alternative vote (AV)

For completeness sake, I include a note about AV, colloquially know as the Preferential Ballot. AV is used in Australia (Lower House) and was used in BC for the 1952 and 1953 elections. It was also used in Manitoba and Alberta in the rural ridings for the provincial elections from the early 1920s to the mid 1950s. In all three provinces, it was abolished in favour of FPTP for political reasons.

AV uses single-seat districts. Voters use numbers to mark their preferences, and a candidate who receives 50 percent or more of first preferences is declared elected. If no candidate achieves an absolute majority of first preferences, the candidate with the fewest votes is eliminated, and that candidate's ballots are reallocated using second preferences. The process is repeated until a candidate is elected.

AV is as disproportional as FPTP. It is often mistakenly assumed that when a majority elects each MLA, a majority elects government. It is theoretically possible to elect a majority government with AV on just 26 percent support.

AV is probably the best system when a single position needs to be filled from a diverse range of candidates. But in a general election, British Columbians need to fill 79 seats and select a government. If the legislature is to reflect the political interests as they exist within the electorate, each interest should be able to capture its proportionate share of seats. AV does not do that any better than FPTP. AV would ensure that the people get the local MLA they want, but it does nothing to ensure they get the government they want. In addition, AV would do little to empower the legislature and reduce the concentration of power in the executive.

There is a further consideration. It is very likely that in BC under AV, the NDP would be excluded from power forever. At first blush, some would find that prospect mighty appealing. But anyone who believes in democracy cannot support an institutional exclusion from participation in the governing function for 40 percent of the electorate.

Objections anticipated

1. STV is often dismissed as too complex. It is true that the formula by which votes are translated into seats is among the most complex, but the process of marking ballots need not be difficult for the voter. Ireland has used STV since 1921, and twice since then the Irish have chosen to stay with it in national referenda. Are the Irish more intelligent than British Columbians?

2. The political left sometimes objects to STV on the basis that it is too individualistic. Wishing to protect the social and communal nature of politics, they fear that STV will weaken, and even undermine political parties. There is no empirical evidence for this, and more importantly, there is nothing in STV that prevents voters from favouring parties

and supporting candidates who will take direction from their parties. If voters are so minded, they can support a strong party regime. The genius of STV is that such choices are left to the voters. If we believe in democracy, our goal is to empower citizens. All voting systems have built-in biases. STV's bias is that it puts the citizen in the driver's seat. In a democracy, no one should object to that.

3.   Jeffrey Simpson and others suggest that PR will institutionalize and legitimize our differences. We may not get a party for every ethnic group, but we might get some, and there will no doubt be a "Beyond Hope" party for the Interior of British Columbia, and perhaps a party for social conservatives. FPTP favours large, catch-all parties. Such parties perform an important brokerage function in bridging our differences and bringing people together. Such pre-election coalitions contribute significantly to a province-wide political identity. Will PR not balkanize the province politically and drive us in separate directions?

The counter argument is as follows. A more proportional voting system will lead to more, not less brokerage, compromise, and bridging of differences. Instead of finding consensus before the election within the confines of partisan politics, under PR compromise, negotiation, and consensus would characterize our governance between elections. These accommodations would be out in the open for all to see on the floor of the legislature. Permanent coalition government would be less adversarial, more cooperative, consensual, and far less hierarchical than our current system. Such a system holds the potential to practice the politics of inclusion. There is more opportunity for all political interests to have a say, even though not all would have their way.

In addition, STV would not lead to as much party proliferation as some list-PR systems. We need just enough proportionality to ensure that the most significant political interests have, on occasion, the opportunity to participate in government, but not so much as to cause perpetual deadlock and undue fragmentation. Proportionality can be fine tuned to suit the particular needs of our province.

It is popularly assumed that Israel's voting system leads to instability. Since Israel imposed a threshold it has had more stability, but if it weren't for that country's PR voting system, the instability would have been much greater. Imagine that the new parliament for Northern Ireland was elected under FPTP (they use STV), and that either the Catholic or Protestant factions could have 100 percent of the powers of government on a minority of the vote. Would that be acceptable on the basis that FPTP induces parties to practice a brokerage function? With a polarized electorate the alleged brokerage function of FPTP is nonexistent.

Would Quebec not be better served under a more proportional system, forcing federalists and separatists to work together to govern after the election? Under FPTP, the separatists, who make up about 40 percent of the voters, are either in total control or totally excluded from government. Neither is healthy. Are politically diverse electorates not better served when governance is a common responsibility? Why seek to bridge our diversity before the election within parties when we can aim to make governance after the election a more communal undertaking? Province-wide political stability demands governing structures that are inclusive. Inducing parties to be inclusive is important, but making government inclusive is more important. Countries with deep divisions and diversities are better governed under coalitions than under majorities manufactured by FPTP. Examples include Switzerland, South Africa, and Belgium.

Some claim that because British Columbia is so diverse, it cannot afford to risk coalition government. Perhaps it is precisely our diversity that demands coalitions. Alberta hardly needs a more proportional voting system: having one would make little difference. BC, on the other hand, needs such a system because it is much more politically diverse. India needs PR badly because of its diversity, as does Canada federally, for the same reason.

Furthermore, the claim that FPTP performs a brokerage function is itself suspect. In theory, FPTP induces parties to seek out the large bulge of voters in the middle, to moderate the extremes, and to avoid polarization. There are instances where the theory works. BC is not one of them. In fact, FPTP has had an opposite effect here; it has exacerbated existing social divisions to produce highly polarized politics.

For 40 years, BC politics was severely polarized between a coalition of the right and a coalition of the left. For most of that time, the Liberals tried to straddle the centre, to be the voice of reason and moderation, to bridge differences, to lessen the polarity. They were defeated by FPTP. W.A.C. Bennett's threat that a vote for the Liberals was a vote for the Socialists carried because of FPTP. Consider the numbers.

Average Votes per Seat for the Seven Elections, 1956-1975	
Social Credit	15,647
CCF/NDP	20,866
Liberals	53,258

On average, the Liberals needed more than three times the number of votes the Socreds needed, per seat. In British Columbia, those who want to built bridges are penalized by FPTP. The claim that FPTP performs a brokerage function does not apply to this province's politics.

Despite the most recent election results, BC politics is and remains diverse and polarized. FPTP cannot accommodate diversity, and in BC's case it exacerbates polarization. If the objective is to lessen polarization, to bring the Interior, for example, into the decision making circle of governance more meaningfully, such objectives can best be obtained through a more proportional voting system that unites us after the election, not before, and that unites us in the act of governing, not within party politics. Unity in governance is a more principled and noble goal than polarization in campaigning.

4. FPTP is said to provide strong government, and coalition government is said to be weak. No doubt about it, good government can be provided by benevolent dictators, but sometimes we get the other kind. Bill VanderZalm tried to stop funding abortions. To his supporters, that was strong government; to others, it was dangerous extremism. Similarly with Glen Clark, actions that were hailed as a virtue by some were a vice to others. In a democracy, there can be no strong government without accountability. In as much as parliamentary accountability is weak in our system, our governance cannot be said to be strong. British Columbians have seen the forced resignation of three premiers. Arguably, greater parliamentary accountability in the system would have prevented such a sorry spectacle, such waste, and such a tarnished image for our province.

The turnover of MPs and MLAs in Canada is higher than most countries worldwide. The 1993 federal election produced 200 rookie MPs and 101 returning MPs. Provincially, the last election in BC produced 47 new members and 32 returning members. British Columbia has its seventh premier in just eleven years, and during the late 1990s, Cabinet was shuffled so frequently it represented a ministrial merry-go-around. The Labour Ministry had eight ministers in just four years. Is this strong government?

Besides, are coalitions indeed weak? They served us well during wartime. Most of Europe is governed by coalitions, and the US congressional system is entirely dependent on successful coalition building for each budget and legislative initiative. Is Europe weakly governed; is the US weak?

But, the argument goes, governmental coalitions in PR systems that are unlike the US congressional legislative coalition system collapse frequently and there is a greater turnover in administrations. That is true. PR administrations have a shorter life span, but governance has greater continuity than under FPTP majority systems. This is because in PR systems, successive Cabinets usually comprise the same coalition partners in a slightly different mix. Because FPTP removes administrations completely and installs a whole new crew, our governments always govern with one eye—or both—on the next election. In contrast, under PR systems, public policy is more informed by the long-term public good than by the short-term partisan interests of the party in power.

Because FPTP gives manufactured majorities 100 percent unfettered power, each new incoming administration has the potential to subject public policies to wild, politically driven lurches. The first major measure of the VanderZalm administration was to overhaul the labour code. Five years later, Premier Harcourt's first act was to undo what Bill VanderZalm had done, just as Mike Harris undid what Bob Rae had done, who had undone what David Peterson had done. Is this strong government? Yes, for the duration of their term, premiers are very strong, but does such strength produce good government over the long-term? The claim that majoritarian systems are strong and coalitions weak is a generalization open to serious challenge.

Summary

There are good reasons to review BC's voting system. British Columbians and often those in other provinces do not get the governments they vote for. Political interests are not fairly represented in the legislature. Forty percent of the voters should not have all the power, nor be completely denied participation. Neither are healthy.

Moreover, BC's legislature is dysfunctional. There is no parliamentary accountability on the powers of the executive. MLAs lack sufficient independence to check the executive; in fact, they have no legislative function. In Canada, FPTP is a significant contributing factor to the excessive concentration of power in the executive.

World wide, most democracies use voting systems under which majorities are earned, not manufactured. British Columbia's unique political culture, history, and geography require a made-in-BC solution. British Columbians first need to find agreement about the objectives a voting system should attain, and then design one to meet those objectives.

Is there public demand for a change to the voting system? It is often not put in those words, but there is an appetite for better, more responsive, and more accountable government. In addition, people do not like the distortion between votes and seats. Ten years ago, the Lortie Commission found that 68 percent of British Columbians would favour two votes, one to select a local candidate, and one to select the government. Last July, Canada West Foundation research found 75 percent of British Columbians—the highest proportion among the Western provinces—support proportional representation.

Improvement is possible. In my opinion, we need to mobilize citizens to make it happen.

Reference cited

Franks, C.E.S. (1987). *The Parliament of Canada*. Toronto: University of Toronto Press, 1987.

CHAPTER 3
The Failings of First-Past-the-Post

Discussion by Andrew Petter

Let me say from the outset that I am substantially in agreement with Nick Loenen's analysis, particularly with respect to the failings of our current first-past-the-post (FPTP) voting system.

One of the things that have most impressed—and depressed—me in recent years is the extent to which our institutions of government at both the federal and provincial level have become disconnected from the people they seek to represent. Like Nick, I believe that FPTP is a big part of the problem. When one looks at the way FPTP works—or doesn't work—is it any wonder that citizens get the impression that their votes don't matter and that governments are unrepresentative of their interests?

introduction or representation paragraph

The first-past-the-post system
- systematically disenfranchises voters by "wasting" the votes of those casting ballots for candidates who do not finish first and "diminishing" the value of votes of those casting ballots for first place candidates who gain more votes than they require to be elected
- creates legislatures that do not reflect the make-up of the electorate, conferring majority powers on parties that are supported by a minority of electors, and reducing or denying representation to those who support smaller parties
- fosters one-party governments in which decision making is centrally controlled and brokered behind closed doors (except in those rare instances of a minority or coalition government)

- Exacerbates regionalism by divvying up representation based upon geographic rather than individual voting preferences.

For these reasons and more, I agree with Nick that FPTP is fundamentally unfair and undermines legislative accountability. I also agree with him that the remedy lies in adopting an electoral system in which there is greater proportionality between citizens' voting preferences and electoral results.

STV versus MMP

Where I differ from Nick is in my choice of mechanism to achieve this result. He favours a single transferable vote (STV) system based upon multi-seat districts. I believe that such a system is a second-best solution in that it requires too great a loss of local representation to achieve too little a gain in proportionality. As Nick himself concedes, STV produces "substantially proportional results" only with districts large enough to elect five or more MLAs, thereby severely compromising local representation. (Indeed, true proportionality could only be guaranteed if there were one electoral district for the whole province.) On the other hand, if local representation were fully protected through the maintenance of single member constituencies, STV would become indistinguishable from an "alternative voting" (AV) system and produce results that Nick acknowledges are "as disproportional as FPTP."

The fact that STV entails a direct and inevitable trade-off between proportionality and local representation means that STV is likely to produce a system that fails on both fronts: one that has insufficient proportionality to overcome the deficiencies of FPTP while sacrificing too much local representation to satisfy the expectations of voters and local communities. Moreover, the convoluted nature of the process through which votes are translated into seats under STV effectively makes the system less transparent and, in my view, would discourage public understanding of and confidence in the electoral system generally. (Say what you will about FPTP, it's easy to understand.)

I believe that these tradeoffs and costs are unnecessary. By moving to a mixed member proportional (MMP) system of the kind used in Germany, and recently adopted by New Zealand, Scotland, and Wales, a greater degree of proportionality can be attained with less reduction in local representation.

Such a system would retain single-member constituencies (albeit likely in somewhat reduced numbers), and would augment constituency representation with names chosen from party lists to produce a greater degree of proportionality between voters' party preferences and legislative representation. This system would certainly be more complex to administer than FPTP, but the process for translating votes into seats would be much more straightforward than STV and would be relatively transparent and easy to understand.

MMP can also be designed to avoid most of the shortcomings ascribed to proportional representation systems. Appropriate minimal voting thresholds can be incorporated to prevent too great a degree of party proliferation; open party lists (i.e., allowing voters to select the candidates they favour from lists provided by parties) can be used to maximize voter choice and curb the power of political parties; and independent candidates can continue to run and be elected at the constituency level.

Legislative reform, political inclusion, and stability

Having focused on the one major point of disagreement I have with Nick, I would like to focus on two of his many other points with which I am in full accord.

The first relates to the relationship between the electoral system and the functioning of legislative democracy. I wholeheartedly agree with Nick that "parliamentary reform can largely be accomplished through electoral reform." The reason for this is that parliamentary democracy—a system in which the legislature is supposed to hold the executive accountable on behalf of the public—has been subverted in Canada through the interaction of FPTP and party structures. This interaction has permitted a minority of voters to elect majority governments in which the premier and Cabinet control the legislative process, rather than the other way around. The result has been top-down decision making made behind closed doors, in an environment that discourages public scrutiny and understanding of the difficult trade-offs involved in public policy making.

Electoral reform can go a long way to remedying this situation. A system that results in more proportional representation of parties in the legislature, in addition to being fairer, is more likely to produce minority or coalition governments that are less susceptible to one-party control, and are subject to a greater degree of legislative scrutiny and influence. Governments that depend upon multi-party support will necessarily be more open and inclusive in their decision making. The result will be a policy making process that is more transparent, and in which the public is better able to see and evaluate the issues at stake and trade-offs made.

A second point on which Nick and I agree relates to the desirability of having a governing structure that encourages greater political inclusion and stability. The polarized nature of British Columbia politics, with radical policy swings between left and right, may make for good entertainment, but it creates a political environment that is costly and detrimental to our long-term economic and social well being. Yet this environment is as much a function of our electoral system as it is of our political culture. If our electoral system produced legislatures that more proportionally reflected the preferences of voters, governments would be forced to be more inclusive and to take account of and mediate amongst a broader range of views. Not only would such governments be more accountable, they would be required to produce policies that, by virtue of this process, would enjoy greater political legitimacy and be more likely to stand the test of time.

The value of political pluralism

Let me offer one closing observation. There is no good reason why British Columbians should be afraid of a political system that encourages and reflects the multiplicity of views within our society. Political pluralism is a positive value that should be fostered, not feared, in our governance structures. I believe it was W.A.C. Bennett who, in explaining differences of opinion within his government, said: "When everyone thinks alike, no one thinks much at all." Whether he meant it or not, Bennett was right. A political system that encourages a broad variety of views and perspectives—and requires governments to navigate amongst those views and perspectives—is likely not only to be more democratic, but also to yield better results.

For this reason, and the others canvassed in Nick Loenen's excellent paper, it's long past time that Canada and British Columbia joined the vast majority of the world's democracies in rejecting FPTP and in embracing a more proportional system of electoral representation.

CHAPTER 4
Q&A for Panel 1:
Selecting Representatives

Question: Nick, referring to your comment here about the Italy's "pizza Parliament," at one of your Vancouver Public Library sessions, someone commented that Italy's Parliament is actually more stable than Canada's. We have this opinion that in Italy there are all sorts of crazy parties running around, but that if you look at the Cabinet ministers, people like the Minister of Defence, or the Minister of Agriculture, that isn't so. Because of the coalitions that have developed, they have more stability in the people running the country than we do. Any comment on that?

Nick Loenen: Italy is an interesting example and it is a myth that they have huge instability. How has this myth formed? Because since the Second World War, every 18 months on average, there is a change in administration. Now about seven or eight years ago, Italy changed its system from a purely proportional system to a mixed system thinking that doing so would create more stability. It has not made any difference. Italy still has this quick turnover.

Interestingly, political scientists are now questioning if the problem with Italian politics isn't actually too much stability. Why? Because under proportional systems, even though you have a changed administration, it's about 80-90 percent of the same faces in the new coalition around the Cabinet table, and that just goes on and on and on. Too much stability breeds corruption, for instance. So the situation is very interesting and often totally completely misunderstood. Even to this day, it's a mystery.

Question: First, I just want to thank Nick for outlining the potential bene-fits of the proportional voting system and explaining the line about better representation for political interests, especially for those "beyond Hope" as being a geographic reference. With apologies to Andrew Petter, I thought he was talking about the NDP.

With respect to electoral reform (and Mr. Petter made this point), we ought to be particularly concerned about including more and more citizens. Most of us understand that very few Canadians (certain studies indicate as few as two percent of the population) are actual card-carrying members of political parties. So one thing we have to be concerned about with the elec-tion legislation is that we look at political parties not as private clubs, but more as public institutions. I've often thought that nomination meetings, for instance, were the democratic equivalent of a fulcrum, because that's where you get the most leverage for the amount of effort expended. So we ought to extend certain principles of electoral reform into those nomina-tions, because that in itself will go a long way to making sure that candi-dates who are ultimately elected are not in fact captives of the party organization.

Andrew Petter: That's why I agree with Nick that an open list sys-tem is far preferable to a closed list system. In my view, you don't want a system in which the party decides who the elected repre-sentatives are to the exclusion of the public. A closed list system tilts the balance too far in that direction. An open list system, on the other hand, allows the public to say, "We want this candidate and not that candidate." It creates a choice for voters within those party lists and thereby curbs the power of party elites, perhaps not quite as much as Nick's preferred model, but sufficiently in my view to overcome the deficiencies of a closed list-PR system.

Question: It seems to me this discussion avoids the value of parties. Some-how the word is often used pejoratively. Parties form no matter what hap-pens. Groups of people get together and develop an approach to politics, to government, and so on, depending upon their philosophical position, or their personal financial interests, or whatever. Parties are terribly impor-tant, and in some, the issues of government and the future of the country are debated very profoundly. You don't examine the electoral system here in terms of how parties perhaps could benefit given more opportunity to do this kind of thing more creatively. And then take that to the legislature.

Nick Loenen: I appreciate your comments. What you say is important. I didn't have enough time to talk about them, but I invite you to read my book *Citizenship and Democracy: A Case for Proportional Representation* because I spend a whole chapter on parties. You are right. We need to strengthen parties. Currently, parties are weak in terms of policy development because they are machines whose job it is to win elections. Because of the dynamics of first-past-the-post, parties try to build as big a tent as possible. In order to do that, they don't want to turn anybody off, so they don't talk about things that are important. Instead, politics becomes geared to the leaders, to the images, to the spin doctors, and on and on it goes. Under a proportional system, you can be more authentic. A party can be more principled. A party can stand up and say, "We know we're not going to catch 40 percent, not 30 percent, but maybe only 20 percent of those voting, but at least those 20 percent will have value and significance. Any society needs to make compromises. But under a proportional system, those compromises take place after the election, not before, and as a result parties are stronger, not weaker.

Andrew Petter: Another point worth noting is that the current electoral system is dysfunctional in the incentives it gives to parties. Parties should be valued according to the amount of support that they garner for their policies, not how well they exploit the defects of the electoral system. In our current system, however, small parties whose support is spread across the country are disadvantaged and receive far less representation than small parties whose support is regionally-based. At the same time, governing parties can be shut out of regions in which they enjoy lower levels of support than regionally-based parties. The result is an electoral system that encourages regionalism in national politics and has diminished and sometimes denied regional representation in national governments. This point is made convincingly by Alan Cairns in his seminal article "The Electoral System and the Party System in Canada, 1921-1965." For these reasons as well, it's important that we adopt an electoral system that gives parties representation based on support for their policies rather than their ability to exploit the pathologies of first-past-the-post politics.

Question: My name is John Richards and I've got British origins. Consequently I'm somewhat still attuned to first-past-the-post and the Westminster System. It ain't all bad. I'm reluctantly coming around to think that maybe Mr. Loenen and Mr. Petter have something to say for themselves, but there are virtues to first-past-the-post. Its great virtue is to get the bastards out. For all those of you who voted against the NDP in May, this first-past-the-post system resoundingly said what you thought about the BC NDP for the last four or five years. In my province, Saskatchewan, the virtues of first-past-the-post was to get rid of those devilish Tories in 1991, and get in the good guys, Roy Romanow and friends. FPTP did it resoundingly simply with no ambiguity and no having Mr. Petter phoning Mr. Loenen for half an hour to figure out how the single transferable vote might work. Our getting rid of Brian Mulroney is another example.

There also seems to be attributed to various proportional representation systems my interpretation of Italian politics—although I'm certainly no expert on it. Part of the reason for the growth of corruption and the inability to contend with the Mafia and various other kinds of criminal elements was really the proportional representation system and the inability of the honest northern Italians to kick the bastards out in Rome in an effective way. All that said, I do think that Canada is in a very sorry state. We do not, particularly at the federal level, have a credible party in waiting to be an alternative to the federal Liberals. And a certain dose of proportional representation might be a useful mechanism to increase voter interest in the process and to begin to reactivate and create more realism.

I don't want to let the political parties off the hook. In the last 10 years at the federal level, non-Liberals, including my party—the NDP—politically regressed, whereas in the 1980s the conservative elements in the country thought seriously about how to reconcile Quebec nationalism with Western fiscal prudence. The Reform party ignored that tension. The New Democrats in the 1980s were a credible component of the worldwide social democratic forum of governments when they came to power in Ontario and British Columbia. With all due respect, former cabinet minister, the NDP governed badly. It regressed. Really, the dominant thought within the federal NDP is "let's regress further and completely abandon any attempt to represent the majority sentiment." So we're left with a one-party state, as we deserve.

Nick Loenen: Thank you John. The virtue is said to be strong government. But you know that's a double-edged sword. Former Premier Bill VanderZalm stopped all funding for abortions. To his supporters, that was strong government. To many others, it was dangerous extremism. The same is true with former Premier Glen Clark. To some, that government was a virtue; to others, it was a disaster. In a democracy, you cannot have strong government unless you have accountable government, government that is responsive to the people but also accountability in terms of parliamentary accountability. It ought to be possible for the people's representatives on the floor of the legislature to say no to the executive, on occasion. That is accountability.

Andrew Petter: Two quick points. First, it's good to have a system that allows you to get the bastards out, but better still to have a system that doesn't create the conditions for governments to act like bastards in the first place. The current system, by allowing parties with less than majority support to govern as political fiefdoms for four years, encourages the very conditions that give rise to the impulse that John's identified. Second, it's very haphazard as to whether the current system works well in getting the bastards out. We've had a number of elections in which about 60 percent of the national electorate has voted to get rid of the federal Liberals as the governing party, but has failed to do so because of the way votes have been distributed and because of the proliferation of parties. For this 60 percent of Canadians who have wanted to change the federal government, the current electoral system has been a major impediment to their doing so.

References cited

Alan C. Cairns (1968). "The Electoral System and the Party System in Canada, 1921-1965." *Canadian Journal of Political Science* 1: 55-80.

Loenen, Nick (1997). *Citizenship and Democracy: A Case for Proportional Representation*. Toronto: Dundurn Press.

Empowering
Representatives

Introduction

Once our representatives are chosen, by whatever means, they must be empowered to actually represent us, both with respect to policy formation and to oversight—measurement and assessment—of government performance. Our current Canadian system provides poorly for this. Indeed, aside from having their heads counted to decide who will be first minister, our representatives are mostly irrelevant until the next election. Elsewhere in the world, this is not the case.

This section offers options for Canada.

CHAPTER 5
The Obstacles to Empowering MPs and MLAs, and What It Would Take To Empower Them

Peter Dobell

An ambition of mine when establishing the Parliamentary Centre was to contribute to a more effective Parliament and to strengthen the role of members of Parliament. While I have contributed to some improvements, progress has been depressingly slow. In the process, however, I have learned a lot about the obstacles to empowering elected officials at the federal and provincial levels and I have examined many procedures adopted by other legislatures that have made a difference.

Since the time allotted is short and there is much ground to cover, I will present my argument in point form and refrain from going into much detail on each point. I'll start by identifying the obstacles to empowerment in Canada, then analyse conditions that would facilitate reform, review practices of other legislatures that have modestly increased the role of their members, and conclude by looking at the current and rather special situation in British Columbia and the prospects that it offers for empowerment.

The obstacles to empowerment

Within their own jurisdictions, first ministers in Canada exert more power than government leaders in other democratic countries. Why are they so powerful?

1. Leaders are beyond the reach of party caucuses

Canadian political parties elect their leaders through party-wide conventions, a practice first adopted by Mackenzie King. This places the leader beyond the reach of the party caucus. Once leaders are chosen, they are virtually immoveable if they are determined to hold on. Witness John Diefenbaker. The trauma recently experienced by the Alliance Party results from the absence in Canada of a procedure enabling a caucus—as distinct from party members—to review its leadership. Here in BC, would Premier Clark have been displaced had he not become the object of police attention? In fact, Premier VanderZalm stands out as the only leader in the last generation in Canada to have been driven from office by sitting members. Compare this record with that of the Conservative party in Great Britain, where first Ted Heath, and later Margaret Thatcher were both forced out of office in less than a month when the governing party caucus felt that a change was necessary. Admittedly, Canadian parties hold leadership reviews, usually at two-year intervals, but they are party-wide and are essentially out of the reach of the parliamentary caucus, particularly if voting is by ballot or by telephone. While Jean Chrétien found himself under pressure to name a date for his departure, it was possible for him to suggest a date 18 months later, not a few weeks later as in Britain. Ironically, the move to elect leaders by mail-in ballot or even by telephone has actually further strengthened the position of party leaders.

2. There is pressure on members to conform

Private members in the federal Parliament are under great pressure to conform to the wishes of their leaders for several reasons:

- Federal and provincial politics are team sports and party members sense that they stand or fall together.
- Party leaders, and especially government leaders, have the power to make all kinds of appointments, and equally, to withdraw those appointments. For example, Warren Allemand, a long time and senior Liberal, was removed from the chair of an important committee because he had voted against the budget.
- It is very difficult to get elected in Canada as an independent. If a member is expelled from a party as John Nunziata was from the federal Liberal party, it is almost impossible to get re-elected as an independent. Nunziata, who had a strong position in his constituency and a sister who represented the same part of Toronto at the municipal level, succeeded once but failed on his second try. There are few safe seats in Canada where a member so inclined could risk with impunity confronting the leadership. In Britain, by contrast, there still are safe seats.
- Under the *Canada Elections Act,* a candidate can only campaign under the party label if his or her nomination papers have been signed by the party leader.
- On top of that, most Canadians vote for the party leader rather than the local candidate. Accordingly, an independent candidate has a modest profile and no party label.

Together these constitute a powerful constraint on independence.

3. The political culture favours party loyalty and discipline

The political culture of a legislature has an extremely important influence on how it operates. To illustrate, the Northwest Territories and Nunavut draw on their aboriginal experience and operate what are essentially *representative* legislatures where every vote, including the election of the government leader, is a free vote. The British Parliament until the middle of the nineteenth century had very little party discipline. It was the struggle in the latter half of the century between Disraeli and Gladstone that gradually led to a premium being placed on party loyalty. Nevertheless, the British Parliament has maintained a more inclusive tradition, manifest in a willingness to try to find a role for private members and to sharing some offices with opposition members. Within Canada, the legislature that has made the greatest effort to accord a larger role to private members and to involve opposition members has been the Quebec's *Assemblée nationale*, probably because of the strong sense of community that Quebeckers feel. In Australia, a very different dynamic has resulted in elected members counting for more than they do in Canada. Although party discipline in their Lower House is strong, coalition governments have not been uncommon, which leads to some inter-party compromise. In addition, their Senate is elected, which gives it a strong sense of legitimacy and, since the single transferrable vote is used in the Upper House, a different balance of party power usually emerges there. As a consequence, the government is frequently obliged to compromise.

Contrast the political culture of these legislatures with that of legislatures in Canada, which strongly emphasize party discipline. The Canadian culture, whose main elements I have described, is so pervasive that many Canadian deputies feel constrained from challenging their party and are readier than in other countries with Westminster-style Parliaments to accept strong party leadership. These instincts are buttressed by our media, which is quick to ascribe any signs of independence by members of a party as evidence of weak leadership, thereby reinforcing the power of party leaders.

New leaders are readier to accept reform

Gordon Gibson, Gary Lauk, Nick Loenen, and Rafe Mair's paper, "Report on the Need for Certain Constitutional Change in British Columbia, and a Mechanism for Developing Specific Proposals," included in this volume, explores possible constitutional and political changes in British Columbia and concludes *inter alia* that "the concentration of political power in the office of the premier is unhealthy and needs to be broken." Unfortunately, this objective is much easier stated than achieved.

I have tried to identify the range of powers and conventions that place power in the hands of government leaders in Canada. It should be only too evident that leaders, particularly after they are well established, very rarely agree to changes in the way their legislature works that would threaten any loss of power. Indeed, it is when new leaders take over that significant changes are most likely to occur. Why are they more ready to initiate and agree to change?

First, potential leaders must campaign for office. Promising to carry out parliamentary reforms appeals to frustrated private members and can build support among members of the party caucus.

Second, there are tangible benefits to be derived from offering private members a larger role, which some new potential leaders may perceive and even encourage:
- Substantial review in committee of draft legislation may lead to amendments that result in legislation that is more sensitive to its impact on the community and ensure that the perspective of officials in the capital does not dominate
- A substantive review of draft legislation in committee can generate greater public understanding and acceptance of it. The hearing process may take longer, but there can be less public resistance or scepticism once the legislation has received royal assent
- A new leader, particularly if he or she has just secured a large majority, is less concerned about possible loss of control, yet is anxious to demonstrate that he or she is head of a team with new ideas

My conclusion, then, is that the best opportunity for private members to gain a larger role is when a new leader is campaigning for office.

It should be noted in passing that if the electorate returns a minority government, the control exercised by the government leader will be significantly reduced, and there may be further opportunities for private members to play a larger role. However, the extent of empowerment that takes place will be affected by whether two or more parties form a coalition. In that event, the leadership of the parties forming the majority may get together and privately decide on the policies to be submitted to the legislature, thereby limiting the opportunity for private members to play a greater role in the chamber and in committees.

This having been said, I do believe that a decision to modify the electoral system in a way that would normally produce minority Parliaments would lead to the substantial empowerment of private members.

The matter of confidence

Central to the argument in Gordon, Gary, Nick, and Rafe's paper is the assertion that confidence is "the central control mechanism by which the premier prevents variations in the proposed laws and budget by the legislature." To illustrate how pervasive is this political culture in Canada, let me review for you two, real life situations. Some time ago, when the federal Liberals only had a majority of seven, Gordon wrote an article challenging any seven disaffected Liberal members to join with the opposition to vote in favour of the election of committee chairs by secret ballot. There were and are lots of frustrated members. So why did it not happen? The first challenge would have been to get the subject on the order paper, which the government controls. True, the opposition could try to use one of their "supply days"[17] to force a vote. But that would up the ante. And why would Liberal members risk excluding themselves from any future party preferment just to achieve a genuine election of chairpersons, when the initial price would probably be their removal from the committees on which they were sitting and their appointment to the committee on the parliamentary library? (Interestingly enough, a year later when the Liberals had a significant majority, an opposition motion calling for the election of committee chairs was approved with over 50 Liberal votes in favour.)

---

17   That is, days when the opposition parties can choose the subject for debate.

Now another illustration. Some years ago, I told a friend who chaired the Liaison Committee—the committee composed of the chairs of all committees—that the analogous committee in Britain regularly submits thoughtful reports recommending change in the way their Parliament functions. "Why not," I asked, "copy your British parent?" "Do you think I'm crazy?" he replied. "I'd soon be removed from the committee that I chair and which I enjoy, and automatically I'd also cease to be on the Liaison Committee." So I trust you can see that the culture causes MPs to police themselves.

Until a change in the political culture can be achieved, which will not be easy, I have no doubt that should a bill be defeated, the opposition, strongly supported by the media, would immediately call for the government to resign. Compare this situation with British practice. While government bills in Westminster are infrequently defeated, when it does happen, as it did on a number of occasions during the tenure of Ted Heath, it is understood and accepted that the bill has been rejected, but the government remains in power. The word "resign" never surfaced. So Gordon's paper rightly recognizes that if the question of confidence were to be modified, it would be necessary for a very determined government to define the limited circumstances in which an adverse vote would constitute its defeat, as distinct from the rejection of a bill. Moreover, for such a decision to be effective, it would be important that members of the opposition and the media be persuaded to refrain from asserting that the government had been defeated when a bill failed to pass. In sum, it would take a very determined government to change the confidence convention since this would require a substantial modification of the political culture.

Changes in the standing orders that could modestly empower members

To assist a new leader who might be ready to agree to changes that would lead to some empowerment of private members, I list below (not in order of importance) a number of practices of other Parliaments that would achieve such a result. Time and space do not permit me to discuss the complexities of some of these practices. The first two would marginally increase the opportunity for private members to break party ranks when voting; the next six could make the work of committees more effective, useful and satisfying; and the last three could generate ideas and support for future reforms and reduce the advantage the governing party enjoys at elections.

1. Rather than the sharp dichotomy between a whipped and a free vote that is common in Canada, the British House has three levels of whipping in addition to free votes. A three-line whip is a signal to party members that the confidence of the government is at stake and failure to vote with the government will have harsh consequences. Two- and one-line whips represent correspondingly lower degrees of pressure to vote for the bill. In effect, the government differentiates between bills of central importance where it is ready to put its fate on the line, and those where rejection of the bill would simply mean that the case for its passage had not been sufficiently persuasive. Naturally all ministers of a government want to see their legislation adopted. However, for the British system to work in Canada, a major change in political culture would be required by members of the legislature, by the media covering the legislature, and even by the broader public.

2. In Britain, the party platform has much more importance than in Canada. When measures called for in the platform come up for vote, they are treated as matters of confidence. However, party members are not similarly bound to support policies not set out in the platform. This practice fits in with the varying levels of whipping.

3. Again in Britain, the House is experimenting with the referral of draft bills to committee before Cabinet has endorsed them. In effect, the responsible minister is asking a committee to hold hearings to determine whether the advice that he or she has received from officials needs modification. It is much easier to do this before the prestige of Cabinet is at stake and it can offer a committee a genuine role.

4.   Many Canadian legislatures revise committee membership every year. In addition, whips even have the power to replace members who are absent from the House, a practice that, incidentally, means that a member who might not follow the party line can easily be removed. Appointing members to a committee for the life of the Parliament increases their knowledge and strengthens their backbones, particularly if the whip cannot replace absent members.

5.   For the same reasons, it would be even more important that committee chairs should serve for the life of a Parliament. It would be good if they could be elected by secret ballot. Alternatively, the Quebec practice could be adopted where chairs are chosen by a double majority, that is, the candidates have to be endorsed by both the government and opposition caucuses. This procedure ensures that the persons chosen to chair committees tend to be senior private members who have demonstrated a capacity to work cooperatively with members of both parties.

6.   The British and Quebec legislatures have adopted the practice of arranging that approximately one third of their committees are chaired by opposition members. They find that this generates a more cooperative relationship between parties in the House.

7.   Until 1985, committees of the federal Parliament needed an order of reference to meet, a requirement that gave ministers the power to block meetings of the committee which was supposed to exercise oversight over their ministry. Committees in Parliament are now free to meet when they wish.

8.   Two committees of Parliament are now televised. Committees provide the best opportunity for private members to make a contribution and they are also a forum where members are seen to be working cooperatively and listening to Canadian citizens who appear as witnesses. The British Parliament has likewise observed that the public finds committee work more impressive than debate in the House.

9.   The British House of Commons encourages the Liaison Committee, which is composed of the chairs of standing committees, to make proposals for reform—and they do so regularly. Quebec established a committee composed of the deputy-speaker and two senior chairpersons to propose improvements in the working methods of the *Assemblée nationale*.

10.   British Columbia has recently adopted a fixed election date. In my judgement, the main attraction of this measure is that it prevents the leader of the government setting an election date so as to avoid the electoral consequences of an unexpected embarrassment. Some have also argued that it also prevents the government leader using the threat of an election to force party members to conform. While this is a widely held view, I think that the primary concern of a government leader is whether the party will win if he calls a vote, so I do not regard it as an effective constraint on private members.

11.   The federal Parliament has increased the time available for debate on private members' bills and their votability. This can be a source of satisfaction to some members.

Since many of these practices could satisfy private members and modestly empower them without the loss of control, some government leaders would be prepared to agree to their introduction. This would be particularly true of more effective committees, since they represent the forum that provides private members with the main opportunity to make a personal contribution.

Possibilities for empowerment in the current situation in British Columbia

British Columbia's recent election has produced a government that dominates the legislature simply because the opposition barely exists. BC also has a new leader who has asserted that he wishes to strengthen the legislature and improve its credibility with the public. To this end he has revived committees, adopted a parliamentary calendar, established a fixed day for elections and for presenting the budget, invited the public to submit questions that can be used in the legislative assembly and, in an interesting innovation, opened some Cabinet meetings to television. Frankly, apart from the move to activate committees, I don't think any of these changes will empower private members. And as the premier is obviously aware, a legislature without an effective opposition faces particular challenges.

Although a government with a huge majority is new to British Columbia, Alberta has lots of experience with that situation. When Peter Lougheed first routed the opposition and faced a legislature without a single opposition member, he devised a system, which the Conservative Party still uses, designed to engage elected members of the government party very actively in policy review. However, the locus of their involvement is the caucus, which, when the legislature is in session, may meet every morning for a couple of hours. It even meets frequently when the House is in recess. Every bill is carefully reviewed in caucus and some 25 percent of bills are returned to the responsible departments for revision before they are tabled in the House. All members of caucus are free to propose motions and votes are held. It even happens that the government leader may sometimes be on the short end of the vote. Not surprisingly, government members feel genuinely engaged in forming party policy. So significant is the involvement of government private members that a man who had been dropped some years ago from the position of deputy-premier to the back benches told me he was quite satisfied with his new role. It is also a system that ensures that the concerns of all parts of the province are fully aired in caucus. However, once a party position has been determined, all members of the caucus must vote with the government. In effect, the caucus becomes the true legislature, and the House proper becomes a rubber stamp where opposition members are powerless.

This is not to say that committees became redundant in Alberta. What is unusual, however, is that ministers sit as members of the committee that monitors their ministry, while opposition members are so stretched that they scarcely attend. Thus committees, which do meet in public, become an additional instrument enabling government private members to hear witnesses and to interact with ministers in a substantive way, which adds to their sense of engagement.

Is the Liberal government in British Columbia likely to go down the road built by Peter Lougheed? It would be surprising if a decision to do so was not welcomed by members of the government caucus because the Alberta practice would offer them substantial empowerment. The Alberta model also tends to generate policies that fit the needs of the whole community. Its main cost is that there is little policy debate in public and the lack of opposition parties can mean that the electorate is not offered alternative policies.

Such a situation could be substantially rectified if the new Liberal government, which has already opened some Cabinet meetings to the cameras (and in effect to the public), were similarly to open meetings of their caucus to the cameras. That would be a truly revolutionary step. But I doubt that it will ever happen and I would not recommend it. Party members need to be free to challenge their leaders in private.

Alternatively, rather than following the requirement of the Lougheed model that party members must support in the House all positions adopted in caucus, I would urge the government to consider the practice which Dalton McGuinty, the leader of the Liberal opposition in Ontario, has proposed, namely, that—except on matters of confidence—private members of a Liberal government would be free to vote against government bills. Because there is, practically speaking, no opposition in the BC legislative assembly at this time, this practice should not present a difficulty. Since it is inconceivable that any bill would be defeated, it is a risk that the government could safely take.

I remember sitting in sessions of the Kenya legislature when Jomo Kenyatta was President. Kenya was a one-party state at the time. It was the most liberated legislature I have ever witnessed. Because everyone belonged to the same party, no one could be accused of being in opposition and the President had made it clear that every private member was free to make up his or her own mind on legislation. It strikes me that such an approach would be more democratic than the Lougheed system. The fact that, when in opposition BC Liberal members were on a few occasions free to vote as they wished, suggests that some ground has already been laid.

If the premier genuinely wishes to improve relations with the public, there has to be debate in the House. Since there is scarcely an opposition, debate would have to come from government members. Discussing questions submitted by the public would not be sufficient. I believe that, if debate were to take place publicly between members of the same party, who obviously could not be perceived as seeking to form an alternative government, the credibility of the legislature should be increased.

With such a large majority, this would be an ideal time to try out such an approach. A successful experiment along these lines could serve as a model for all of Canada and could even contribute to transforming the political culture of the country.

It is good that committees are meeting once again, hearing from the public, and travelling around the province. The absence of opposition members might even offer an advantage since that would eliminate the partisan tension that can on occasion seriously diminish effective inquiries by committees. The participation of ministers is also a good development, since it exposes them to another source of opinion than that offered by their officials. In Britain, ministers join a committee as a member, not as a witness, when it is reviewing their legislation. The interchange can be good for ministers and for private members alike. My one concern is that I have been told that BC's committees meet with some frequency *in camera*. Except when preparing a report, I think it important that committees meet in public. If the proceedings are carried on television, so much the better, since the public appreciates the less partisan environment in committee meetings.

CHAPTER 6
Thoughts on Empowerment

Discussions by Gary Lauk,
Jack Weisgerber, & Ted White

The Substance of Reform
by Gary Lauk

When I heard the presentations earlier about changing the electoral system, and now a discussion of the political power structure in Canada, I realized that one thing was missing, and that is personalities. No system can work unless we have a thorough sense of personalities. The idea of individual courage, the idea of review, the idea of independence, is the main additive to any system that we develop in this province or in this country.

We can talk about a caucus system of choosing and dismissing the leader, and in Bill VanderZalm's case it worked. He was fired. But also there is something that few people noticed. In Glen Clark's case, he also made it work. He was able to get rid of Mike Harcourt through his own caucus. That subterranean method didn't hit the front pages, did it? But the fact is, it happened. We got rid of a sensitive, democratic, consensus-building premier who was about to devolve power and decision to individual members of the legislature, and he was removed by—is "tyrant" too strong a word? He was removed by an individual who wanted power for himself, and wanted to control and direct the government in his own way, on a more ideological level than Mr. Harcourt felt was necessary.

This kind of power game goes on all the time. If you defy the prime minister, you don't get the nomination in the next election. You're off your committees, you may even be out of Cabinet and so forth, no matter how powerful you are, frequently. That kind of power at the top is completely repugnant to a democratic system. I like the old parliamentary system, the blood and guts, the cut and thrust among members, blood up to your ankles—that sort of thing—the adversarial system in the House. It's fun. Some MPs enjoy that sort of thing, and so did I. Indeed, the fact is, what is wrong with democracy is that there is not enough democracy.

Some of the elements in Mr. Dobell's paper are extremely important. We have heard them before on many occasions, and as Nick said, "Saying it isn't good enough." We need some fundamental changes to the power structure. We need an open, formal procedure for the caucus to dismiss its leader without the backstabbing and the corridor problems, as is the case in Britain, where MPs can challenge a leader on legitimate grounds. I hope changes don't altogether do away with the cut and thrust of politics, because that's a part of the business. If you're going to go into politics, you're going to see a little bit of bloodshed, but a more formalized process for removing the leader, and checking his or her power, has to be instituted in Canada.

As the other speakers have indicated, our system has reached a crisis here. One party that had a grassroots movement, an ideological commitment, and an intellectual leader—a great Canadian from Alberta—is now in disarray. The NDP has lost its way because it's been fossilized in its own ideology. The party in power has no ideology at all. The national governing party is totally without principles except holding onto government, and they have been tremendously successful. What kind of a lesson is that to our children?

If we are a democracy, we have to adopt, at the very least, the program of reform that is being set forth by Mr. Dobell, and some combination of electoral reform as set forth by Mr. Loenen and Mr. Petter. Gordon Gibson, Mr. Loenen, Mr. Mair, and I have put together such a program (please see the appendix to this book). We're asking that the government adopt some sort of an assembly of citizens to look at the whole provincial constitution, including parliamentary reform, and so on. I don't think politicians should be excluded necessarily from such a process, but politicians should be reluctant to participate directly as representatives in that assembly, which should come up with these reforms. I think that the legislature should immediately appoint a Commissioner for Reform who would be the key civil servant to develop that assembly, to encourage its work, to bring it to a conclusion, and to present to the people of British Columbia an electoral system that is second to none in the world. *[Editor's Note: The legislative assembly has since provided for a Citizens' Assembly on Electoral Reform.]* This is the place to start. Mr. Dobell and others have also made significant recommendations that should be adopted.

The only criticism I have of Mr. Dobell's comments is that there is some element of elitism in the Peter Lougheed approach. Elitism hardly can be avoided when there is absolutely no opposition, but it is elitism nevertheless. If that is the only solution in this jurisdiction, fine, but I would like to see a more representative electoral system. I argued for these changes long before the current electoral results; I am not a recent convert.

Changing the Way we Run our Parliamentary System
by Jack Weisgerber

My 15 years in the legislature have given me a really keen sense of the need for reform, for changes in the way we manage our Parliament, our government.

I have been a government backbencher, I've been a Cabinet minister, I've led an opposition party, and I've been an independent member, so I have sat in all quadrants of the House. I've seen the legislature function from a number of different perspectives. A couple of years ago, I had the ability and privilege to be able to commission a study on some aspect of our democratic system. I decided to look at parliamentary reform. I decided not to look at electoral reform because I knew that Gordon Gibson, Nick Loenen, Rafe Mair, and others were engaged in that. I thought that we needed to look at the way we run our parliamentary system. This is an issue that the federal Reform party has also been very keen on.

I looked at a number of things. First, I examined changes that have been adopted in other British parliamentary governments. I didn't want to be copying the US model, or trying to adopt a method that had been used in some system that was incompatible with ours. I looked at ways of balancing power between the premier—the leader—and elected representatives. I believe that a leader—whether a premier or a prime minister—needs to have a significant amount of authority. The problem is: that power is absolute in Canada. It's not a balance of power. It's not a weighted power between the different participants, but, as has been discussed, it is absolute. With David Marley's help, I was very fortunate to find Jay Schlosar, who actually did the research and prepared the paper (entitled *Towards Greater Efficacy for the Private Member: Possibilities for the Reform of the British Columbia Legislative Assembly*). We focused on five primary areas.

We looked at the experience of free votes in parliamentary governments, the proper use of the committee process, the importance of time allocation to backbench members (it is certainly important for members who want to fix their schedules), the significance of fixed election dates and a parliamentary calendar, and finally, how Cabinet ministers are appointed. One motive was to try to encourage the incoming Liberal government in British Columbia to follow through with reforms to Parliament.

All of us in opposition are keen for change. We all can see the blemishes and the blisters on the system. Rarely when we make the transformation to government do we follow through with our ideas for change. All of a sudden, the warts appear to be great advantages—which they are because those warts give the leader all the power. Once you become the leader, your enthusiasm to change diminishes dramatically. Because of that, I'm delighted with the changes that Gordon Campbell and the BC Liberals have adopted.

They have, in fact, looked at and adopted a fixed election date law. That can be done, and is done regularly in New Zealand and Australia by convention, not necessarily requiring a change to the constitution.

The adoption of a parliamentary calendar, too, is incredibly important to the individual backbench member. If there is no such calendar, they simply swing in the wind. They don't know if they can plan a meeting of their constituency association. They don't know if they can plan a vacation. They don't know if they can plan a trip, or examine issues. Governments understand that. They like that power so much that they put their own members through the excruciating exercise of being unable to plan their own lives so that they can punish those in opposition and keep them off step. I don't want for a moment to minimize the importance of having adopted a parliamentary calendar. I think it's a very good change and one that will stay in place now that it's here in British Columbia.

The committee system, given the constraints of the government having 77 of 79 members *[Editor's Note: The number has since been slightly reduced]*, has been changed to the extent that it can be. I understand that members are out traveling, looking at policy questions, talking about issues, and looking at ministry budgets. Indeed, I am advised that between the tabling of bills in the Spring session and their second reading, government committees will examine legislation before it is finally moved forward to committee stage in the House. Again, that is a huge improvement.

The fourth item—and I think the jury is out on this matter—is with respect to free votes. When a party is in opposition, free votes are relatively painless. They can be managed in a way that really doesn't challenge the leader. They can be shown to make a party inclusive, and welcoming of diversity. But free votes are much, much more difficult when your party forms the government. It has been noted that the media, the public, and opposition members jump on any division within the government party as a sign of weakness, as a sign of dissatisfaction with the leader. We need to change that.

The group of people attending this conference has an obligation—a responsibility—to help with this change. When contentious issues arise and when government (whether backbench
members or others) shows the fortitude to vote against a bill for
regional or personal reasons—we must help ensure that the system does not steamroll over them. We should support their stand
by writing columns, calling in to talk shows, etc. I don't think we
see enough of this type of support. Neither should we expect bills
to be defeated in the BC legislature, not with the government's
overwhelming majority, not with bills that are properly discussed
in caucus. A minister, a premier, would have to be a damn fool
having gone to Cabinet, and seeing that he doesn't have a majority
support for legislation, to then introduce it. But you will find that
you can't get consensus from everybody. Indeed, some pieces of
legislation will have regional connotations and backbench members from a certain geographic area who represent a certain ideological bent *should* vote against it. They should be permitted to
vote against it. I'm waiting to see whether this will happen in this
current legislature, but from what we have seen in other areas, the
chances are pretty good there.

Two final areas haven't received a lot of attention. One is the
amount of legislative time that's available to backbench MLAs,
particularly government members. Both in our Parliament and in
the federal Parliament, backbench members have often been
referred to as "trained seals," and been told that their only job is to
be in their seats and to leap to their feet at the appropriate time to
support the government. The government doesn't want to hear
from you when legislation is being debated. It doesn't want to
hear from you during question period. They don't want to hear
from you at all. We need to change the system to accommodate
backbench members.

Question period in BC is classic: it lasts for only 15 minutes. I
used to take a perverse pride in question period, because it's the
real blood-and-guts of politics—it's the cut and thrust. But there
are only a very select number of players: Cabinet ministers, and
usually a select number of Cabinet ministers, and an A-team in
the opposition. Nobody else gets to play. The backbencher
watches the ping-pong match, watches the ball go back and forth.

On those rare occasions when they do get a question, it is such an event that they usually screw it up.

They've got one minute to shine. Their voice fails them, their hands tremble, their paper shakes—and they are written off. No more questions.

I have had the privilege of having regular access to question period. In a good, effective question period, members should be raising constituency issues: "What's happening to my hospital?" "Why has the highway to Dawson Creek not been fixed?" There should be a sensible, reasonable exchange of ideas. In British Columbia, our current government has a marvelous opportunity to extend question period to 45 minutes, perhaps an hour as is common in most jurisdictions. I think it's one area where we could make a significant reform.

Finally, I want to talk about the selection of Cabinet ministers. Everybody wants to be in Cabinet, and that, in my experience, is the biggest single club that any leader has: the ability to put someone in Cabinet or take then out. If you're in, you want to stay. If you're not in, you want to get in. The effect of that is to cause everybody to go along with the leadership.

What I am proposing, and what has been practiced by labour parties in the UK, in Australia, and in New Zealand, is for caucus, rather than the Leader, to select opposition critics while in opposition. Tony Blair and others lost their enthusiasm for that when they got into government in the UK, but in Australia and New Zealand, the caucus in government also selects the *ministers*—not the specific *portfolio*, but who will be ministers. The premier says, "I need 20, 15, or 10 ministers" or whatever the number is. Then caucus votes, and selects the team. The leader still has the ability to make someone the minister of finance and someone else the minister of wastebaskets and libraries.

So there is still a balance of power there. But think about how differently Cabinets would operate if this system were in place. Cabinet ministers would relate more to their constituencies and to the individual MLAs if they knew that every once in a while they were

going to face a vote, and knew that if it wasn't going to be the premier who put them on or took them off the team, it was going to
be their colleagues. Quite honestly, when I was in the system, I
didn't have much of an appetite for the way these things were
done. I thought that it was interesting, but kind of quirky. I would
like to be able to have a voice in selecting the team. This is one of
those issues that we should start to think about and talk about.

That said, I'm excited about what's happened so far in British
Columbia. We've had a number of changes. We've got a premier
who seems to understand the need for change. We should support
those changes that have been made, and continue to push for
more. To all BC MLAs: push the system, push for the kind of
change you'd like to see. I believe change will serve us all well.

Freedom of the MP Within a Party Structure
by Ted White

It would be easy to jump to the conclusion that everybody here
supports the idea of their representative having more influence,
but maybe some of you don't think so. I believe, though, that all of
us would agree that if we were to try to get more representative
ability for MPs and MLAs, it would require a multi-faceted
approach, and that was illustrated well in Peter's remarks.

In conferences that I have participated in during my years as an
MP, I have often spoken in broad terms about the contribution
that direct democracy could make to such reforms. My contribution today, though, focuses exclusively on the straitjacket of party
control worn by members of Parliament. That straitjacket con-
stricts them in the ways that they vote, make public comments,
and express themselves in their speeches in the House itself.

As one of the very early members of the Reform Party, I was anxious, as were a lot of the other early members, to find a way to
address this problem. We tried to formulate a solution in the
direct democracy direction. We said that if we have citizens' ini-

tiatives, referendums, and recall, it really does make MPs directly accountable to their constituents, and does put some constraints on the members of Parliament. It forces them to obey the will of their constituency.

In practical terms though, as we later discovered, controlling the power of the leader is essential if MPs are going to be free to accurately represent their constituencies in a truly democratic fashion. This is true regardless of the type of electoral system that is chosen. There really isn't much that an individual member of Parliament can do when the leader has tremendous power within the system.

The Reform Party did adopt a very important, but little known, restriction on the power of the leader, and it has worked well in terms of encouraging free votes by Reform, and now Canadian Alliance MPs. This control of the leader did not, however, come without an internal struggle.

That struggle occurred back in 1988, when a very controversial and colourful columnist, the late Doug Collins, was chosen by the West Vancouver Reform Party Association to be their candidate for the 1988 election. The constitution of the Reform Party gave the members of the local association the sole right to choose a candidate. This rule had been included in the constitution in order to prevent the leader, or the party administration, from parachuting in candidates or from directing the association whom to choose. However, the leader of the party at the time, Preston Manning, was unhappy with the choice and announced that he would not sign the candidate nomination papers unless Doug agreed to a set of conditions in writing related to his controversial views. Doug refused, so his papers were never signed, and a new candidate had to be chosen.

The local riding association was furious with Preston, and made sure that party members across the country recognized the Collins incident as highlighting a problem in the party structure that we had not foreseen. I should note that under the provisions of the *Canada Elections Act,* the leader *is* required to sign a candidate's nomination papers, so in a traditional party structure, the leader has absolute control over who becomes a candidate. In the Reform Party though, a resolution was put forward at the party convention following the Collins nomination. That resolution was adopted. It changed the party constitution so that the leader could not refuse to sign the nomination papers of any candidate who had been endorsed by a majority of national council, which is the body of party members (until recently fully elected from the grass-roots members), who are responsible for the running of the party.

I have to say that this part of the constitution has turned out to be somewhat empowering for incumbent Reform and CA MPs. A number of observers believe, for example, that Preston would have liked to have had some of the incumbent Reform and CA MPs replaced at the time of the 1997 and 2000 elections.

The reasons why he may have wanted to see some of us replaced are of little relevance to this discussion. Much more important is the fact that it was impossible for him to orchestrate such a change because party members had made it clear to the national council that they considered their incumbents to be doing a good job. National council therefore voted to endorse the nominations, and this forced the leader to sign our papers.

Now clearly this is not a cure-all measure in terms of MP empowerment, because any MP wanting a political career, such as a major critic role in opposition, or a ministerial appointment in government, still needs to be careful not to upset the leader. But for those of us who are more interested in striving to accurately represent the will of our constituents, and who support significant changes to the political system in Canada more than we want to be career politicians, this one tiny change to the party constitution protects us completely from removal by the leader. It leaves us free to vote in the House against the wishes of the leader and/or caucus whenever we feel that it is justified and appropriate to do so. It has also encouraged a culture within the caucus, *inclusive* of the leader incidentally, which is very tolerant of such voting. In fact it is more than a *tolerant* culture because contrary voting, properly and logically justified, is fully *encouraged*. The only requirement is that there be reasonable evidence that an MP's constituents want him or her to vote against a majority caucus position.

We've also established a variation on the three-line whipping system mentioned elsewhere by Peter Dobell, in that we have a way of grading the bills on a scale that relates not only to levels of oppositional support for the bill, but also the importance of being there to vote on the bill, and whether or not it will be a freer vote than at some other level. We've experimented with these sorts of changes; they're not written in stone at this stage, but the experimentation has been going on. These are really healthy things to be doing at the caucus level, although progress is incremental. Obviously in this volume we are engaged in a wide-ranging discussion of significant and comprehensive measures that can be taken to improve the system, but what I wanted to illustrate is the important contribution that can flow from small changes in party administrative practices.

Let me give another example. In New Zealand, the National Party caucus selects its leader from amongst the elected MPs. There is then a regularly-scheduled secret ballot of caucus members—I believe it is at least once a month—to reaffirm confidence in the leader. As an MP friend of mine from New Zealand told me, a leader who is losing the confidence of the caucus cannot ignore the exponentially increasing numbers of *nay* votes over two or three ballots, and usually resigns before things become too embarrassing. I have no doubt that a tiny change like this in the way our Canadian caucuses operate would significantly reduce the amount of power concentrated in the offices of the party leaders. Those nasty little secret ballots would ensure that the input from MPs was taken seriously, at least most of the time, otherwise discontent would quickly lead to a palace coup. The problem for a party like my own, which has a totally membership-based method for electing a leader, is: how do you mesh the two ways of choosing a leader? The membership wants a say in how the leader is chosen, yet there are real advantages for representation in terms of performance if the MPs themselves have a bit more control over whom the leader is, and how long that leader can stay there.

The bottom line for me is that I don't think it matters terribly much what type of electoral system we have. In my view, it is more critical that we establish ways to reduce the power the leader has over the representative, and establish ways to increase the amount of power the voters have over the representative. That way, the representatives can tell the leader what to do a bit more, and the voters can tell the representatives what to do a bit more. I certainly still support the idea of more direct democracy involvement, specifically workable recall legislation (not the type that British Columbia has), as offering a tremendous incentive for members of Parliament to represent their constituents.

Although I strongly support the idea of a move from our present first-past-the-post system to something more representative of the actual voting preferences of Canadians, I do not believe that such a change is necessary in order to get better and more accurate representation for the voters in Parliament. I am convinced that accurate representation would flow automatically, regardless of the peculiarities of the electoral system, if minor changes, like those mentioned above, were made within the parties, and if voters had the power of citizens' initiated referenda and the right to recall their MPs. In other words, self-interest would ensure that MPs—and party leaders—did their jobs in a more representative manner than they now do, if their decisions could be over-ruled, and their careers ended, by the people who pay their salaries.

Reference cited

Schlosar, Jay (2000). *Towards Greater Efficacy for the Private Member: Possibilities for the Reform of the British Columbia Legislative Assembly.* Paper commissioned by Jack Weisgerber, MLA, Peace River South (August). Available digitally at *www.pris.bc.ca/mla-prs/ParliamentaryReform.pdf*

CHAPTER 7
Q&A for Panel 2:
Empowering Representatives

Question: Mr. Dobell and Mr. Weisgerber made an observation about the reluctance of leaders once in office to make changes; I thought that made this an appropriate time to put something important on the public record. I think it was in June of '87 that the Globe and Mail ran an editorial in which they reminded Jean Chretien that in 1985 he had said, "If ever I am prime minister, the first thing I will do is bring in proportional representation."

Gordon Gibson: Is that before or after he promised to eliminate GST? *[laughter]*

Question: I am Philip Mayfield, member of Parliament. The conversation has been very interesting this morning, about things that backbenchers and opposition members think about every day, if not every minute. Power is a dynamic process, as we know, and we can talk about what has happened in the Alliance Party as it has struggled over leadership issues. But also it's a dynamic process within the government.

Once I was working on a private member's bill and was talking with the legal people who were assisting me. One of them said that he was really concerned about the shift in government legislation, which will push future amendments of such legislation to Order-in-Council provisions and thus diminish Parliament. I was interested in your remark, Peter [Dobell], that you really don't see how the government leader's power can be diminished, since once he has power, he's not going to voluntarily relinquish it. Even opposition leaders, if they do become prime minister, take up the same dynamics, as Jack [Weisgerber] explained. The question on my mind, given that there seems to be no resolution to the problem of not only the power, but the increasing power of the leader, is what will be the consequences for our province, for the Parliament of Canada, and for our country? I'm really concerned because historically, I don't think there has been such a thing as an immovable object. Something will always cause it to burst it free sooner or later; some of the exciting stories of history involve that kind of explosive confrontation. Have you given any thought to where this is leading if there is no orderly resolution of the problem?

Peter Dobell: I'd like to begin first by addressing the first part of the question you raised. A new leader, as distinct from a leader already established in office, is ready to make change for a couple of reasons. He or she will have run the campaign to get to become the party leader, and in the process will have appealed to the people in their own party who they know to be frustrated and who want change. That's one factor.

The second thing is, before you've tasted that degree of power, you see the advantages that come from having party support that is more moderate and that recognizes that committees can actually improve legislation, rather that simply voting the way they've been told to do, so I think new leaders are prepared to consider change if you can get them right at the beginning. Then they're locked in.

I think I disagree with you that power is increasing. In the past, what made one huge difference was that in Ottawa until 1955, and later in the provinces, the ministers used to sit in the House. Prime Minister McKenzie King attended almost every debate. What really killed the power of the private member was polling, because government ministers no longer had to listen to their colleagues to find out what the people of Canada thought. They now turn to the polls and they get that information from them.

Jack Weisgerber: I think what happens is that various governments push each other. Up until very recently, British Columbia was by far the furthest behind in terms of parliamentary reform and change. Following the recent BC election, and very much in line with Peter's remarks, I think the new leader provided a dramatic shift. British Columbia now is a least in the game with other parliamentary democracies and arguably is prepared to move into a leadership role. That will, in turn, drag other governments along, just as we were influenced by what has happened in Alberta (but not greatly, I hope, by what happens in Ottawa). We move forward that way. I don't think we're ever in a "time warp"; we always get pushed forward, which, I think, is what's happening now. That's why these kinds of conferences are so useful. Hopefully we move forward as a result of these debates.

Ted White: Philip, your question really was, "What will be the future?" And reluctantly and sadly, I think more of the same. The reason I say that, is if we really look at where there are significant and major changes to the electoral system and the way leaders have their power, it takes some sort of crisis for there to be a change. In recent times, New Zealand completely changed its system in 1993-94 after a fiscal crisis. Another recent example is Scotland, which took some sort of political crisis. We had the potential for a political crisis in Canada based on the threat of Quebec separation in the mid '90s, but that has now evaporated. I don't know when the next opportunity will come in Canada. Maybe with our leadership race, I don't know. I'll keep my fingers crossed. But my prediction for the moment is more of the same.

Question: I'm Herb Grubel. I'm concerned about a problem raised often in connection with free votes and it is this: you could easily get lots and lots of votes for programs that involve spending, or regulation, or the distribution of benefits to interest groups. But then when it comes to paying for these programs, everybody will withdraw, because it will cost them votes. Isn't it a serious problem that you cannot, in fact, have the kind of accountability that exists in a system with strict party discipline?

Ted White: I think the worldwide evidence is exactly the opposite. You just have to look at the initiative and referendum powers in California to see that there is a wide range of decisions made by voters. Those decisions range from sometimes increasing their taxes to pay for things like new veterans' homes, all the way to Proposition Thirteen. There's a whole range of sensible, conservative-type positions that voters take. On top of that, look at the situation in New Zealand when the labour government came in there. The government started cutting and changing, getting rid of marketing boards, and so on. There was tremendous public appetite for more and more and more. Even though it often hurt, people felt it had to be done.

Herb Grubel: You are talking about public initiative. And you are talking about the government. I asked a specific question regarding MPs having completely free votes.

Ted White: If the MPs are voting according to their constituents' wishes, that's the result you get.

Peter Dobell: I've often been concerned if we moved to a federal Parliament with a really free vote, everything that Ontario and Quebec wanted would be approved, and what the West or the Maritimes wanted probably wouldn't be approved.

Question: Ted, in your earlier response to Peter Dobell's paper, you support a move away from the present, first-past-the-post electoral system, and touch on direct democracy. Is it your opinion, from your New Zealand and other experience, that a direct-democracy type system could take this to where we all do our digital democracy voting from our computers every night, and wouldn't that be total chaos?

Ted White: If we were to vote from our computer every night, it would be total chaos. Nobody who seriously considers direct democracy as a tool to help representation would ever, ever suggest that. There *are* good models around the world that indicate how direct democracy can be used well. California is a good model, but even closer to home, in Washington State and Oregon, you can see citizens making decisions that the politicians refuse to make, or are unwilling to make. Decriminalization of marijuana is an example. Politicians don't want to touch that with a 40-foot pole, but the citizens are willing to take that to some sort of initiative, and make a decision one way or the other. So no, I would never promote the idea of nightly votes, but I think there's a very, very good role to play for citizens' initiatives.

Question: We are now ruled by the friendly dictator, but the prime minister does not really act alone; he has a large number of strong people who advise him continuously. Many of them are not in Parliament. They're the lobbyists. What do you think?

Ted White: Lobby groups are tremendously powerful. We had a recent example in our own caucus where the critic adopted a position on a bill to do with free trade with Costa Rica based mainly on the very strong lobby from the sugar industry. Only when the discussions came up in caucus, and some of the rest of us brought reality back to the situation, did we change our position on the bill. So lobby groups are very, very powerful. Within my own riding, I handle the situation by insisting that when a lobby group wants to come and meet with me, they sign a register in my office, and print the reasons why they came to meet with me. They don't come to visit me anymore, because they don't want my constituents reading this book while they're sitting in the waiting room and seeing all the lobby groups who came and wanted money. So there are ways of taking away the some of the power of the lobby groups, but you're right, they are tremendously powerful.

Interjection: I wouldn't call them powerful; I'd call them influential.

Gary Lauk: I just want to comment on individuality. In my view, we don't elect MPs and MLAs to reflect the will of their constituency. I disagree entirely with this predominant theme from the Reform and Alliance parties. I never once was influenced by the majority will in my constituency, and yet I never lost an election. In fact, I always increased my majority vote. The fact is, I must do what I think is right, and I must avoid what I think is wrong. One of the central themes that Preston Manning, and Tommy Douglas, and a whole variety of other great Canadians have taken is that the central problem with modern life is that we have no moral centre. We've got decide between right and wrong, and that's primarily why we're elected. By the way, people do not elect MLAs and MPs because they're brilliant or they're great economists. They elect their representatives because they feel that these people have a sense of what is right and wrong.

Gordon Gibson: We're here to set an agenda. Responsible representation is absolutely central on the agenda. Thank you for concluding in that fashion.

Powers Reserved
to the Electorate

Introduction

Some things must be done by and *only* by voters directly. The
selection of representatives is an obvious example. Ratification
of constitutional amendments is, by convention, and in some
provinces by law, approaching that status. But how far should
this direct democracy concept be advanced in a Westminster system? And are there legal limits? These issues are canvassed in
this section.

CHAPTER 8
Limitations and Ambiguities

Barry Cooper

> It is, of course, an exaggeration to say that political science without constitutional law is blind, and constitutional law without political science is empty, but it is only an exaggeration.
> —K.C. Wheare

In this chapter I would like to make three major points. The most important is that constitutional formalities limit the effectiveness of direct democracy measures. I will call this the Constitution, and it is found chiefly in the schedule appended to s.52 of the *Constitution Act*, 1982. Second, there is, notwithstanding these Constitutional formalities, a longstanding substantive tradition of effective (but not formal) popular sovereignty, the origins of which can be documented at great length as stemming from the Confederation period, behind which lay the much longer British constitutional development. I will refer to this as the constitution. Third, even if direct democracy could be more widely practiced in Canada today than in the past, because of improvements in communications technology, for example, any legislation that supports such measures on solid constitutional grounds must also take into account the limits imposed by Constitutional formalities. And, if this is properly done, politicians will find it difficult to ignore expressions of effective popular sovereignty even while they live and move and have their being within a Constitution that vests sovereignty in the Crown—the Crown in right of Canada, the Crown in right of British Columbia, or of Newfoundland, but the Crown nevertheless.

First, then, the Constitution.

The Constitution

In July 1994, the government of British Columbia passed the *Recall and Initiative Act* (RSBC, 1996, C.398). It is entirely appropriate that the same act contain provisions for establishing procedures to recall elected members and to initiate legislation inasmuch as these two measures, along with the referendum, comprise the three aspects of what is usually referred to as "direct democracy" or "direct legislation." At the same time, it is unquestionably true that such procedures originated not in a parliamentary system, but in a congressional one. The two types of government are sometimes lumped together as varieties of constitutional democracy, which is accurate enough; but it is equally, perhaps more, important to focus on the formal differences between the two in order to determine the limitations and ambiguities indicated by my title.

The Canadian regime is usually identified by the term "responsible government," which we may take as synonymous with parliamentary government. Both terms refer to agreed-upon procedures, as to *how* we are governed, and not to broader purposes and goals, for which more capacious terms such as "liberal democracy" are available. Procedures determine why in a parliamentary regime the legislative assembly or the "House" is not, as in the United States, a congress. The problem, however, which is exemplified in the popularity of procedures such as recall, is that many Canadians, including Canadian political leaders, look upon the House as a congress. The history of the development of a parliamentary regime can dispel this misconception, but that history is, as Jack Granatstein observed in a larger context, not well known (Granatstein, 1998, p. xiv).

To simplify somewhat, the distinction between the formal and legal Constitution, and the political, traditional, and practical constitution, is less easily made in a congressional system. In a parliamentary regime, the legal head or sovereign follows the advice of political leaders; in a congressional regime those elected by the citizens do not offer advice to a sovereign governor, but govern themselves. "Here," wrote Canadian Senator John Stewart, "we have the essence of congressionalism: the body that represents the people is legally the government" (Stewart, 1977, p. 2). Despite the modifications that the American system of congressional government has undergone since the eighteenth century, including the popular election of senators and of the president, and the effective participation of the courts in the governance of the United States, the notion of "government by the people" remains a political, but more important, a legal force in that country that it has never had in Canada. In a congressional regime, the formal procedures associated with direct democracy can be made compatible with representative democracy largely as a result of the legal doctrine and the political reality of popular sovereignty. In a parliamentary regime, the procedures associated with direct democracy, including the recall, cannot easily or simply be made compatible with responsible government, nor with the forms of constitutional monarchy. Partly this is a consequence of the legal and political doctrine of parliamentary supremacy (modified by the principles of federalism),[18] and partly it is a consequence of the constitutional conventions that regulate the actual operations of responsible government.

In a parliamentary regime, the government is both representative and responsible.[19] The House is *representative* because it is a legal body composed of individuals summoned from the constituencies where they were elected. They are charged with the task not of governing, but of supporting a government. The House does not

---

18   In *Hodge v. the Queen* (1883-4) 9 AC 117, the Judicial Committee of the Privy Council ruled that the federal Parliament and the provincial legislatures had received powers as "plenary and ample" as those of the UK. Necessarily this is still true under the Charter, either because of s.33, which allows for the limited legislative abridgment of rights guaranteed elsewhere in the Charter, or because of the possibility of constitutional amendment.

19   A thorough discussion of these terms can be found in Birch, 1964.

choose a government; that task is performed by the electorate, usually by means of returning one political party to the House with a majority of members. Officers of the Crown, or ministers, and their subordinate servants, the civil service, undertake the actual governing, and do so by submitting their administrative and legislative activity to scrutiny by the House. All of these procedures are well known. In contrast, *responsibility* formally defines the link between the assembly and the government. In a parliamentary regime the government is *in* and *with* the members of the House but does not govern *by* the House. As noted above, the purpose of the House is not to govern, but to support the government. This means that Cabinet ministers exercise formal executive authority or power, are responsible for the actions of the officials in their several ministries, and are also responsible for the overall direction of government. A second meaning of responsible is the common sense notion that governments are expected to be trustworthy in the sense that they will, in fact, guide the affairs of the realm, the electorate, or the nation.[20] Third, ministers "are not only responsible *for* the use of these powers, but are also responsible and accountable *to* parliament" (Franks, 1987, p. 11; Dawson and Ward, 1964, ch. 4).

It will be necessary to refer again to the matter of responsibility and to the necessity of ensuring that the sovereign is present in Parliament or in the legislative assembly for it to operate. It may bear repeating that the executive authority reposes in the sovereign or the representative of the sovereign, namely, the lieutenant-governor in the example of a province, and that this authority acts upon the advice of his or her executive council in nearly all instances. Considered from the perspective of political science, these constitutional practices are matters of convention.

---

20   This does not mean that they will guide the affairs of the realm the way they promised to do in the election campaign, but rather, that the *government*, and not some other body (such as the House or the electorate), will, in fact, guide the realm.

Origins of direct legislation

It may be useful to begin this account of the origins of direct legislation with some definitions. The meaning of the three major terms, initiative, referendum, and recall, are identical in the US and Canada. The *initiative* allows voters to propose either legislative measures or constitutional amendments. The *referendum* refers a proposed law or constitutional amendment to voters for their approval or rejection.[21] The *recall* allows voters to remove an elected public official from office by filing a petition demanding a vote to determine the official's continued tenure. To the extent that legislation, parliamentary privileges, and constitutional conventions and laws govern elections, the operation of a recall amounts to an initiative insofar as voter action overrides existing practices and forms. As Zimmerman observed, "the recall is a natural extension to the petition referendum and the initiative," as a kind of completion to the populist understanding of representation as agency (Zimmerman, 1986, p. 105).

Besides the usual or conventional ways of replacing representatives, namely in elections, there are other modes available in both congressional and parliamentary regimes. In the US, officials may be removed by ordinary judicial process, by legislative address, by executive action, and by impeachment. In British common law, impeachment is a criminal proceeding, with the House of Commons serving as prosecutor and the House of Lords as judge. In the federal government of the United States, the House of Representatives initiates the proceedings and the Senate acts as judge. In the US, every state except Oregon has impeachment procedures, but they are seldom invoked; in Britain impeachment has not been used since 1806. As a judicial procedure, impeachment requires both proof and legislative action to remove an offending representative or official.[22]

---

21 Sometimes a distinction is drawn between a plebiscite and a referendum, the difference between the two being that a plebiscite is non-binding, which is to say it is little more than a public opinion poll administered by government.

22 I have been unable to find reference to a single instance of impeachment in Canada.

The great difference between impeachment and recall is indicated by the observation that the latter requires neither proof nor legislative action. So far as recall is concerned, neither establishing the truth nor the merit of charges of misconduct is an issue, which is to say it is primarily, and often entirely, a political rather than a judicial procedure (Cronin, 1989, p. 2).[23] One of the reasons for the popularity of recall procedures in the US is that impeachment is both difficult and cumbersome. "High crimes and misdemeanors" are not easily proven, and "low" crimes such as may be covered up by corrupt-practices regulations in Canada, or by provisions of the Criminal Code, are not usually considered sufficient grounds to initiate an impeachment process. As Patrick Boyer observed:

> In Canada, provisions in statutes such as the *Senate and the House of Commons Act,* or the various provincial statutes pertaining to the legislative assemblies and provincial constitutions, govern disqualification from office of an elected representative. Legislation relating to conflict of interest may also serve to remove elected officials who have breached the rules of conduct related to holding office. In either case, it should be strongly emphasized that these provisions for removal apply to legal procedures of impeachment, not to political procedures of recall. (Boyer, 1992a, p. 30)

An additional matter, not mentioned by Boyer, is that, in a parliamentary regime, one of the privileges of a legislature is to determine its own composition. In the American system the voters elect representatives and senators to the two chambers and they

---

23   Article 2(8) of the Constitution of Michigan explicitly acknowledges that, "the sufficiency of any statement of reason or grounds procedurally required [for recall] shall be a political rather than a judicial question" (quoted in Cronin, 1989, p. 127). The political basis for recall is an American approximation to what in a parliamentary regime would be called a privilege. As with "presidential immunity" from congressional scrutiny (apart from impeachment and trial) the emphasis on politics rather than law is justified on separation-of-powers grounds; such grounds cannot exist in a parliamentary regime when the government, the executive, sit as members of the House, nor when the legislature includes the Crown or its representative.

become members by reason of their election. In Canada, as early as 1759, the Speaker of the Legislative Assembly of Nova Scotia asked the governor for an assurance that the "usual privileges" would be granted, directly conforming to the precedent and convention of Britain. The most basic corporate privilege of the House concerns its composition. That is, the assembly has the unquestioned ability to decide whether a duly elected individual has the right to sit as a member of the House. Just as a member may be expelled for refusing to abide by the rules of the House, so the House may refuse to admit a member in the first place, a rejection that may be repeated if the member is re-elected (Maingot, 1982, ch. 11).[24] In short, the *Canada Elections Act* or its provincial counterparts provides the structure for the election of members, and may deal with disputed elections and practices, but the corporate body of the House determines its own membership. Even if a member is convicted of treason or any lesser indictable offence, it still requires a formal resolution of the House to unseat a member.

Recall was discussed during the American founding as a kind of revival of ancient Athenian ostracism. Article 5 of the Articles of [US] Confederation and Perpetual Union contained a recall provision. During the debates over these Articles, which led to the eventual drafting of the US Constitution, it quietly died from lack of support. During the 1890s, American socialists and populists advocated the procedure as a means of resisting "corruption" by the wealthy—a theme that reappeared in Canada shortly thereafter.

As in the United States, proponents of direct democracy in Canada have chiefly been westerners. The reason for western populism was obvious: "parliamentary institutions had not brought satisfactory federal policy" (Laycock, 1960, p. 37; Morton, 1944,

---

24   Louis Riel, for example, was twice expelled from the House of Commons; in 1946 Fred Rose, a Communist MP and convicted spy, was languishing in jail after his election. The Speaker then declared him "incapable of sitting or voting in this House" and issued his warrant to the chief electoral officer "to make out a new writ for the election of a new member" (House of Commons, 1947, p. 2). Likewise, an elected member who was insane could probably have his seat declared vacant (see Ward, 1950, pp. 75-6). This condition actually took place in the Ontario Legislature in 1884.

p. 292). The first legislative enactment of recall in North America was in 1903, as part of the charter of the city of Los Angeles (Bird and Ryan, 1930, pp. 2-3). Generally speaking, the American Progressives sought to enact the initiative and referendum to check the legislature, the direct primary to check the power of the party organization, and the recall to check the power of elected officials. All of this checking and balancing of interests, place, and ambition, was part of the climate of opinion that prevailed during the period of the American founding, the greatest expression of which can be found in *The Federalist*. Canadian politicians were familiar enough with the American arguments. During the Confederation period, they were debated in a language thoroughly akin to that of *The Federalist* (Hamilton *et al.*, 1961). A few decades later, when similar arguments emerged from politicians from western Canada, they were rebutted dogmatically, by invoking the language of constitutional monarchy, a formality that was scarcely considered in Canada during the 1860s.

It is true, of course, that both for parliamentary and for congressional regimes there is a common historical and, indeed, "philosophical" origin to the doctrine of balance and equipoise in government that may be traced to the historical experiences of the Italians during the fourteenth and fifteenth centuries.[25] We must emphasize, however, that notwithstanding similar regionally-based interests in Canada and the US directed historically against eastern interests, the legal and constitutional forms assumed by the quest for balanced interests, and the legal, constitutional, and conventional procedures that put that common quest for balance into operation, is different in Canada than it is in the United States. Hence the distinction made above between responsible, Cabinet, or parliamentary government and congressional, presidential, or republican government.[26] In this respect, the different

---

25   The "balance of power" among the fourteenth-century Italian city-states was reproduced in the succeeding centuries north of the Alps among the national states; the balance of the "most serene republic" of the Venetians was subsequently found to have been transferred to Britain by Harrington in the seventeenth century, from which it was translated to the British colonies (see Pocock, 1975).

political language of the two countries both reflected and developed the two distinct constitutional forms.

Moreover, even in the United States, notwithstanding the legal compatibility of its constitutional forms with direct democracy, critics have nevertheless argued that populist procedures go against sound republican principles, which hold that good legislators ought to be allowed to govern, which is to say, to lead and direct; it is contradicted as well by the principles of representative government, which emphasize the need to "refine" and "elevate" public opinion, to use the terms of *The Federalist*, rather than simply to reflect it (Simon, 1984, p. 11; Fountiane, 1988, pp. 733-76; *Federalist* 10 and 39 are particularly pertinent; Epstein, 1984, chs. 3, 6). In Canada, direct democracy runs afoul not of intellectual reservations and institutional counter weights[27] but of legal and Constitutional barriers. Chief among them is the position of the Crown.

The Crown

The Crown is not simply the presence of the sovereign in government but is, as David Smith said, the "organizing force" behind the executive, the legislature, the judiciary and the administration—in short, of all the organs of governance. The problem both for political science and for citizens, including most contemporary politicians, is that the influence of the Crown "remains largely invisible behind the shield of responsible government," the chief characteristic of which has come to be executive domination of the assembly (Smith, 1995, p. x; Savoie, 1999). The problem of making visible and articulate the formal reality of modern executive power lies in the fact that it is always exercised in the name of something else—of the Crown in Canada, of the people in the US.

---

26   There are many subtle distinctions that might be made on theoretical, historical, and even legal grounds regarding all these terms; for the moment all that is intended is a general textbook distinction (see, for instance, Dickerson and Flanagan, 1988, ch. 19).

27   A typical US study, for example, listed six arguments in favour of recall legislation and twelve against (see Zimmerman, 1986, pp. 123-29).

This does not mean that the executive is an errand boy. Far from it: it means precisely that executives exercise their real power by hiding it. Unmasking what is hidden and operates best when hidden is always a delicate business. In the fall of 1945, when the memory of wartime executive power was still fresh and the implications of its continuance, because of the cold war, were becoming apparent, an important debate, all but forgotten today, took place in the House of Commons. The Prime Minister was absent, in Washington discussing defence policy with the chief executives of Britain and the US, and the opposition mounted an attack upon executive rule and government by order-in-council. The leader of the opposition, Gordon Graydon, made the assertion that Cabinet was nothing but a "committee" of the House and that "Canada is governed by the House of Commons." The acting prime minister, J.L. Ilsley, corrected Mr. Graydon. Graydon was neither "historically nor constitutionally correct.... The authority of the government is not delegated by the House of Commons; [it] is received from the Crown," which is the head of the executive, and is advised by members of Cabinet. The CCF leader, M.J. Coldwell, dismissed this "fiction" with the same contempt shown by Mr. Graydon, who had called it "medieval," and declared: "real power is derived from the people of Canada" (House of Commons, 1945a, p. 2020; 1945b, pp. 2075-78). Ilsley, not Graydon nor Coldwell, was correct, but their objections pointed to a genuine problem, which Ilsley did not address.

A few years later, the Prime Minister of the day, Louis St. Laurent, recalled Ilsley's remarks and observed: "it is well to have the truth as one's inspiration, but it is sometimes wise to express only as much of it as one's supporters can be expected to accept" (National Archives of Canada, 1949, quoted in Smith, 1995, pp. 72, 206). This aspect of the ambivalence of the Canadian executive, Smith said, "proved a distinctly unseizable concept to explain" because it seemed to contradict "a much more entrenched view of responsible government." For this reason, if for no other, there have been very few attempts by ministers of the Crown to explain to the House of Commons and to the country that executive power is, in fact, derived downward from the Crown, not upward from the House or from the people (Smith, 1995, p. 72).

On the other side of the issue, the first Canadian parliamentarian to sign a recall resignation statement was O.R. Gould, elected after the 1919 by-election in Assiniboia. In the spring of 1920, the issue was debated at some length in the House of Commons. In April the following discussion took place:

> Mr. Gould: We believe in the principle of direct legislation. We also believe that with the initiative and the referendum you may have the recall. That is one of the planks of our platform, it is one of the things we discussed in our local. An agreement does exist between my committee, whose names I have read, and myself. Forty percent of the number of electors who voted at my election may, if I refuse to do what this committee asks me to do on the floor of this House—and that committee must meet very often and find out what public opinion is in the district of Assiniboia—if they advise me and I refuse to do that they can apply the recall, and ask me to go back. In going back I have the right of appearing before the people and giving an explanation of my attitude...
>
> Mr. Edwards: How many are on that committee?
>
> Mr. Gould: It is a committee of fifteen that was appointed by a general gathering of the people from all over the electoral district. Everybody was welcome, and they got together and appointed that committee and told them to proceed.
>
> Mr. Edwards: Did my hon. friend place his written resignation in the hands of that committee?
>
> Mr. Gould: To call the document I have placed in the hands of the committee a resignation is a misnomer. I did not place my resignation in the hands of the committee. That would be a very difficult thing to do in practice. It is an idea that has gradually attached itself to the principle of the recall. It is not correct to say that you place your resignation in the hands of a committee. I have not been asked to do that. Some of the members of my committee did put it that way, but after an explana-

tion they could all see the reason why such a thing could not exist.

Mr. Edwards: Would my hon. friend be good enough to place that agreement on Hansard for the information of the House?

Mr. Gould: The committee hold that agreement. I also have a copy, but I haven't it here. It is something that I would not be afraid to place on Hansard, and yet I do not think it absolutely necessary. I do not see what object it would serve. We take the stand that any individual can make whatever agreement he likes. Nothing can prevent you having your private agreement with a committee or a man. I am very pleased to say that some planks of our platform have been adopted by this Government, and the day will come when the recall will also be adopted. Public opinion will oblige whatever Government is in power to adopt that principle. (House of Commons, 1920, p. 1181)

The admission that he had, in effect, signed a recall notice three weeks later led to a motion to make the practice illegal under the Dominion Franchise Bill, which was then before the House (Dawson, 1933, pp. 189-90). There was no discussion of the effect of the recall on Constitutional forms; there was nothing said of the monarchic nature of parliamentary government; the larger issues raised in *The Federalist* were not considered either. Instead, the "scheme" was discussed in terms of its political wisdom, a highly elastic notion, and of its generally unparliamentary character. In the event, after the 1921 general election, many if not most of those elected from the west on the Progressive ticket were subject to recall. For opponents, recall remained simply a means of punishing instructed delegates for disobedience, which was contrary to their political or constitutional understanding of what a member of Parliament was. It was not until the *Dominion Elections Act* was revised during the spring of 1938 that any extensive discussion of the nature of representation by members of Parliament took place.

Mr. C.G. "Chubby" Power, Minister of Pensions and National Health, introduced the bill on April 5, 1938. In the course of defending changes to make the recall illegal under the act, he remarked:

> Another suggestion is to curb, if not to eradicate entirely, the practice which has grown up in recent years of submitting candidates to what I personally call a perfect plague of questionnaires, pledges and written undertakings that he will take such and such a course of action if elected... Our contention is that this forces a candidate to make a pronouncement, under duress, so to speak, on matters of which he cannot, during the election period, have had time to make a comprehensive study. It takes away from him and from the people themselves certain rights and is to some extent a negation of our democratic system of government whereby every member of this house represents all the people of Canada and not any individual class or section. (House of Commons, 1938a, p. 2040)

A few weeks later, when the bill was discussed in committee, Power again made the argument that the MP is "a representative of the whole dominion" and not "a mere delegate of a class or group or section" (House of Commons, 1938b, pp. 4393-4). Here he was on solid formal Constitutional as well as practical constitutional grounds. Elected members of the House of Commons are members *of* Parliament, not merely deputies or quasi-ambassadors *from* Assiniboia, as Gould seemed to assume. At the same time, however, one cannot help notice that Power was arguing in favour of a substantive political practice using the language of procedure and form. By the 1930s, it would seem, debate on the nature of representation, which is highly ambiguous, had hardened into a kind of doctrine or dogma. Members of the opposition thought there was something false in Power's argument, and they were right. But they were unable to state their objections in persuasive constitutional language. Power won, even if he did not win over, because he spoke for the government.

Direct democracy in the west

Federalism, John Stuart Mill once argued, allows for experiments in governing, much as liberal democracy allows for experiments in living. It is no great surprise to learn that the governments of the western provinces, as well as MPs from the west, tried to introduce direct democracy measures. In 1912, in Saskatchewan, the Liberal government of Premier Walter Scott introduced the *Direct Legislation Act* (S.S., 1912-13, c. 3). It provided for a 90-day interval following the close of a legislative session for a referendum petition to be submitted asking that a specific measure be referred to a vote of the electorate, excepting only measures granting supply. Some acts could be declared exempt from this provision if explicitly so identified, passed by a two-thirds majority, assented to, and proclaimed. A parallel initiative provision was also included.

Argument in favour of these measures was usually made in the language of democratization, familiar from the House of Commons, and of an alleged historical shift of the locus of sovereignty away from the king and onto the people. No concern was voiced regarding the formalities of parliamentary government. Nothing was said of the Crown as a safeguard of constitutional liberties, nor of the limitation upon government action that the existence of the Crown entails.[28] As Elizabeth Chambers remarked in her extensive analysis of the legislation, "little concern was expressed for the effect that the proposed system would have on the role of the lieutenant-governor or the Cabinet, or how the parliamentary system of government would function without strong political parties" (Chambers, 1968, p. 62). The premier had grave doubts about the constitutionality of the bill, notwithstanding the great political appeal of "increased democratization." He then decided to submit the direct legislation package itself to a referendum and set a double threshold: 30 percent of the electorate was required to take part, and a majority had to approve the proposal.[29] The

28 For a discussion of the constitutional importance of these questions see, besides Smith (1995), MacKinnon, 1976. See also the more polemical book by Farthing, 1957.

29 An Act to Submit to the Electors the Question of the Adoption of the *Direct Legislation Act*, S.S., 1912-13, c. 3.

high level of support required for passage and the low level of publicity accorded the referendum ensured its defeat, notwithstanding the five-to-one vote in its favour.[30] As a result, the *Direct Legislation Act* was repealed at the next session.

Alberta, not Manitoba, had the most extensive experience with direct democracy and gave this political doctrine the most extensive statutory expression. However, it was in the province of Manitoba that the incompatibility of populist measures and direct democracy with the Constitutional forms of responsible government was first decided in the courts. Manitobans climbed aboard the direct legislation bandwagon rolling across the prairies in 1916, but they had been flirting with the idea for some time before that, chiefly in the pages of the *Grain Growers' Guide*. In 1910, and again in 1914, the Liberals included direct legislation in their election platform, but they were unsuccessful at the polls. In the spring of 1912, Premier R.P. Roblin delivered a speech, famous in its day, denouncing direct legislation as "a denial of responsible government and a form of degenerate republicanism" that was being advocated by Liberals, who were "inflammatory demagogues, in order to pull the underpinning out from the British Empire." The conservative party, he thundered, "will have none of it!" (Manitoba *Free Press*, April 12, 1912. Also quoted in Morton, 1944, p. 285; Boyer, 1992b, p. 88; Adamson, 1980, p. 51).

In January 1914, an opposition Liberal MLA, C.D. McPherson, introduced a resolution calling for direct legislation, claiming the measure "is in direct accord with the British principles of government" (Manitoba Free Press, January 21, 1914). The government opposed the measure and nothing happened until the Roblin government fell in 1915 and was replaced by the Liberals who promptly passed the *Initiative and Referendum Act* (S.M. 1916, c. 59). As might be expected, the act was hailed in the assembly as a triumph of democracy, popular sovereignty, and the common sense of the common people (Manitoba *Free Press*, January 25, 1916).

---

30   In the referendum, 26,696 of 161,561 eligible voted in favour, and 4,897 voted against. This amounted to 16.52 percent of the vote, just over half the required number. See Smith, 1975, pp. 70-1.

Section 7 of the act gave the electors the power of making laws and s.11, in conjunction with s.9 (1), provided for the submission of laws to the electorate for censure and repeal. The essential feature was that the legislative assembly had passed a law that made it possible for a body other than itself, namely the electors of Manitoba, to pass and repeal laws. Once the Legislature of Manitoba passed this measure, however, the Cabinet had second thoughts and decided to refer the act to the courts for a ruling on its constitutionality.

Litigation in Manitoba

By agreement of all sides there was no argument at trial and the Chief Justice of the Court of King's Bench upheld the legislation. In the Manitoba Court of Appeal it was ruled unconstitutional, a judgement ultimately upheld by the Judicial Committee of the Privy Council in a decision written by Lord Haldane.

In rendering their unanimous decision, Chief Justice Howell, speaking with the rhetoric of a political scientist as much as with the rhetoric of a jurist, began by rehearsing the forms and conventions of parliamentary government. Sections 69 and 71 of the *BNA Act* (1867) and s.9 of the *Manitoba Act* (1870) make it clear that "the King shall be a part of each legislative body," though his duties remained unspecified and, therefore, must be found in convention and "the unwritten law and history" (1 WWR, 1012 at 1015-16). Whatever those duties may be, he said,

> If the proposed Act is within the powers of the Legislature, then all powers of legislation could be taken from the Legislative Assembly and given to the democracy and the Assembly could be wiped out. Representative Government would cease to exist and there would be a reign of pure democracy, and yet, into it there must be placed the power of the King as the chief executive and as part of the legislature.

Warming to his theme, Howell, CJ, continued:

The Crown is a vital portion of the legislative power, and there is no provision for the representative of the King having any part in this proposed legislation, and apparently there might be legislation in defiance of s.53 and s.54. The law apparently is to take effect without the assent of the Crown. Who is to advise the Lieutenant-Governor as to these bills which are voted on, and who is to be responsible for the legislation? If a bill was passed which did not meet with the approval of the Chief Minister, the Lieutenant-Governor would be without an adviser, and there would be no representative of the people responsible for the legislation. This, it seems to me, would be legislation regarding the office of the Lieutenant-Governor.

Then and now, altering the office of the lieutenant-governor is beyond the legislative competence of any province or of the federal government; in 1919, it would have required a piece of imperial legislation, and today it requires a constitutional amendment taken under s. 41 of the *Constitution Act* (1982), which requires unanimity.

Howell's colleague, Justice Richards, agreed in even stronger language:

In Canada there is no sovereignty in the people. So far as we are concerned it is in the Parliament at Westminster, and our powers to legislate are such, and only such, as that Parliament has given us... Our legislature consists of the Lieutenant-Governor and the Legislative Assembly. To substitute the popular vote for that of the Legislative Assembly would leave us without a legislature.

The other judges, in offering their reasons for judgement, agreed the legislation was *ultra vires* the Legislature of Manitoba.

In short, the Manitoba Court of Appeal confirmed a number of well known Constitutional forms regarding the nature of the legislature in a parliamentary regime. The Crown is an integral part of the legislature and its representative, the lieutenant-governor, has to fulfill specified procedural duties in order that legislation be passed. In addition, however, the practical or substantive purpose of the legislative assembly as a forum for debate, deliberation, and amendment was also mentioned. Both substantive and formal aspects of the legislature and the Legislative Assembly of Manitoba were attacked in the "direct democracy" legislation.

On appeal to the Judicial Committee, Lord Haldane confirmed the reasoning of the Manitoba court, adding that the purpose of the constitution of Canada was "to form... a Dominion with a constitution similar in principle to that of the United Kingdom" (3 WWR, 1919, 1 at 4. These were, of course, the well-known words of the preamble to the *BNA Act*). Their main point, however, was that

> Their Lordships are of opinion that the language of the Act cannot be construed otherwise than as intended seriously to affect the position of the Lieutenant-Governor as an integral part of the Legislature, and to detract from rights which are important in the legal theory of that position. For if the Act is valid it compels him to submit a proposed law to a body of voters totally distinct from the Legislature of which he is the constitutional head, and renders him powerless to prevent its becoming an actual law if approved by a majority of these voters... Thus the Lieutenant-Governor appears to be wholly excluded from the new legislative authority.

These considerations are sufficient to establish the *ultra vires* character of the act.

Legal commentary

The legal argument as well as the political evidence laid before the JCPC seem to be conclusive. However, as with other seemingly authoritative decisions, where lawyers and law professors are involved, nothing is conclusive. It is no surprise, therefore, that this decision by the JCPC has been challenged in the law journals, though not in the courts.[31]

Most of this commentary fails to accord sufficient weight to forms and procedures. To take but one example: at the same time as Peter Hogg accused their lordships of deciding the issue on weak grounds, namely the formal role of the lieutenant-governor, he said they overlooked the stronger grounds to rule the *Initiative and Referendum Act* invalid. "A more substantial objection could be made to legislation by initiative and referendum," he said, "and that is, that the process bypasses the province's legislative assembly" (Hogg, 1992, 14.2(e), pp. 14-12. See also Morton, 1944, p. 288; Dawson, 1933, p. 58. On the other side, Cheffins and Johnson, 1986, pp. 74-5). If by "substantial" Hogg means that such an objection may be rhetorically powerful because it appeals directly to popular understanding of the assembly as an organ of self-government and democracy, that is, as a congress, there is probably great merit to his words. However, the assembly, in a parliamentary form of government, is but one element of the legislature. Just as it is impossible for a legislature to function without an executive council and without the Crown, so too, it cannot function without the assembly (except in emergencies when by convention it is possible to govern by order-in-council). In other words, Hogg's objection to a process that "bypasses the province's legislative assembly," applies equally to a process that bypasses Cabinet or the lieutenant-governor. The formal composition of the legislature includes all three elements.

So far as the issue of powers reserved to the electorate is concerned, the importance of the Manitoba Initiative and Referendum Reference is twofold. First, it brought to light very clearly the formal conflict between the institutions of parliamentary representative government and the requirements of direct or populist

---

31 See Scott, 1966-67, pp. 550-56; Boyer, 1982, p. 36. Boyer cited in agreement Whyte and Lederman, 1977, pp. 1-27. See also Hogg, 1992, 14.2(d), 14-10. This position was reiterated by Conacher, 1991, p. 188, who was a strong supporter of "popular sovereignty" and considers it to be, in some respects, compatible with parliamentary government. See also Mallory, 1984, p. 23.

democracy. Second and more broadly, it illustrated the conflict between the populist desire to exercise the power of government against, not through, its formal institutions using whatever agency is available to give effect to the popular will, whether or not that agency is formally and legally compatible with existing institutions. For this reason, notwithstanding the arguments as well as the ruling of the JCPC, populist direct democrats continued to argue that "democracy" is not served by the institutions of responsible and parliamentary government. This argument involves both constitutional and Constitutional forms, which is to say that the Manitoba reference indicated clearly that the conflict between direct democracy and representative government is a formal conflict before it is anything else.

Direct democracy in Alberta

Turning to Alberta: between March 1913 and April 1916, the Alberta legislature enacted three laws providing for the initiative and referendum (R.S.A. 1922, c. 6. Further amendments took place throughout the 1920s and 1930s: R.S.A. 1941, c. 7). The impetus for these measures came from the United Farmers of Alberta, the most powerful social and political organization in the province. Liberal premier A.L. Sifton introduced the bills and the Conservative opposition was able only to criticize the details (see Thomas, 1959, pp. 134-40). The operation of the act was nearly identical to the proposals introduced in Saskatchewan. It was used chiefly to obtain the views of the electorate regarding the controversial question of prohibition.

In 1915, a petition was presented to the legislative assembly praying that a bill be passed prohibiting the sale of liquor. In 1916, the *Alberta Liquor Act* was passed, the terms of which were practically identical to the wording of a referendum that, in turn, was supported by a majority of those voting for it. Four years later, Nat Bell Liquors, Ltd., was charged with violating the *Liquor Act* and fined $200. The company appealed its conviction on two grounds and eventually was heard by the Judicial Committee of the Privy Council, Lord Sumner delivering the judgement (2 A.C., 1922, 128-68). Unlike the Manitoba Reference, however, the JCPC found the Alberta act constitutional because it had been passed according to the required forms and procedures, even though it deferred "to the will of the people" inasmuch as it was adopted "without material alteration" of language used in the petition. In fact, the provisions of the *Direct Legislation Act* required that the language used in the petition be reproduced in the legislation, which is to say, the act imposed a statutory duty on the provincial legislature. As Berriedale Keith remarked,

> the reasoning of the judicial committee seems to over-look one vital point: the procedure under the act de-prives the legislature of any deliberative function whatever, and turns it into a mere machine for register-ing the decrees of the people. It deprives the legislature of the whole business of shaping a law, since it is not permitted to make any substantial change, and it de-prives the people of the profit to be derived from the in-telligent discussion of the proposed measure by the legislature. There is nothing in the judgement to show that this aspect of the case was present to the Court, and it is, of course, wholly contrary to British political views to treat a member of the legislature as sent there simply to carry out the instructions of his constituents (Keith, 1922, pp. 240-1. See also Scott, 1966-67, which essen-tially echoes Keith's objections).

In addition, as Peter Hogg pointed out, the effect of the law was to require future legislatures "to enact whatever policies were deter-mined upon by the initiative and referendum process," which clearly violated the rule that no legislature can bind its successor (Hogg, 1992, 14.2 (e), pp. 14-13, 14; see also Conacher, 1992, pp. 188-9). In the event, the *Direct Legislation Act* was never again used and, in 1958, was repealed "as a result of someone making inqui-ries about the possibility of using it" (Boyer, 1982, p. 34). Ordi-nary political practice proved more decisive than the legal reasoning of their lordships or criticism of it.

In April 1936, the Legislative Assembly of Alberta passed the *Social Credit Measures Act* along with "the first recall bill ever to be passed in the British Empire" (Mallory, 1954, p. 67). The story of the passage of the *Recall Act* and its first use, against the premier, has often been told, usually with glee by individuals who were opposed not only to Social Credit and William Aberhart, but to the spirit of self-sufficiency and initiative that the Social Credit legislation symbolized to Albertans.[32] The Social Credit legislation, nearly all of which was either disallowed or reserved by the lieutenant-governor, was inspired by the same doctrines of representation as was the *Recall Act*. The lesson would appear to be that, for different reasons, the complex of laws intended to implement direct democracy and institute populism were withdrawn because they proved incompatible with the practices, conventions, and forms of parliamentary government. Chubby Power knew this beforehand. William Aberhart found out the harder way.

Direct democracy in BC

That left only British Columbia. In fulfillment of an election promise by Liberal premier John Oliver, late in March 1919, British Columbia passed an *Act to Provide for the Initiation and Approval of Legislation by the Electors* (SBC, 1919, c. 21). It was not proclaimed after being passed, however, pending the outcome of the Manitoba case. When the judicial committee handed down its decision in July, the law was not proclaimed at all. The reason, according to the attorney general of the day, Mr. J.W. de B. Farris, was because of "the uncertainty as to its constitutional validity" (Adams, 1958, ch. 1, fn. 14, p. 166). It was listed in the *Statutes of British Columbia* until 1923 but was not included in the *Revised Statutes of B.C.* of 1924, except as a note indicating it was never in force. The act remained on the statute books, never having been repealed and, as Patrick Boyer observed in 1992, "could become law if proclaimed by the lieutenant-governor" (Boyer, 1992b, p. 93).

Over the years, several plebiscites have been organized in BC under provisions of the *Elections Act*, most of which involved beer, wine, or daylight savings time. On July 5, 1990, shortly after the

---

32   A fairly balanced account of this peculiar episode in Alberta's political history is found in McCormick, 1991, pp. 269-300.

demise of the Meech Lake Accord, the Social Credit government of William VanderZalm introduced Bill 55, the *BC Referendum Act*, for first reading (RSBC, 1990, c. 400). The government went out of its way to ensure that the legislation was compatible with the traditions of Parliament. Sections 4 and 5 explicitly indicated that the results were advisory only for the government that enacted it.

After expressing a certain amount of misgiving, both from the Social Credit government and from the NDP opposition, two questions were submitted to voters in conjunction with the October 17, 1991 general election (BC Legislative Assembly, 1990, pp. 11294-5). The first dealt with the citizens' right to initiate a referendum and the second asked whether voters were in favour of a right of recall. Both questions received very strong support from the electorate, though the government that sponsored them was defeated and the NDP was left to deal with the results. Eventually the new government appointed a committee to look into the kind of process that British Columbians wished to see in place, and in late November 1993, they produced their *Report on Recall and Initiative*.

A tone of reluctance permeates the report. At one point the committee echoed Patrick Boyer and said, "it must be acknowledged that the concepts of recall and initiative are alien to our parliamentary system of government." If, nevertheless, support for such measures was widespread, this "may be a symptom of the anger and resentment that many Canadians feel towards the institutions of our contemporary political systems" (British Columbia Legislative Assembly, 1993, p. 10).[33] Notwithstanding the reservations of the committee and, no doubt, of the government of

---

33 There was a similar reluctance to be found in the Reform Party, notwithstanding the populism that inspired its success. In *The New Canada* (pp. 325-6), for example, Preston Manning advocated the introduction of a special initiative to recall members of the House, but with a "quite high" threshold "so as not to result in recall being used simply as a partisan device for unseating political opponents." Since that is precisely what a recall is designed and intended to do, and since there are already ample means of expelling "corrupt" members of the House, one wonders why Reformers bother with recall at all, since they do not also advocate changing the regime.

Michael Harcourt, the required legislation was quickly passed (RSBC, 1996, c. 398). The recall provisions have, in fact, been invoked. Whether the legislation has been a political success is a matter for the citizens of BC to determine. Formally, the law certainly looks to be constitutional. Were it ever tested in the courts, an adverse judgement would probably turn on the weight accorded conventions and privilege, aspects of the constitution that courts are reluctant to examine. On the other hand, in the New Brunswick Broadcasting case, Canadian courts have shown no reluctance at all in ruling on questions of privilege (*New Brunswick Broadcasting Co. vs. Nova Scotia* [1993] 1 S.C.R. 319), so no one can say with confidence what the courts might say, in this area as in so many others.

Let me turn briefly, to my second point, the existence of a genuine tradition of popular sovereignty within the formal Constitutional structure that assumes the sovereignty of the Crown.

Popular sovereignty and confederation

It has become an interpretative commonplace that the Fathers of Confederation were primarily dealmakers, not philosophers like the American Founding Fathers. Jefferson, Madison, Hamilton, they say, were philosophers; Macdonald and Galt and Cartier surely were not. John Ibbitson wrote not long ago in the *Globe and Mail*: "The Americans rightly revere their founding fathers; the American constitution is a magnificent thing. The Fathers of Confederation, on the other hand, should have been horsewhipped... Maybe it was the champagne at Charlottetown, or the rain at Quebec. But the framers of the *British North America Act* bequeathed Canada one of the democratic world's worst constitutions" (Ibbitson, 2000, p. A4). Academics are usually more evasive than journalists and would never dream of declaring the Canadian constitution one of the worst. Instead they damn with the faintest of praise.

In 1962, for example, Peter Waite, in his classic study, *The Life and Times of Confederation*, remarked that "Confederation had a fundamentally empirical character" (1962, p. 24). A year later, Frank

Underhill announced in his Massey Lectures, "the Canadian Fathers [of Confederation] in contrast to the US Founders, were ignorant of philosophy" (1964, ch. 1).[34] According to Ed Black, "Confederation was born in pragmatism without the attendance of a readily definable philosophic rationale" (1975, p. 4). Donald Smiley agreed: "Unlike Americans in the eighteenth century... Canadians have never experienced the kind of decisive break with their political past, which would have impelled them to debate and resolve fundamental political questions" (1980, p. 185). In 1987, Phil Resnick had the temerity to suggest that the Fathers of Confederation might actually have read a few books and applied some of the insights of Montesquieu to the development of the constitution (1987, pp. 97-115. See also Ajzenstat, 1987a, pp. 117-120; Preece, 1987, pp. 121-24; and Resnick's reply, 1987, pp. 125-29). A decade later, however, commentators had strongly restored the old orthodoxy (Martin, 1995), and as late as 2000, Ramsay Cook could magisterially sum up a generation of opinion: "It is well known that the Fathers of Confederation were pragmatic lawyers for the most part, more given to fine tuning the details of a constitutional act than waxing philosophical about human rights or national goals" (2000, p. 82).

Cook's opinion was clearly untenable when he wrote it, chiefly as a result of the outstanding restorative analyses of Janet Ajzenstat (1999; 1987b; and forthcoming). The Fathers of Confederation were not just empirical, pragmatic lawyers, devoid of coherent opinions, ideas, or political vision, which is all that is usually meant in this context by the term "philosophy."

As Ajzenstat said, "if we were to rely only on what we know of the Fathers from the Charlottetown and Quebec Conferences, it would be easy to conclude there's no philosophy in our founding. The meetings were held behind closed doors; we have records, though not complete ones. What we have indeed seems to show a pragmatic group of men with their minds on business, doing a deal. There's no philosophy on parade" (Ajzenstat, *et al.*, 1999, pp. 2-3). But when we look at the debates over accepting or rejecting

---

34   A few years earlier, he was lamenting the absence of a Canadian Burke or Mill or even of a Jefferson or Hamilton. See Underhill, 1960, pp. 6-7.

the deal, or the "treaty" as Macdonald liked to call it, a different picture emerges.

In this context they *thought* about ratification and about how to legitimate the new body politic. The issues of legitimating and of founding a new regime go to the heart of political philosophy. Whether they wanted to or not, legislators in every one of the assemblies in British North America were driven to philosophize about the new government. They spoke of liberty, political participation, the duties of representatives, of ambition and how to keep it within bounds, of loyalty and patriotism, of political obligation and obedience to law. Most importantly, they were compelled to address the central question in the issue of ratification: will legislative resolutions suffice to legitimize the founding of the new nation or must the sovereign people be consulted directly?

Because they have focussed so strongly on the formalities and doctrines of the Constitution and on a simple and abstract tale of evolution, "from colony to nation," Canadian historians and political scientists have simply accepted, in Peter Russell's words, that "at Canada's founding its people were not sovereign, and there was not even a sense that a constituent sovereign people would have to be invented" (1993, p. 5). But as Ajzenstat proves beyond question, this is not so. Conservative or Liberal, pro- or anti-Confederation, the starting point was that the people are the repository of rightful constituent power. Here's one statement, uncontradicted because it was so widely assumed to be true: the "people are the only rightful source of all political power," said James O'Halloran, in the Canadian Legislative Assembly, on March 8, 1865 (reprinted in Ajzenstat, *et al.*, 1999, p. 449). The only issue of moment was: how were the people to make their wishes known?

One side, mostly anti-Confederation, argued for consultation by referendum or a single-issue election in each province. "The principle which lies at the foundation of our constitution," said William Lawrence of Nova Scotia, "is that which declares the people to be the source of political power" (reprinted in Ajzenstat, *et al.*, 1999, p. 385). O'Halloran in the Canadian Legislative Assembly agreed: "If we [legislators] do not consult the people, we arrogate to ourselves a right never conferred upon us, and our act is a usurpation" (reprinted in Ajzenstat, *et al.*, 1999, p. 45). William Gilbert of New Brunswick sounded a lot like Locke: "The only way in which the constitution of a free, intelligent and independent people can be changed at all," he said, "is by revolution or the consent of the people" (reprinted in Ajzenstat, *et al.*, 1999, p. 408). By implication, in Gilbert's view, Confederation was a Canadian Revolution. Gilbert was not alone in his opinion. J.S. Helmcken of BC declared, "it is for the people to say whether they will have confederation or not" (reprinted in Ajzenstat, *et al.*, 1999, p. 411). On the other side of the continent, Thomas Glen of Newfoundland said: "The constitution was granted, not to the House of Assembly, but to the people of Newfoundland," and he considered the people were entitled to be consulted before the House of Assembly came to a decision (reprinted in Ajzenstat, *et al.*, 1999, p. 394).

These appeals to popular sovereignty, it nearly goes without saying, were passionate and principled because the individuals involved on all sides of the issue thought that a great deal was at stake. James Currie of Canada said the new arrangement would "vote away our whole constitution" (Reprinted in Ajzenstat, *et al.*, eds., 1999, p. 439). George Sinclair of Newfoundland said the delegates at Quebec City had "signed away our rights" (reprinted in Ajzenstat, *et al.*, 1999, p. 401). These were sentiments that expressed a clear sense that what was happening could not be undone. This was a *constitution* they were debating and constitutions are intended to endure. Said Benjamin Seymour of Canada: "Here you propose to change the constitution—to change the whole fabric of society—in fact to revolutionize society, without asking the consent of the people, and without the possibility—at any rate the reasonable possibility—of this important change ever being reconsidered" (reprinted in Ajzenstat, *et al.*, 1999, p. 431). Stewart Campbell of Nova Scotia was concerned that, if the measure were passed now, "it will be passed forever—the doom of Nova Scotia will then be sealed" (reprinted in Ajzenstat, *et al.*, 1999, p. 375).

The other side, mostly pro-Confederation, said that Parliament *is* the people and parliamentary resolutions are enough. John Mercer Johnson of New Brunswick remarked: "The legislature when they meet are the people, and they have the power to deal with all questions that may occur during their existence. They are the people for all legislative purposes" (reprinted in Ajzenstat, *et al.*, 1999, p. 411). David Christie of Canada said: " Submitting a statute to the popular vote in order to give it force of law is unheard of in British constitutional practice." Many, many others agreed with the sentiment that direct consultation was simply "un-British" (reprinted in Ajzenstat, *et al.*, 1999, p. 438).

But an appeal to tradition is a very weak appeal, and the parliamentary party buttressed their argument with criticism of what they called unbridled democracy, mob rule, or extreme democracy. They had in mind, and many could recall, the populist excesses of Papineau and Mackenzie in 1837. Thus Sir John A. remarked:

> Sir, a reference to the people—a direct reference to the people—of a question of this kind may be the means by which a despot, an absolute monarch, may get that popular confirmation and approval which he desires for the laws necessary to support a continuation of his usurpation. It may be the means by which a despot, at the point of the bayonet, may ask the people to vote yea or nay on a measure he proposes; but in every free country where there is a constitution at all, the vote must be taken by the constituted authorities, the representatives of the people, and not become a mere form and cover to tyranny, but a measure which accords with the calm and deliberate judgements of the people, as expressed through their representatives. (Reprinted in Ajzenstat, *et al.*, 1999, p. 459)

We note in passing not only that Macdonald sought "the calm and deliberate judgements of the people, as expressed through their representatives," but that the judgement of the people was final. Such sentiments and arguments would be entirely at home in *The Federalist Papers*.

Moreover, Macdonald was suspicious of direct consultation because a referendum *cannot* represent the people or their calm and deliberate judgement. All it can do is represent the majority of the moment—what older contemporaries, J.S. Mill and Tocqueville, feared as the tyranny of the majority. In contrast, Parliament protects all the people by protecting the opposition as well as the ministry. Here is Macdonald's description of the proposed federal Parliament:

> We will enjoy here that which is the great test of constitutional freedom—we will have the rights of the minority respected. In all countries the rights of the majority take care of themselves, but it is only in countries like England, enjoying constitutional liberty, and safe from the tyranny of a single despot or of an unbridled democracy that the rights of minorities are regarded. (Reprinted in Ajzenstat, *et al.*, 1999, p. 206)

The minorities Macdonald was concerned with were *political* minorities, not religious, or ethnic or visible minorities, and Parliament, he said, respects minorities better than referendums. Better to make constitutions by Parliaments, he said—to say nothing of ordinary legislation—because Parliaments better respect the opposition, and so better respect the sovereign people.

So there are the two genuine sides to the debate over the constitution, the one fearing the destruction of existing liberties if the new constitution were adopted, the other promising that liberties best will be protected if this same constitution were adopted; the one appealing directly to the people because a revolution is happening, the other appealing to Parliament because it is the best way to forestall the disorder of violent revolution. Unlike the dogmatic certainties of their successors, where "democracy" was evoked in opposition to "Parliament," the political minds of the Confederation period understood the need to harmonize practice and principle, substance and form.

Conclusion

Machiavelli once said: "a country that is compelled to change its constitution is unhappy." In the present context we must wonder whether the appeal to direct democracy today is akin to the appeal of 90 years ago in Western Canada: the present constitution has usurped liberties and must be changed; the present constitution cannot make visible and reconcile our interests and our pride. On the contrary, it is a source of shame and frustration. If, indeed, British Columbians or Albertans do feel that way, then the only remedy is Locke's "appeal to heaven," which as Gilbert and Seymour well knew from the words just quoted, meant revolution—or as we say nowadays, "rebalancing the federation" or even "reconfederation."

That is, perhaps, the only remedy for the usurpation of liberty. Readers of Donald Savoie's *Governing from the Centre,* or those who have read the report of the "Citizens Forum on Canada's Future," will know a case can be made that liberties have been usurped. The only question is: can a change of regime in the direction of direct democracy restore them? Or will it lead to precisely the kind of tyranny that Macdonald feared? These are questions for citizens, not political scientists, to consider, even though an answer can appear only in the hard realm of political action, where many sparrows fall.

My third point, then, can be stated with brevity: if Canadians, or perhaps only British Columbians, or Albertans, or Quebeckers, seek to exercise directly those powers reserved to the electorate, they will have to confront and deal with inhibiting Constitutional formalities as well as a more encouraging constitutional substance.

References

Adams, Audrey Marilyn (1958). Letter from Senator Farris (as he then was) to Adams on April 12, 1956. Quoted in *A Study of the Use of Plebiscites and Referendums by the Province of British Columbia.* MA Thesis. Vancouver: University of British Columbia.

Adamson, Agar (1980). "We Were Here Before: The Referendum in Canadian Experience." *Policy Options* (March).

Ajzenstat, Janet (1987a). "Comment: The Separation of Powers in 1867." *Canadian Journal of Political Science* 20: 117-120.

_____ (1987b). *The Political Thought of Lord Durham*. Montreal: McGill-Queen's University Press.

_____ (forthcoming, 2003). *The Once and Future Canadian Democracy*. Montreal and Kingston: McGill Queen's University Press.

Ajzenstat, Janet, Paul Romney, Ian Gentles, and William D. Gairdner, eds. (1999). *Canada's Founding Debates*. Toronto: Stoddart.

Birch, A.H. (1964). *Representative and Responsible Government*. London: Allen and Unwin.

Bird, Frederick L. and Frances M. Ryan (1930). *The Recall of Public Officers: A Study of the Operation of the Recall in California*. New York: Macmillan.

Black, Edwin R. (1975). *Divided Loyalties*. Montreal: McGill-Queen's University Press.

Boyer, J. Patrick (1982). *Lawmaking by the People: Referendums and Plebiscites in Canada*. Toronto: Butterworths.

_____ (1992a). *The People's Mandate: Referendums and a More Democratic Canada*. Toronto: Dundurn.

_____ (1992b). *Direct Democracy in Canada: The History and Future of Referendums*. Toronto: Dundurn.

British Columbia Legislative Assembly (1990). *Debates*. 34th Parliament, 4th Session, vol. 19 (July 24): 11294-5.

British Columbia Legislative Assembly (1993). Select Standing Committee on Parliamentary Reform, Ethical Conduct, Standing Orders and Private Bills. *Report on Recall and Initiative*. Ujjal Dosanjh, MLA, Chairperson. (November 23).

Chambers, Elizabeth (1968). "The Referendum and the Plebiscite." In Norman Ward and Duff Spafford, eds. *Politics in Saskatchewan*. Toronto: Longmans.

Cheffins, R.I. and P.A. Johnson (1986). *The Revised Canadian Constitution: Politics as Law*. Toronto: McGraw Hill.

Conacher, Duff (1991). "Power to the People: Initiative, Referendum, Recall and the Possibility of Popular Sovereignty in Canada." *University of Toronto Faculty of Law Review* 49/2.

Cook, Ramsay (2000). "Canada 2000: Towards a Post-Nationalist Canada," *Cité Libre* (Fall).

Cronin, Thomas E. (1989). *Direct Democracy: The Politics of Initiative, Referendum and Recall*. Cambridge: Harvard University Press.

Dawson, Robert MacGregor, ed. (1933). *Constitutional Issues in Canada: 1900-31*. Toronto: Oxford University Press.

Dawson, R. MacGregor and Norman Ward (1964). *The Government of Canada*, 4th ed. Toronto: University of Toronto Press.

Dickerson, Mark O. and Thomas Flanagan (1988). "Parliamentary and Presidential Systems." Chapter 19 in *An Introduction to Government and Politics*, 2nd edition. Toronto: Nelson Canada.

Epstein, David E. (1984). *The Political Theory of the Federalist*. Chicago: University of Chicago Press, chs. 3, 6.

Farthing, John (1957). *Freedom Wears a Crown*. Judith Robinson, ed. Introduction by E.D. Fulton, M.P. Toronto: Kingswood House.

Franks, C.E.S. (1987). *The Parliament of Canada*. Toronto: University of Toronto Press.

Fountaine, C.L. (1988). "Lousy Lawmaking: Questioning the Desirability and Constitutionality of Legislating by Initiative." *Southern California Law Review* 61: 733-76.

Granatstein, Jack L. (1998). *Who Killed Canadian History?* Toronto: Harper Collins.

Hamilton, Alexander, James Madison, and John Jay (1961). *The Federalist*. Jacob E. Cooke, ed. Middletown: Wesleyan University Press.

Hogg, Peter (1992). *Constitutional Law of Canada*, 3rd ed. 2 vols. Toronto: Carswell.

House of Commons (1920). *Debates* (April13). Reprinted in Dawson, 1933, pp. 188-89.

_____ (1938a). *Debates* (April 5).

_____ (1938b). *Debates* (June 29).

_____ (1945a). *Debates* (November 12).

_____ (1945b). *Debates* (November 13).

_____ (1947). *Debates* (January 30).

Ibbitson, John (2000). "BNA Act Spawned 113 Years of Complaints." *The Globe and Mail* (August 17): A4.

Keith, Berriedale (1922). "Notes on Imperial Constitutional Law." *Journal of Comparative Legislation and International Law* 4.

Laycock, David (1960). *Populism and Democratic Thought in the Canadian Prairies: 1910-1945*. Toronto: University of Toronto Press.

MacKinnon, Frank (1976). *The Crown in Canada*. Calgary: McClelland Stewart West.

Maingot, Joseph (1982). *Parliamentary Privilege in Canada*. Toronto: Butterworths.

Manitoba *Free Press*, various issues, 1912-1916.

Mallory, J.R. (1954). *Social Credit and the Federal Power in Canada*. Toronto: University of Toronto Press.

Manning Preston (1992). *The New Canada*. Toronto: Macmillan.

Martin, Ged (1995). *Britain and the Origins of Canadian Confederation, 1837-67*. Vancouver: UBC Press.

McCormick, Peter (1991). "Provision for the Recall of Elected Officials: Parameters and Prospects." In Michael Cassidy, ed., *Democratic Rights and Electoral Reform in Canada*. Royal Commission on Electoral Reform and Party Financing. Research Studies. Vol. 10. Toronto: Dundurn.

_____ (1984). *The Structure of Canadian Government*, rev. ed. Toronto: Gage.

Morton, W.L. (1944). "Direct Legislation and the Origins of the Progressive Movement." *Canadian Historical Review* 25.

National Archives of Canada, St. Laurent Papers. Letter from Louis St. Laurent to Alan Macnaughton.[b]No. it is a letter from Louis St Laurent to Alan Macnaughton, dated 28 October, 1949, quoted in Smith's book; the original is in the National Archives. Dated October 28, 1949. N-10-5 (a) "National Status." Quoted in Smith, *The Invisible Crown*, 72, 206.

Pocock, J.G.A. (1975). *The Machiavellian Moment: Florentine Political Thought and the Atlantic Republican Tradition*. Princeton: Princeton University Press.

Preece, Rod (1987). "Comment: Montesquieuan Principles of Canadian Politics?" *Canadian Journal of Political Science* 20: 121-24.

Resnick, Philip (1987). "Montesquieu Revisited, or The Mixed Constitution and the Separation of Powers in Canada." *Canadian Journal of Political Science* 20: 97-115 and 125-29.

Russell, Peter (1993). *Constitutional Odyssey: Can Canadians Become a Sovereign People?* 2nd ed. Toronto: University of Toronto Press.

Savoie, Donald J. (1999). *Governing From the Centre: The Concentration of Power in Canadian Politics*. Toronto: University of Toronto Press.

Scott, Stephen (1966-67). "Constituent Authority and the Canadian Provinces." *McGill Law Journal* 12.

Simon, Lucinda (1984). "Representative Democracy Challenged." *State Legislatures* 10: 11.

Smiley, Donald (1980). *Canada in Question: Federalism in the Eighties*, 3rd. ed. Toronto: McGraw-Hill Ryerson.

Smith, David E. (1975). *Prairie Liberalism: The Liberal Party in Saskatchewan, 1905-71*. Toronto: University of Toronto Press.

_____ (1995). *The Invisible Crown: The First Principle of Canadian Government*. Toronto: University of Toronto Press.

Stewart, John B. (1977). *The Canadian House of Commons: Procedure and Reform*. Montreal: McGill-Queen's University Press.

Thomas, L.G. (1959). *The Liberal Party in Alberta: A History of Politics in the Province of Alberta, 1905-21*. Toronto: University of Toronto Press.

Underhill, Frank (1960). *In Search of Canadian Liberalism*. Toronto: Macmillan.

_____ (1964). *The Image of Confederation*. Toronto: CBC, ch. 1.

Waite, Peter (1962). *The Life and Times of Confederation, 1967-1867: Politics, Newspapers and the Union of British North America*. Toronto: University of Toronto Press.

Ward, Norman (1950). *The Canadian House of Commons: Representation*. Toronto: University of Toronto Press.

Whyte, John D. and William R. Lederman (1977). *Canadian Constitutional Law: Cases, Notes and Materials*, 2nd edition. Toronto: Butterworths.

Zimmerman, Joseph F. (1986). *Participatory Democracy: Populism Revived*. New York: Praeger.

CHAPTER 9
The Substance of Reform

Discussion by Scott Reid, MP

Let me start by going through a number of the themes that Professor Cooper has hit upon. He started by making reference to the Constitution of Canada, which he says is not as favourable towards the introduction of direct democratic measures as the US Constitution.

I might rephrase that slightly. I don't think I would be wrong in saying that the written constitution in Canada would seem to be unfavourable towards direct legislation, whereas the unwritten constitution allows more freedom. This is curious because our written constitution is really the American-style part of our constitution, and the unwritten part of it is the British-style part of our constitution. This, in itself, reflects the fact that we have evolved from our British roots. We were really the first society within the British context, aside from the American colonies, that actually had any form of written constitutional framework. This indicates the flexibility of that particular system.

I will break Barry Cooper's chief premises into three.

Parliamentary system hinders direct democracy

The first is that Canada's monarchial/parliamentary system is not as congenial to direct democracy as is the US congressional system, for a variety of highly technical reasons that are based on the nominal derivation of sovereignty in Canada and in all British societies from the Crown, rather than from the people. This is the essence of the reference decision in Manitoba, and also of the countering decision in the Nat Bell liquor case that decided that Alberta's direct legislation law was, in fact, constitutional. This is the source of the distinction Prof. Cooper makes—quite a good distinction between "directory" versus "mandatory" referenda. Directory referenda are those that offer direction to the government, but do not actually force it to act in a certain way. The more common parlance for distinguishing between these two type of referenda is: "advisory" versus "mandatory." We would find that advisory referenda are permissible; mandatory referenda are not constitutionally permissible. Note, however, that "Nothing is conclusive where lawyers are involved," and the Manitoba and Alberta jurisprudence has been challenged in the law journals, if not in the courts.

Indeed the argument in favour of direct democracy, and of the validity of direct democracy, goes back much earlier than the Manitoba and Alberta cases, to Albert Venn Dicey, the great British constitutionalist. He wrote in favour of Swiss-style referenda and their legality in the British constitution in his *Introduction to the Study of the Law of the Constitution*. This view is also something that has appeared in our own jurisprudence as recently as the Supreme Court reference regarding Quebec sovereignty, in which the Court decided that a provincial referendum on sovereignty could impose a federal obligation to negotiate.

What they meant, of course, was ambiguous. I'm almost the only person in Canada who seems to be prepared to say that this was a very poor decision, and not just this part. It was a poor decision in general, reflecting the generally low quality of Supreme Court decisions in Canada. But it was a decision nonetheless that could mean that the federal government is required to come to the table in good faith to negotiate sovereignty, or to negotiate a number of other things that could be put forward in a provincially-sponsored referendum. This implies that some federal sovereignty is being moved to another locus of power, and if it can be moved to a provincial electoral body, then surely it could be moved to other sources of sovereignty.

In consequence of the Supreme Court ruling in the Quebec Secession Reference case, both the Parti Québécois and the Liberal Party of Quebec have been considering the possibility of a referendum that they expect would force the federal government to negotiate on such issues as transfers of tax points. I was in the House of Commons recently asking a question on just this matter. The so-called "firewall" group, consisting of Ken Boessenkool, Stephen Harper, Andy Crooks, and a few other people, also has made reference to this Supreme Court decision in suggesting that Alberta could hold a referendum on compliance with the *Canada Health Act.* So there is, in fact, some movement there both prior to, and since, the two decisions to which Prof. Cooper refers.

I also want to indicate that when we deal with the written text of our constitution (which is widely seen as being tremendously conservative, and presenting tremendously high formal barriers to change), we actually see remarkable flexibility. This has been true both of our own constitution and of the constitutions of British-style parliamentary democracies over the past century. The most striking example of this flexibility is the concept of the divisibility of the Crown. In a process of constitutional evolution that started at about the time of the First World War, and came to fruition in 1931 in *The Statute of Westminster* and in the late 1940s with the creation of an Indian Republic within the Commonwealth the divisibility of the Crown was established. The unity of the Crown, which was the central guiding constitutional principle of British parliamentary democracy, was completely abrogated, and the idea of a plural Crown was formed, so that the Queen of Canada is an entirely different person, legally, from the Queen of England, notwithstanding the fact the same individual holds both offices. Britain could become a republic; Canada would still be a monarchy. That's an indication of the kind of flexibility that the Westminster style of parliamentary democracy shows on a much more technically difficult question than this one.

Structural differences between Canadian and US systems

Turning from that issue, Professor Cooper says that Canada's parliamentary system is structurally different from the congressional system that we see in the United States (and also in Switzerland), in ways that make direct legislation very difficult. I'm going to quote here from Professor Cooper's paper at some length, because I think this lays out the argument very clearly.

> Direct legislation originated not in a parliamentary system, but in a congressional one, the essence of which is that the body that represents the people is legally the government. In a parliamentary regime, the House is simply a legal body, charged with the task, not of governing, but of supporting a government. The House does not choose a government. That task is performed by the electorate, usually by means of returning one political body to the House with a majority of members. All of these procedures constitute a set of procedural forms that cannot be easily accommodated to the procedures of direct democracy. [_Editor's note: This is a quote from Prof. Cooper's shorter paper as actually presented to the conference. This argument is amplified in the previous chapter._]

I am going to take issue with this, and suggest that on this particular point, Professor Cooper is incorrect. I can't identify what the mechanisms he's referring to might be. It seems to me that the inclusion of the government in the House of Commons is entirely a convention in this country, and is in no way formally constitutionalized. The House is not formally subsumed in the government, and is not formally a part of the government. Now the converse of this—but it is a reinforcing point—is that in a congressional system, the House of Representatives and the Senate are not part of the government either, or to use the American term, they are not part of the "Executive." Remember, in strict, legal, Canadian language, the government is what the Americans refer to as the Executive. The House of Representatives and the Senate are the legislative branch of government, whereas the president and the various offices that he appoints are the government in the term we would understand it, or the Executive branch of the state. Thus, rightly understood, the legislative branches in Canada and in the US are on roughly equal footing.

Empirically, this is why it has been so easy to adopt referenda in a couple of other parliamentary systems. In Australia, the constitution is amended exclusively by popular vote in referenda. In New Zealand, we see citizen-initiated referenda very firmly taking hold, and becoming an important part of that country's political process.

Direct democracy is not culturally unsuitable for Canadians

Professor Cooper's final point is, I think, his strongest and most insightful. He rightly notes that a bogus argument is frequently presented. It's almost a truism among Canadian political commentators that Canadians are culturally unsuited to direct legislation because we are more deferential and less individualistic than Americans. This is what I would describe as the "Margaret Atwood/June Callwood/Pierre Berton/Edgar Friedenberg/Seymour Martin Lipset/John Ralston Saul/CBC/ *Toronto Star/ Maclean's*" view of Canada. It is nonsense. I thank him for making that point.

The particular version of the extraordinary myth that Prof. Cooper takes on is the claim made by Ramsey Cook, Frank Underhill, and a thousand lesser lights, that the original intent of Canada's founders was to produce an elite-driven, consociational representative system in which direct legislation is firmly rejected. Mr. Cooper cites the brilliant work of Janet Ajzenstat in this matter. I assume that his reference was primarily to the book *Canada's Founding Debates,* which is edited by her, a book that I would recommend everyone read. It contains the edited Confederation debates of the various provincial legislatures that took place in the 1860s, which demonstrate that individualism and popular sovereignty were quite central to the political culture of Canada at the time. He quotes some excellent examples; many more could be cited.

I've done my own research in this area, and it confirms exactly what Professor Cooper is saying. You can see a piece on my web site that was printed in the *National Post* in August or September of 2000 called "Individualists from Day One," which makes a similar argument based upon similar archival research.

To make the point as well from a different source, I have here a copy of a pamphlet that was written by D'Arcy McGee. It's been out of print for 137 years. The only copy, other than the one I have in my hand, is the one on my hard disk, plus the original copy in the National Archives. We have not, in Canada, done ourselves any great service in terms of collecting our founding documents. Let me read what D'Arcy McGee said, because it reinforces what Professor Cooper is saying. McGee says:

> We have in British America the same problem to solve that was put before the Greeks. To the vast majority of our population, the monarchial idea is respectable if not venerable, is full of the promise of permanency, without being considered, in any respect, incompatible with the largest liberty. The vast majority either born amidst or long-accustomed to the greater equality of fortunes and greater laxity of manners which characterize those like all American communities when compared with European countries, have necessarily very decided democratic tendencies working within them. To regulate this two-fold movement of our public mind, to see that freedom suffers nothing while authority is exalted would seem to be our task in the times on which we have fallen.

I think that greatly strengthens his case.

But in addition, there is further strength to the argument Professor Cooper is making in the fact that when one looks at America's founding documents, one discovers that they were not, in fact, written by a group of people who favoured direct democratic measures. Quite the contrary; in America in the 1780s there was a much stronger movement against direct democracy than in this country in the 1860s. One need only read Madison's commentaries in *The Federalist Papers* to get a sense of how the greatest American constitutionalist felt about direct democracy. The most famous thing Madison said on this subject was: "Had every Athenian citizen been a Socrates, every Athenian assembly would still have been a mob."

Even more striking than that is the utter absence of proposals for direct democracy during the American ratification debates. During these debates, many resolutions were put forward as to amendments that should be made to the American constitution. Some States said, "We will not ratify unless we know that a Bill of Rights, including a variety of amendments, is included."

Among the amendments which are contained in Edward Dumbauld's documentary review of the ratification process are 90 different proposed amendments on such subjects as: double jeopardy, self-incrimination, due process of law, just compensation, excessive bail, the retained rights of the States, re-examination of the facts before second trial, grand jury trials, freedom of speech, quartering soldiers, the right to bear arms, and religious freedoms. Out of 90 proposals, many of which were repeated in 10 or 11 different ratification assemblies, not one refers to direct democracy.

So I'm inclined to think that if the Americans were able make the leap from a process that was emphatically in favour of exclusively representative democracy, and which completely rejected direct democracy, then it seems entirely possible that Canadians could do so as well.

References cited

Dicey, Albert Venn (1982 [1915]). *Introduction to the Study of the Law of the Constitution.* Indianapolis: The Liberty Fund.

Dumbauld, Edward (1957). *The Bill of Rights and What it Means Today.* Norman, Oklahoma: University of Oklahoma Press.

Hamilton, Alexander, John Jay, James Madison (1950 [1787-88]). *The Federalist.* New York: Random House.

McGee, Thomas D'Arcy (1865). *Notes on Federal Governments.* Ottawa.

CHAPTER 10
Q&A for Panel 3: Powers Reserved to the Electorate

Gordon Gibson: I had a fascinating discussion with Scott Reid when he was considering coming to this conference. In that conversation, he reflected on how much trouble the matter of initiatives had been for his party in the last federal election, particularly the question of the threshold needed to activate initiative legislation. Would you care to tell us a bit about that, Scott?

Scott Reid: I suppose everybody knows the context. You may recall that during the last federal election, the issue came up as to whether extreme measures would wind up being promoted by means of citizen-initiated referenda. People were particularly concerned about the question of the threshold. For years, the Reform Party had a policy that said if three percent of the population initiates a referendum by means of a petition, then a referendum must be held. This was dropped from our policy platform, but became part of the background documentation. Our new policy simply said that when an issue is important enough, some form of initiative should take place. So of course what happened was that when the background documentation found its way into Liberal hands, they presented this as part of the nefarious hidden agenda of the Canadian Alliance Party and it was darkly suggested that this would lead to referenda on a whole series of policies that were unacceptable to average Canadians. The most notable of these would be, of course, a referendum on abortion.

In this discussion, Gordon was really asking how one overcomes this problem. Isn't it going to come back and haunt you? In a sense, if you advocate citizen-initiated referenda, something like this can always come back to haunt you for the simple reason that as long as there is such a thing as a petition, and it is signed by three, five, or ten percent of the population—or whatever number you happen to choose—it is always conceivable that you can have a referendum on question that will have been placed by an unrepresentative minority. So, if ten percent of Canadians feel strongly enough about something to sign up on it, but ninety percent of Canadians oppose it, you will end up with a referendum on an issue that most people oppose.

The Liberals were very skilled at presenting the suggestion that somehow this potential scenario would lead to extreme minority points of view being foisted upon the Canadian public and upon our public policy. Of course this is nonsense. The proper answer to a question like this one, when someone brings up "Won't there be a referendum on …?" (whatever it is that comes up) is simply to say that nothing can get approved by referendum that is not approved by 50 percent of participating voters.

I was asked this question repeatedly during the eight debates we had in my constituency during the election. Of course, seeing that this was supposed to be a weak point, my opponents would always have someone get up and ask a question like, "Remember, this is a rural constituency. Well, wouldn't it be the case that we would have referenda on questions such as completely banning firearms? After all, most Canadians are urban." (Or they'd ask a question on whatever the issue was that they thought would resonate best with the people present.) I would always come back with an example, such as Switzerland, which has direct legislation, yet hasn't banned firearms.

The real point I would drive at is that people should think very carefully when they're talking about extreme measures. Direct democracy is very different from what happens when legislation goes through Parliament. In an election, about 60 percent of Canadians participate, maybe a little bit less in the last election. About 40 percent of participating voters cast ballots for the governing party. Party discipline is then applied to force that group to accept decisions that are actually the will of a smaller group within the parliamentary caucus. So legislation can be passed that has the support of a very tiny percentage of the population. In fact, that is the standard way in which our legislation is made. Tyranny comes very much from our elite-driven system of representative government—not at all from direct democracy.

Question: Just on picking up on the referendum idea. Scott raised it and Barry Cooper might want to comment. You mentioned the federal court decision regarding a referendum vote in Quebec, and that if the majority had voted for separation, then the federal government would have had to negotiate with Quebec. You just left it there. I was wondering two things. First, does that mean that the federal government would be forced to negotiate, but that Quebec could leave anyway, or does it simply mean that we would have some discussions, the outcome of which could go either way? Second, what then happens to the rest of Canada? (We just picked Quebec. Quebec is a good example, but there could be other referendums, on, for instance, what happens to the rest of Canada—something that we might view as a national issue, although the province would view it as a particular provincial issue.)

Scott Reid: Quite frankly, the court was remiss not to put something like that in its decision in order to clarify it. What it did instead was say, "Well, democracy consists of the following things ..." and then put in a whole series of things that have nothing to do with democracy (although they are fine principles, such as minority rights, and so on).

With regard to this question, the Supreme Court decision simply said there was an obligation to negotiate (section 88 of the decision). It didn't say that it was an obligation to negotiate in good faith, or that it was an obligation to negotiate so that you will come to a conclusion. At some point in negotiations—real negotiations—there are two possible outcomes. We can work towards achieving a compromise, or one or the other of us can pick up our marbles and go home. So an obligation to negotiate is actually nonsensical, in my opinion, and it is a reflection of just how poor the quality of thought is in our Supreme Court that this is out there.

What the court should have done is said in an *obiter dicta*, that is, in the non-binding part of their decision, "We, using our position as senior people within the society, using our moral suasion, indicate that you ought to follow some of these rules," as opposed to saying, "We, in our capacity as interpreters of the constitution, tell you, you must follow this rule which we will not bother to define for you."

Barry Cooper: I have two responses. One is a quote from Hegel that the owl Minerva flies at dusk, and political scientists can say what happened in the past but we don't like to look forward to the future. The other is a quotation from Mike Walker who says we should never be political in The Fraser Institute and I take that *obiter* very seriously as well. I would say, however, that the Supreme Court of Canada's advisory decision in that particular case opens up some absolutely fascinating possibilities about other provinces acting in exactly the same way as the province of Quebec did to force constitutional changes. I certainly agree with Scott about the low level of intellectual rigour in the Supreme Court of Canada. This, I think, proves it at least as much as Delgamuukw.

Question: I wanted to bring up two points relating to citizen-initiated referenda for legislation. The first is that a peer of Prof. Cooper's who teaches political science at the University of Hawaii said in an article in the **Encyclopaedia Americana** *that the Weimar Republic had citizen-initiated referenda from 1919, and West Germany ripped that out of their constitution in 1949 precisely because of the role that kind of citizen-initiated legislation had in the rise of the Nazis to power. The second was with regard to the role of citizen-initiated referenda in California. In the 2000 election, a dot-com millionaire in California proposed an initiative for parental choice in education. He said he was going to put $25 million of his money behind this initiative. The California Teachers Association said they were going to put $30 million behind a campaign to oppose it. So the whole campaign on that issue ceased to be one of reasoned argument and became a question of who could buy the most expensive advertising agency and the most television time for heart-wrenching commercials to manipulate public opinion emotionally. Reasoned debate goes out of the question when that becomes a dominant theme. Could both of you comment on those two issues?*

Scott Reid: This argument comes up all the time—that there are these fact-free discussions in referendum debates, and this, I suppose, would be as opposed to Canadian federal election campaigns, which are models of representative democracy. Tongue in cheek, I note that nobody would ever suggest in the midst of an election campaign that the official opposition consists of "holocaust deniers, prominent bigots, and racists." Elinor Caplin, a member of the Liberal Cabinet, did this on November 14, 2000, in the midst of an election campaign. This kind of demonization goes on in Canadian representative politics. Such nonsense could never be successfully employed in a referendum campaign. We know this because in 1992 the federal government tried to use fear-mongering in a national referendum to do just that. It tried to stage a referendum in which all the money would be on the "Yes" side. It would form a consensus and browbeat people into submission both in the government party and in the opposition parties. It completely failed. People can see through that stuff. The whole debate on educational choice in the United States is becoming a more and more informed debate over time—precisely because the avenue of citizen-initiated referendum is available in so many states. We are starting to see some movement in this area that we're not seeing in Canada.

With respect to the Weimar Republic (and I could be wrong on this as I'm not a German historian), I believe that at no point was the citizen-initiated referendum ever actually used in the period either between 1919 and 1933 when Hitler came to power, or in the period afterwards. Hitler did, of course, stage a revolution, but he clothed it in constitutional terms and claimed that in fact he'd always acted constitutionally and legally, and then proceeded to carry out a series of bogus referenda which were about as free as the sorts of elections that the Soviets used to conduct. The result was overwhelming majorities in favour of his quite rapid erosion of constitutional barriers. It was in removing such barriers that, as a by-product, the initiative was removed from the Weimar constitution. Other powers in Europe in the interwar period in the Baltic States had initiatives, and (I stand to be corrected again) I think in one or two cases initiatives may have gone forward. I think they provided a more benign model than the Weimar model.

Barry Cooper: You can make the abstract observation that no rules will ever ensure you have decent politics—I think that's absolutely true. Decent politics depend on virtue, and character, and so on. But this is not a major problem right now in Canada. It might have been a problem in Weimar Germany. But that was then, and this is now. Right now, it seems to me, initiatives—however they're crafted—will benefit Canadians and will probably improve our political order.

Andrew Petter: It strikes me in talking about direct democracy that we shouldn't neglect opportunities to bring decisions that are currently situated within legislative processes closer to the people. Most of what we've been talking about with initiatives and referenda and recall is giving citizens more influence on the legislative process. But there are a number of ways in which we might take decisions that are currently located within the legislative process and relocate them within the citizenry. It seems to me that these strategies may be more productive, because they don't suffer from some of the impediments—constitutional and otherwise—that have been discussed here.

Let me offer three examples. One is to engage individuals directly in government decision making. There was, for example, a very successful effort by the Harcourt government to bring citizens to the table to resolve land use issues. The constituent or citizens' assembly that Geoff Plant has talked about is another example of an attempt to do that, albeit in a representative way.

A second is to devolve power. I suppose at The Fraser Institute, the most obvious example would be to turn decisions over to the market place, but from a social democratic point of view, there are other alternatives. The creation of community resource boards to make decisions about the allocation of local resources and the way they're managed is an alternative strategy that involves citizens making decisions that have often been poorly handled in the legislative arena.

A third, which has a lot of history in Europe, is the use of institutions—co-ops in particular—to enable those people most affected by government programs to assume direct responsibility for their design and delivery. In Northern Italy, for example, many social services are provided by co-ops made up of the people to whom those services are delivered. Operating within fixed budgets, they are in a much better position than legislators to determine how those services can best be delivered. In this province, for example, some Crown corporations might be turned into citizen co-ops. Citizens would have a direct say in the running and functioning of those Crowns in a way that would entail more accountability than the current structure and more social responsibility than if they were privatized.

The general point I want to make is that, when we talk about direct democracy, we should not leave off the table the full range of creative possibilities, including those that turn decision-making power directly over to citizens rather than merely trying to make the legislative process itself more accountable.

Scott Reid: I note everything that Andrew pointed to. He is quite right about co-operatives and decentralization of power in the case of provinces, municipalities, and so on. But I do have some reservations about the whole question of constituent assemblies. I had opportunity when I was living in Australia to attend the Australian constituent assembly in which the issue of turning the country into a republic was debated. The proposals put forward by the assembly were then sent off to the voters, and a referendum was held in 1999 in which, ultimately, the proposals were rejected. The assembly was elected by a mail-in ballot. It produced quite intelligent delegates on all sides, and a document was produced at the end of it. But then, under the rules that had been put forward, the bureaucrats got hold of the document and proceeded to turn some of the rather good proposals that the assembly had had for a moderate, thoughtful, consensual sort of republic into something that would have, in fact, gutted Parliament and given the PM virtually dictatorial strengths. The Australian voters, being intelligent people, rejected this in a national referendum. In fact, it was defeated in every state. So, thank goodness referendums were there to limit the power of constituent assemblies.

The BC Government's View

Introduction

A fundamental reason for this book and the conference on which it is based has been the fact that the new government elected in British Columbia in the spring of 2001 had a specific agenda of commitments on democratic reform, quite unique in Canada. These commitments gave an air of tangible possibility to many ideas for the improvement of our democracy that are usually, alas, discussed with just about no hope of implementation.

Accordingly, it was appropriate to have the keynote presentation given by the Minister Responsible for democratic reform, Hon. Geoff Plant. The commitments, some already fulfilled and others still promised, place British Columbia at the forefront of the development of democratic governance in this country. This chapter gives the BC government's philosophy in this area.

CHAPTER 11
Reforming Government

Geoff Plant

I want to congratulate The Fraser Institute for sponsoring this conference on an important but marvellously intractable subject: reforming politics. The subject is important, obviously, because politics comprises the institutions, the rules, and the practices that permit and limit access to state power. Politics, if you will, is the space between the citizen and the state. But the subject of politics is also intractable, in the *Oxford Dictionary* sense of "not docile." Politics is the thing we instantly recognize but cannot define. It is elusive and ever-changing and is capable of seemingly infinite expansion. In my former professional discipline as a lawyer, for example, one of the great debates of the last quarter century has been the argument that this thing called "legal reasoning" is actually just politics practiced under a different label. If all law is politics, then so, too, no doubt, sooner or later, is geology, bird-watching, and Mariano Rivera's splitter. But enough about baseball. (There's actually never enough about baseball, but I am here to talk about reforming politics.) It was W.H. Auden who said, "There is no such thing as the perfect democratic state, good for all time." Our political institutions will change, even when we're not paying attention to them. But as circumstances change, so, too, will our attention focus from time to time on the need to embrace more consciously the project of political reform. For my part, this particular story begins on election night in British Columbia in 1996.

On May 28, 1996, the BC Liberal Party, of which I am a member, lost a provincial election by six seats, despite winning the popular vote. The election may, in fact, have marked a turning point in BC's political history, because the outcome prompted people of every political stripe—even people not committed to any political party—to take a good, long look at their electoral system. Some said the system had failed us. Others argued the will of the people had not been served. There was a call for electoral reform. That call has really never ended. Fast forward, then, to 2001. We, that is, the BC Liberals, went into the most recent provincial election promising to create the most open, accountable, and democratic government in Canada—with an implicit message that to meet this goal we would need a complete review of how we run our elections. In the run-up to the campaign, I told the voters of the constituency that I sought to represent that I believed it was time for change. Not just a change in the cast of governors, but change in the way government works, and change even in the institutions of government themselves.

Our campaign platform—the *New Era* document—laid out a roadmap for institutional change. We committed to change the public service, the operations of government, and to open up a for-mal discussion about electoral reform through the mechanism of a citizens' assembly on electoral reform.

The job of this assembly would be to assess all possible models for electing MLAs—things like preferential ballots, proportional rep-resentation, and even the status quo. We also promised to give the citizens' assembly a mandate to hold public hearings through-out BC and, if it recommended changes to the current electoral system, to put those recommendations to the people through a province-wide referendum. We were elected to keep these com-mitments and we intend to keep them. But the results of the last election have, for some, and perhaps only temporarily, shifted the focus of the debate on electoral reform, because in the election of 2001, a strong majority of the popular vote translated in to a mas-sive majority for one party in the legislature. The corollary was that as a result, parties like, for example, the Green Party, received a significant number of votes, but elected no representatives. The question of electoral reform, raised in 1996, has not been answered, but it may have been redefined. At times, it seems to me, the current debate has begun to focus excessively on ways of ensuring that political parties are happy with the number of seats they get on Election Day.

But surely the fundamental goal of elections and electoral reform is not to serve the needs of political parties. Rather, the goal of elections and electoral reform is to give citizens a voice in choosing their government. Thus, the urgent question for 1996, for 2001, and for all elections yet to come, is this: How do we create a system that better serves all of the people of British Columbia? The history of electoral reform in British Columbia has traditionally focused not on enfranchising political parties, but rather on enfranchising voters. In 1876, for example, British Columbia dropped property ownership as a qualification to vote, thereby expanding the franchise. Forty years later, the province extended voting rights to women. And then in the late 1950s, British Columbia's voting age from dropped from 21 to 19, and then in 1992, was reduced still further to 18 to conform to national standards. Even the most significant changes in the last 10 years of our political history have tended to focus primarily on reforming politics to better serve the interests of voters. For example, the 1995 *Recall and Initiative Act* represented an attempt to put more power in the hands of voters. Of course there is also a legislative history in British Columbia of regulating political parties. That history culminated in 1995 in a new *Election Act*—a statute about which I'll have more to say in a minute or two—that prescribes in 160 pages of mind-numbing detail the ways in which we are, and are not, permitted to engage in electoral democracy.

The *Election Act* speaks to political parties, but the main focus of electoral reform is and ought to be, not the political party, but the voter. The challenge is to find ways to ensure that citizens are satisfied with the politicians they have elected, and with the process used to elect those politicians. It is not an easy task. I believe we need to ensure that our inquiry is not limited to a mindset that automatically identifies partisan representation as the benchmark of a successful electoral system. The debate about electoral reform, about government reform, is broader than the debate about ensuring that the political parties are adequately represented in the legislature. In the months since last spring's election, the new government in British Columbia has moved to implement a range of reforms to the way we are governed. In his speech at the Cabinet swearing-in ceremony on June 5, Premier Gordon Campbell elaborated on his vision for open, accountable, and democratic government when he said that he wanted BC's new government (and these are his words) "to reflect a fundamental change in attitude." As he said, "The legislature is there to serve the people, and the Cabinet is there to serve the legislature." He went on to say, " Our legislature will be open. It will be a place where we all learn from one another. It will be a place where we strive to reflect the values of British Columbians and to unite our province in common purpose." Simply put, the government has embraced the challenge of earning back some measure of trust and respect for political leaders. One measure of political credibility must surely be the extent to which elected leaders keep the commitments they made in seeking public office. We have been working hard to fulfill our commitments. One of the first acts of the new government was to honour the *New Era* commitment for fixed election dates. So we have amended the *Constitution Act* of British Columbia to provide that the next provincial election will be held on Tuesday, May 17, 2005. Thereafter, barring dissolution for loss of confidence, provincial elections will be held on the second Tuesday in May every four years. The intention behind this change is to disperse power from the premier's office by ensuring that the timing of elections can no longer be manipulated for political or partisan purposes. The enactment of a fixed election date means everyone in British Columbia knows that we, in government, have four years to keep our commitments, and that in May 2005, the citizens of British Columbia will be able to hold us to account for our record.

Similarly, we have followed up the fixed election date reform with laws establishing a fixed date for the tabling of the provincial budget and a set legislative calendar—reforms that were long overdue—all with the goal of increasing public accountability. We have introduced lobbyist registration legislation, not to regulate the profession of lobbying, but to provide a measure of public disclosure of the significant volume of political persuasion and influence that takes place behind closed doors along the corridors of power. We have also committed to free votes in the legislature to permit MLAs to vote freely on behalf of their constituents on all matters not specifically identified as a vote of confidence for a *New Era* platform commitment. Free votes help decentralize the power base. Free votes, and an expanded role in government policy making through the use of government caucus committees, help give individual MLAs a real voice in the decision making process of government—an opportunity to exercise individual judgement. As well, they give the electors of constituency MLAs a more direct voice in the legislature through their elected representatives. Free votes is a reform that looks forward but does so by recalling a past in which the firm hand of the whip played a less intrusive role in the control of parliamentary governments. Free votes, government caucus committees, fixed budget dates, three year ministerial service plans, and a new approach to ministerial accountability that creates personal financial incentives for ministers to meet their government-wide and individual ministerial budgets are all part of the toolkit for dispersing power away from the premier's office, out to ministers, and beyond them to the private members of the legislature and the voters they were elected to serve. Reforming recall and initiative legislation—another platform commitment—will make it easier for citizens to hold MLAs accountable to the people of this province. We are also working on legislation to honour additional commitments targeting electoral reform.

I said we would come back to the *Election Act*. In the *New Era* document, we promised to amend the *Election Act* to eliminate loopholes on disclosures of financial contributions to parties and to include donations of labour, as well as to outlaw donations from charities to political parties. These commitments represent a response to some specific issues identified as problems with the 1995 *Election Act*. But in arguing for and expressing my commitment to these particular reforms, I do not want to impose unreasonable constraints on a public discussion concerning our regulation of elections. I recently came across a marvellous speech given in 1999 at Dalhousie by Roderick Macdonald when he was president of the Law Commission of Canada. In that speech Professor Macdonald talked about the limits of prescriptive regulation as a tool for social change. He identified as one of the misconceptions that has afflicted the law for the last half-century (and these are his words) "the belief that it is possible to make people better by detailed Parliamentary prescription." The following is another passage from that speech:

> Sustaining these misconceptions of law are two debatable suppositions about the motives and capacities of human beings. One is that people are not able to function in society without the assistance of public officials staffing specialized regulatory bodies. The other supposition is that people are naturally inclined to exploit one another and will always try to extract disproportionate advantage in situations of conflict.

From this perspective, and the perspective of those observations, I believe it may be both timely and appropriate to encourage a broader discussion about reforming the regulation of elections themselves. Do we really need a 160-page *Election Act*? This brings me back to the citizens' assembly, which is, I believe, a noble idea, but obviously one not without its practical challenges. British Columbia is a unique political entity. We are neither New Zealand, nor Germany, nor Israel, nor anywhere else. Our population is widely dispersed and diverse. Our expectations of elected representatives are sometimes less than clear. And we cannot redesign our electoral system without asking ourselves the question: what is it that we expect our elected MLAs to do?

The fundamental objective of the citizens' assembly takes us back to the fundamental objective of electoral reform, that is, to create a system that better serves all of the people. To achieve this, the government of which I am a member believes that it is necessary to take the question of electoral reform out of the hands of politicians and place it in the hands of the people we are elected to serve. The challenge, therefore, is to find a way to create a citizens' assembly that effectively represents the citizens of this province and gives voice to their concerns.

Premier Campbell has suggested that the citizens' assembly should be selected randomly, as are members of a jury. I've heard objections to this proposal. Among them, of course, is the familiar objection that we might not end up with citizens with the expertise needed to address these complex issues. Well, that's an interesting dilemma. It presupposes that democracy has become incomprehensible to the citizens it is intended to serve. I am unwilling to accept that contention. In truth, while I confess that I might personally want to be at the front of the line at the first congress of philosopher kings, we had better figure out how to ensure that a system of government that is intended to work for ordinary citizens is comprehensible to them.

But that is only the beginning of the list of questions about the selection and process—and even about the idea itself—of a citizens' assembly, many of which, I am certain, you will have been discussing and will continue to discuss here today. I am here to reaffirm the commitment of the government of British Columbia to political reform, and to a process that will engage citizens in a dialogue about the difficult question of whether we should change the way we vote for those who govern us. There is much that each of you can add to the discussions about how to implement the commitments we have made and intend to keep. I look forward to hearing the results of your deliberations.

Questions for Geoff Plant

Ted White: Minister, I attended a meeting you were guest speaker at just a few weeks ago, and I asked you questions about the referendum on Native land claims. I was very buoyed by your answers and felt you had a commitment to it. So I'm a little disturbed to hear the news reports in the last few days that some research has been done into comparing a mail-in ballot with a true electoral type of ballot for this referendum. Now keeping in mind that the results of this ballot have to been seen to be valid and perceived to be valid, what on earth was the thinking behind any idea that you could run a mail-in ballot for this process? [Editor's note: The referendum has since been held, by mail-in ballot.]

Geoff Plant: I don't think you can make good public policy decisions, particularly expensive public policy decisions, without canvassing the options. The objective of the referendum is to give all citizens of British Columbia a one-time opportunity in the form of a vote on the principles that should guide the province's treaty negotiators as they sit down and negotiate treaties. The government is questioning what is the most effective, efficient, fair, and affordable way to give affect to that commitment. In that regard, we imposed upon the folks at Elections BC to give us a sense of what the cost would be of some of the options, and we were much assisted by their work in giving us a sense of what the range of costs are.

Ted White: Minister, please do not throw away $8 million and have a worthless result. Please consider very carefully that you need to produce an electorally sound referendum.

Geoff Plant: The state of Oregon does electorally sound voting by mail, so it's not something that is completely unique. But thank you for that.

David Elton: I've been working on direct democracy and parliamentary reform issues for 30 years. This is the first time I've heard as clear a declaration of intent on this issue in that period, and I thank you very much for it. I think this is a window of opportunity that British Columbians should take and seize and act on very quickly. We've never had anything quite like this in Alberta.

My question, however, deals with a comment that was made this morning. In all of these kinds of issues, the devil is in the details. So I want you to tell us how your government is dealing with one issue that you indicated has already been implemented, and that's the issue of non-confidence votes. It's easy to say we're going to provide a free vote for all non-confidence votes, but then make all subsequent votes confidence votes. As a minister, how are you going to determine which issues that come from your department are to be confidence votes, and which one of them will not be?

Geoff Plant: The starting point is that confidence votes include those things that are traditionally confidence votes, such as the address and reply to the Throne and the budget. We have also determined that it did not make much sense to encourage people to run for office on the *New Era* platform, and then to say they could vote against elements of that platform when they became elected. It seems to me hard to figure out how they could have run for office on that basis. But when you examine the *New Era* document itself, you will see that some of the commitments in that document are expressed in precise terms, while some are expressed more as principles or objectives. A precise manner of implementing those objectives may well be something that will be a subject of debate within the larger society, and even within the caucus. You said that the devil was in the details. That's right, although I would put the point differently. The test of a commitment to free votes lies in the reality of its implementation. That's a long way of saying "time will tell." As an opposition party for the five years between 1996 and 2001, we did implement free votes on a number of matters. I could wish that the headlines the morning after each of the days we did that were, "Liberals bravely embrace concept of free votes." Interestingly enough, the headlines were usually, "Liberals greatly divided on important and difficult issues." I think all of us citizens, media, academics, and participants are going to have to get used to a few more of those headlines, because the premier continues to say that if it isn't a vote on the budget, the address and reply to the Throne or *New Era* commitments, then it's not a confidence vote. Now, that isn't to say that from time to time other issues of confidence may arise. Clearly, on May 17, 2005, the voters of British Columbia will be able to assess the credibility of our claim against our record, but the goal is to make it real.

Peter Dobell: Minister, I was encouraged by your statement, as it referred to free votes. I was also encouraged by your response to David Elton's very appropriate question. I was a little disturbed when you described the conditions under which a member might be free to vote against: you said if his constituents wished it or thought it appropriate. I hope that it also includes just disagreeing with the policy. One of the challenges I think you face as a government with really no opposition is that the credibility of the legislature will depend on the extent to which there is debate in the chamber, so I hope that the courage that your government is displaying will go so far as to actually promote division or debate between members of the party in the chamber. If you are successful in doing that, then I do believe you could become a model for the reform of the political culture of Canada.

Geoff Plant: Thank you for that comment. I had intended to say that the way in which free votes would work was to help give individual MLAs a real voice in the decision making process of government and the opportunity to exercise individual judgement. This would give the electors of constituency MLAs a more direct voice in the legislature through their elected representatives. I tried to cover all bases there. I know that there is a debate about what the role of elected MLAs should be in a representative democracy, whether the MLA is a mere delegate of the wishes of his constituents, or, in traditional Burkean terms, has the authority to exercise independent judgment on their behalf. I'm not sure that we've achieved any greater clarity on that subject in the two centuries since Burke. Clearly, each individual MLA is going to have to figure out their rationale for making decisions, and I think the toolkit, if you will, or the range of options, ought to include simple disagreement with the policy of government. I'm not, by the way, suggesting that none of my caucus colleagues who are not members of government would be permitted to exercise free votes without conducting constituency polls, for example. I don't advocate that. Probably the best way of putting it is that they can do whatever they want.

Constitutional Constraints

Introduction

However responsive, representative, or efficient governments may be made by various reforms, we still have reason to fear them. They are, after all, and by definition, enormous bureaucratic organizations based on monopoly power and coercion. Indeed, from a certain point of view, the "better" governments are in terms of popularity and efficiency, the more they are to be feared. The same may be said of brilliant, charismatic leaders. The more power accumulates, the bigger the mistakes that may be made. The more the crowd is pleased, the more certain individuals may suffer. Thus, thoughtful political philosophers have always warned about the need for constraints and limits on government. Usual discussion of "democratic reform," which, after all, is about making government more user-friendly and attractive, ignores this darker side of the democratic dilemma.

For this reason, the focus of this section on constraints on government pays particular attention to (arguably) the two most important and least well defended in Canada, namely, freedom of information and private property. Others of our political and personal rights and freedoms are well recognized and defended. These two are not.

CHAPTER 12
Limits to the Power of the People

Herbert G. Grubel

Most of the papers in this volume present ideas on how to give "power to the people" through appropriate reforms of existing political institutions.[35] My contribution to the discussion will be the argument that we also need to consider "limits to the power of the people" exercised through the legislature.[36]

It is not obvious that such limits are needed. After all, the ideal political system and institutions give power to the people and therefore, almost by definition, legislation reflects their collective will. When we combine this system with the notion that the people are always right and act in the best interest of all citizens, why do we need limits on legislative power?

There are those who answer that we do not have a defensible position. But for my taste, such an answer relies too much on faith. My interpretation of human nature and history suggests that this faith is not warranted. The theories of public choice and bureaucracy imply that the motives of governments are driven by more than the desire to maximize the public good.[37] At any rate, there

---

35 I thank Gordon Gibson for his many discussions of the subject and his thoughtful comments on an earlier draft of this paper.

36 My analysis draws on an earlier paper I had published on this subject (Grubel, 1992). A thorough historic review of balanced budget legislation in the United States is found in Uhler, 1989. There are many references to related publications and legislation in US states.

are some influential people who have held the same views as I do. The fathers of the US Constitution and the advocates of the Canadian Charter of Rights and Freedoms have not only held these views, but were successful in getting them translated into fundamental documents that limit the power of the US and Canadian legislatures.

Protection of human rights

Limits are needed because there is a risk that legislatures will pass laws that violate certain fundamental human rights and subject the minority to the tyranny of the majority. Equality before the law, the right to trial by a jury of peers, free speech, and the right to bear arms are not safe from legislatures interested in the advancement of their political agendas.

Most modern states have imposed such limits on their legislatures. In the United States, they are embodied in the constitution and later amendments. In Canada, they are spelled out in the Charter of Rights and Freedoms.

In practice, questions arise periodically whether specific pieces of legislation are in violation of these limits. In both countries, Supreme Courts are required to rule on these questions and their decisions are binding on the legislatures.

In a dynamic, evolving, and growing world, limits can become obsolete or need to be added to. The problem is that such changes to the limits must be possible, but not so easy that determined legislatures could severely limit their effectiveness. For these reasons, changes to the limits require super-majorities in the legisla-

---

37   Readers requiring a detailed explanation of public choice theory are referred to the MSN internet search engine, which lists over 474,000 references to publications containing the words "public choice theory." Most prominent in these listings are the names of James Buchanan, Gordon Tullock, and Mancur Olson. Some interesting extensions of the basic theory involve the study of bureaucracies (William Niskanen) and rent-seeking (Anne Krueger), whose work is also referenced and partly accessible through the internet.

tures, assent from partner (or junior) governments in the federations, or both. In addition, some countries allow for referenda to initiate and ratify constitutional amendments.

It is probably correct to suggest that most Canadians are happy with the limits that the Charter of Rights and Freedoms has put on the legislature, even if some would prefer the British common law tradition and its history of organically evolving limits. Such a general consensus is consistent with considerable opposition to the role given to the Supreme Court in interpreting some of the limits, especially as they apply to the issue of group versus individual rights and the rights of accused criminals against those of victims and society as a whole. Many experts believe that most of the problems with the Charter are due to the fact that its designers left many of the details so vague that it opened the door to judicial activism by a Supreme Court inclined to advance the political agenda of the social democratic left.

The need for the protection of property rights

I share the presumed majority view on the merit of the Canadian Charter of Rights and Freedoms. The main theme of my paper is that the Charter focuses exclusively on human rights and does not protect property rights. During the drafting of the Charter the inclusion of these rights was considered seriously. However, in the end, they were omitted because of the opposition of provincial NDP governments, which threatened to veto the patriation if they did not get their way.

Social democratic parties like the NDP and their governments are ideologically inclined to oppose the constitutional entrenchment of property rights because they fear that such rights would limit their ability to manage the economy and redistribute income and wealth. I confess that for analogous ideological reasons I believe that the public interest would be well served by such limits.

My ideology is rooted in economic theory and empirical evidence from history and around the world. Secure property rights encourage investors and entrepreneurs to create capital and produce innovative products and technology. Capital and innovation are mainsprings of economic growth and prosperity. In addition, property rights are a dimension of human freedom, which includes the freedom of the person as well of possessions. Many value these freedoms in their own right and independent of any economic benefits.

The issue of private property rights historically first arose when sovereigns simply confiscated property without compensation, be it capriciously to support their own life-styles, or to finance defense and military adventures. The right to be compensated for such "takings" was one of the most important clauses in the Magna Carta. It was upheld and strengthened by the British parliaments and has been considered to have contributed to the success of the Industrial Revolution.

However, in modern times, protection from outright takings is not as important as is protection from a wide variety of other government policies that are not designed explicitly to take away property, but do so more or less incidentally. I now discuss these policies individually by considering how they affect property, what current policies are, and how property can be protected.

The right to stable prices

Inflation reduces the value of a country's currency domestically and abroad. It often leads to the redistribution of wealth from creditors to debtors or the government. Future generations are forced to service the debt with their taxes without receiving corresponding benefits. Efficiency, and therefore property, is lost for society as a whole as inflation induces the public to adjust their behavior in order to minimize its harmful effects on their conditions.

The need to curb inflation has already been accepted by the Bank of Canada, presumably with the consent of the federal government. Since the early 1990s, the Bank of Canada has set targets for inflation near zero. This commitment has been driven by the realization that the inflation of the 1970s and 1980s had not brought the lower unemployment and higher economic growth promised by Keynesian economic theory.

The problem with the current practice of the Bank of Canada is that it has been adopted unilaterally. Therefore, it also can be abandoned unilaterally. The whims of economic theory and the political establishment are unpredictable. For these reasons, I suggest that the Bank of Canada be forced to pursue price stability through an appropriate clause in the property rights section of the Charter.

Alternatively, as I have suggested in another study (Grubel, 1999), monetary policy can be removed entirely from the control of Canadian politicians through the creation of a North American Central Bank operating under a constitution that makes it independent of the governments of the member countries and requires it to pursue price stability. My proposal was stimulated by the creation of the European Monetary Union, which was motivated to a considerable degree by the desire of politicians in the member countries to eliminate the historic bouts with inflation caused by the actions of their central banks. To assure price stability in Europe, the European Central Bank in Frankfurt has been required under its constitution to pursue price stability only, not full employment. Its operations and staffing policies have been removed from the political influences of national governments and the legislative and oversight bodies of the European Economic Community.

The adoption of the European model in North America would not only provide the limits on the power of legislatures that is the focus of the present paper. It would also bring a host of other benefits, such as lower interest rates and transactions costs in international trade. As a result of these direct benefits, economic growth and prosperity would rise.

Right to balanced budgets

Budget deficits lead to a growing debt, which needs to be serviced through interest payments. The money for these interest payments has to be collected through taxes, which damage incentives to work and invest and cause inefficiencies. As a result, income levels and wealth are reduced and, in effect, the property rights of Canadians are violated. Most importantly and unfairly, this damage is done to the young without a voting franchise and unborn future generations of Canadians, who have to service or retire this debt during their own lifetimes. In a sense, these future generations are a "minority," much like the other minorities whose human rights are protected by the Charter.

Because of the longer-run damages done by deficits, many US states have constitutional prohibitions against them. Attempts to introduce the same restrictions on the federal government in the United States have failed by narrow margins on several occasions. It is interesting to note that studies of the experience of US states with and without the limits show that the prohibition of deficits has the expected economic benefits—states with these limits have superior economic performance to those without them.[38]

While I was a member of Parliament in Ottawa in 1995, I introduced a private member's bill that would have prohibited deficits.[39] My experience illustrates the premises underlying many of the papers presented at this conference. The government responded the way it responds to virtually all such private bills. I was given the opportunity to present my idea in the House of Commons at the end of a day when the House was empty except for the Speaker and two members from the government. The latter read out papers prepared for them by the department of finance setting out why my ideas were stupid, though they never quite used these words. After all, we have to uphold the legendary standards of Canadian politeness. My proposals were never con-

---

38   Uhler (1989) reviews some of these studies.

39   See House of Commons (1996) for an exact reference to the bill as it was tabled and can be found in the Government of Canada reference section of many libraries. In 1996, Scott Reid, now an Alliance MP, was on the Reform Party of Canada's research staff. He helped me with the concepts and specific proposals underlying my bill. The legal staff of the House of Commons provided very useful help to make the bill logically consistent and legally sound.

sidered in committee, debated in the full House, or voted on. I had to console myself with the comments from the two government members after the debate. They told me privately that they quite liked my ideas after they had listened to me explain them. Of course, they may have just been nice to me, knowing first-hand the frustrations surrounding private members' bills they may well have experienced themselves.

Since 1994, the Liberal government, with Paul Martin as the minister of finance, has committed itself to balancing the budget. Like the commitment to price stability, though, this laudable policy initiative suffers from the fact that it can be reversed at the whim of this or future governments. To protect the property rights of present—and especially future—generations, balanced budget requirements need to be enshrined in the Canadian Charter of Rights and Freedoms.

Again, membership in a supra-national organization can achieve the same goals. As is well known, the European Economic Community has imposed fiscal responsibility on its members. If, under the stimulus of the events on September 11, 2001, a closer union and common perimeter for the NAFTA countries would be considered officially, the inclusion of a fiscal responsibility clause should be given serious consideration and support by the government of Canada.

Right to free trade and capital flows

Tariffs, quotas, red tape, limits on the holding of foreign assets in retirement portfolios, and other restrictions on international dealings reduce the property of many Canadians and increase that of others. These policies also induce Canadians to change their behavior to reduce the impact of such restrictions or maximize their benefits. These induced changes in behavior lower the wealth of all Canadians through lower efficiency.

The general public widely appreciates the damaging effects of restrictions on trade and capital flows. Politicians have embraced the ideas and, in spite of the well-known risks of punishment at the ballot box by those organized groups losing from free trade, have negotiated treaties aimed at creating free trade. NAFTA regionally, and the WTO globally, are the lasting monuments to these courageous political initiatives. However, the job is not complete as there are still many restrictions on the free flow of capital, and host governments still discriminate against foreign investors.

The commitment to free trade through international treaties represents an important limit on the freedom of legislatures. While politicians in principle always can withdraw from such treaties, in practice such withdrawal is very difficult. Therefore, protection against legislated interference in free trade would be stronger if it were enshrined in the Charter.

The right to optimal government size

Until the 1960s, economic models assumed that all government policies were in the public interest, and that they were put into place only after a careful benefit/cost calculus had established their merit. More recently, public choice theory and the theory of bureaucracy have shown that the selfish motives of politicians and bureaucrats play important roles in the creation of many spending and taxation programs. As a result, government is larger than warranted for the maximization of national income and welfare.

Econometric studies involving the history of government spending and economic growth in Canada and some other countries have shown clearly that spending is excessively high in this country. In the early years of the twentieth century, when spending as a percent of national income in Canada was low, economic growth was below its maximum. The growth rate was maximized in the early years after the Second World War when spending reached 33 percent of national income. During the last 3 decades or so, spending has exceeded this optimal level, and economic growth has been below its maximum.

The historic relationship between spending and growth can be explained partly by the amount of spending on the bureaucracy and the large number of regulations it passed, a quantity that burdens the productive effort of the private sector. Economic growth also suffered from the detrimental effects on incentives created by social spending, which has been increased beyond its optimal levels by politicians currying the favor of voters in elections. In addition and most importantly, the taxation needed to finance this spending has reduced incentives to work, invest, take risks, and become educated.

The excessively high levels of taxation and spending during the last 30 years have also been blamed for another important problem, the decrease by about one third of the value of the Canadian against the US dollar. In this context, it is important to remember that the fall of the Canadian dollar cannot be explained by the traditional purchasing power parity theory because Canadian and US price levels increased by virtually the same amount. Falling commodity prices in the world are associated statistically with declines in the value of the Canadian dollar. But this association does not explain why ever-lower returns in the commodity-producing sector have not resulted in a larger shift of resources into the high tech and other growing sectors of the economy. The main villain is high Canadian taxes, which have reduced Canada's attractiveness as a place to invest. American money that did not come to Canada, and Canadian money that did go to the United States caused an increase in the demand for US dollars and the observed depreciation of the Canadian dollar.

All of the negative effects of excessive Canadian spending and taxation have lowered overall economic growth and the purchasing power of Canadians abroad. In this sense, excessive spending and taxation have reduced the property of Canadians.

If my analysis is correct, there should be limits on the size of total government spending. The appropriate limits need to be determined after more studies and wide public discussion. My own work has convinced me that a limit for government spending at one third of national income is about right. Such a limit would not only maximize economic growth, but also assure the stability of the currency's external value.

Limits through legislation, international treaties, and the Charter

In the preceding analysis I have referred to three ways to limit the power of legislatures in Canada: laws enacted by parliament, treaties creating internationally binding agreements, and the enshrinement of property rights in the Charter. Let me now discuss briefly the relative merit of these three approaches.

As already mentioned, limits adopted unilaterally by Parliament or the Bank of Canada and the Minister of Finance are easiest to achieve, but also equally easy to abandon. They therefore are the least desirable, though better than having no limits at all.

International treaties are more difficult to negotiate and to abandon or change; on my scale, they rank second in terms of desirability. However, they have some disadvantages. Institutions charged with adjudicating disputes arising under these treaties are often cumbersome and, some say, ineffective. This fact may be illustrated by the many rounds of WTO complaints and rulings that have not yet resulted in any significant changes to Canada's system of agricultural supply management.

In addition, all treaties have escape clauses that allow countries to assert their national interest under certain circumstances. One of these circumstances is when a country believes damage is being done to an industry by deliberate policies of a foreign government. The Americans have invoked this clause in the case of softwood lumber imports from Canada.

Unfortunately, no countries can be expected to sign international treaties that do not allow them some room to manoeuvre if there is a sufficiently important threat to "the national interest." The resultant provisions in the treaties will always be subject to some abuse.

The enshrinement of rights in the Canadian Charter (just like amendments to the US Constitution) involves a cumbersome procedure, deliberately and rightly designed to assure success only of amendments that have a broad and deep political backing. However, for the same reasons that it is difficult to amend the Charter, once property rights are enshrined, they are very difficult to change. This fact makes amendments to the Charter the best alternative for the introduction of limits on the power of the people and their deliberate or inadvertent encroachment on private property rights.

However, the Charter route also has some shortcomings, the most important of which is the role played by the Supreme Court of Canada in interpreting and implicitly extending the impact of the clause through its rulings. This problem is aggravated by the fact that all vacancies on the bench are appointed by the prime minister without the need to seek approval by Parliament or its relevant committees. Therefore, the Canadian Supreme Court is much more likely to reflect the ideology of Canada's ruling government than the US Supreme Court does the United States government.

Because of the political background of the Supreme Court in Canada, the design of the property rights clause must avoid leaving too much room for the Court to put its stamp on the way in which the clause is implemented. Many analysts argue that political biases have influenced the Court's interpretations of the human rights clauses of the Charter, yet many Canadians oppose those interpretations. A repeat of this record in the interpretation of the property rights clause is a real possibility. Unfortunately, the writers of the property rights clause face an ever-present dilemma associated with such work. If the wording is too precise, it avoids interference from the Supreme Court, but it also limits the ability of the clause to accommodate changes in the economy and social conditions that are certain to occur in the future.

Arguments against limits

Opposition to the imposition of limits on the power of the people comes from those who believe that a truly representative legislature can do no wrong. Their view may be summarized by the slogan, "the people are always right." I have already noted that I am skeptical of this position because of the theories of public choice and bureaucracy as well as my interpretation of history. However, even if one accepts the need for limits on the power of the people, there are many devils in the details on how to specify and operate these limits. One of these details is the time period over which the requirements need to be met. Should inflation be zero, the budget balanced, the level of spending at one third of national income every day, month, quarter, or year? Or is the full business cycle the appropriate length of time over which the goals have to be achieved?

Another issue arises from the fact that deviation from the required targets may be due to unforeseen developments beyond the control of Canadian policy makers, as when there are natural disasters or man-made problems due to wars or economic policies of foreign governments. Missing targets specified in the Charter may not only be inevitable, it may even be desirable to assure the well being of all Canadians. The imposition of trade barriers under certain circumstances may similarly be in the national interest.

These objections to limits on the power of the people must be taken seriously. However, in principle, the objections can be met by properly designing the rules guiding the application of the limits. These rules would be different for each policy area and the details need to be settled only after careful consideration by economists and lawyers. The following analysis presents some examples of such detailed rules.

Target ranges and averaging

In practice, the Bank of Canada is committed to maintaining price stability defined as a target of, say 2 percent annually. It allows itself an acceptable range around the target of 1 to 3 percent. The property rights clause of the Charter concerning the required conduct of monetary policy could be specified in the same way.

However, the Bank has not dealt with the problem that even if inflation is within the allowed range, lengthy periods above the target can result in average inflation higher than the target. To deal with this problem, it may be necessary to require inflation to be below and above the target for some periods so that the target can be attained as an average over a certain length of time. The desirable length of the averaging period is important and needs detailed study. The business cycle should be one candidate for the appropriate averaging period.

The requirement to balance budgets can be specified similarly with allowable ranges around the target of full balance. The business cycle may also be the best period over which, on average, the target must be achieved.

But ranges around targets and averaging are not the only method for making the limits as flexible as possible without interfering seriously with their functioning. During the 1990s, the Canadian minister of finance, Paul Martin, developed an excellent tool designed to ensure that, with a high probability, annual budgets are balanced. The tool consists of a contingency spending reserve, which is part of the planned expenditure side of the budget but for which there are no explicit spending plans. If at the end of the budget year actual spending and revenues on the regular items in the budget are exactly as planned, the reserve is not needed, and all of it is used for debt reduction. If the actual outlays and revenues on the other budget items result in what traditionally would be considered a deficit that draws down the contingency reserve finances, the reserve and debt reduction are correspondingly smaller.

In principle, the size of the contingency can be large enough to cover all but the most extreme cases where actual spending exceeds actual revenues. The tool Martin used has, in effect, redefined the nature of the policy target from a balance in planned budget items to the zero borrowing requirements. The use of this tool over the last 7 years has been a very positive experience, though it remains to be seen how well it works when the economy goes through a recession. The tool certainly has enough promise to be a serious candidate for inclusion in the part of the proposed property rights clause in the Charter that specifies operating procedures. If this tool were adopted, the use targets and ranges of the sort discussed above would not be necessary.

Emergencies and super-majorities

The use of targets, zones, averaging provisions and contingency reserves may not be adequate to deal with cases of genuine emergencies caused by national or international events beyond the control of Canadian policy makers and resulting in the breach of the required limits or targets. There is an obvious way to deal with such emergencies. Parliament can suspend the proposed limits through super-majority voting.

In my private member's bill I proposed that deficits could be made legal if 75 percent of the MPs present vote to approve the necessary resolution. The appropriate super-majorities required might be more or less than 75 percent, depending on the results of studies of their merit and the political consensus about what would be best for Canada. Similar rules can be applied to make legally acceptable deviations from targets for other policies stipulated in the Charter. In principle, therefore, the operation of the government during genuine national emergencies can proceed without hindrances from the proposed limits imposed by the property rights clause of the Charter.

History shows that super-majorities are very difficult to obtain in democratically-elected legislatures. However, I have faith that politicians have the integrity to set aside narrow self-interests and ideology if and when genuine national emergencies require such super-majorities. At the same time, I am also confident that narrow party interests are strong enough to prevent the abuse of the over-riding rule on occasions when no true national emergencies exist.

The proposed super-majority voting rule does not work when a government holds virtually all the seats, as has happened occasionally in the legislatures of some Canadian provinces, including British Columbia after the 2001 election. I welcome suggestions for overcoming this problem. Presumably, the ideal political institutions discussed in this volume would make it rather unlikely that majorities holding more than two thirds or three quarters of all seats would dominate Canadian legislatures. In other words, the issue would become insignificant after the adoption of appropriate electoral reforms.

Manipulation of data

Another devil in the details lies in the need to ensure that the government does not "fudge the books" to meet targets set out under the proposed property rights clause of the Charter. The temptation to do so is strong, even in the absence of the Charter limits. For example, in recent years British Columbia's NDP government has managed to achieve balanced budgets (or smaller deficits) by defining some infrastructure spending as "investment." This practice removed the spending from the ordinary budget, where it would have contributed to the deficit, and shifted it into the capital budget, where it was financed automatically by an increase in the debt and did not contribute to a deficit defined conventionally.

Many economists support the NDP's change in budgeting procedures because economic efficiency and the intertemporal allocation of capital are improved if all additions to society's capital stock are financed through borrowing. This practice sends appropriate signals to capital markets and the resultant interest rates induce the efficient amount of savings and private investment. Future generations will face a higher debt, but it will be matched by a correspondingly higher capital stock, which increases productivity and facilitates the financing of the debt service charges.

The problem with this economic argument is that it neglects the fact that capital also depreciates, and that capital markets should be used only to finance net additions to the stock. Health care and education, representing about two thirds of total spending, result in the formation of human capital, which, in principle, like infrastructure spending, should be financed through borrowing. But while some people are educated and made healthier, others become chronically ill or die. Much of people's education becomes obsolete through time. The size of this depreciation and obsolescence is difficult to ascertain and is certainly subject to manipulation by politicians.

Another way that accounting manipulations can disguise problems encountered in meeting the targets specified in the Charter's property rights clause involves shifting spending and taxation between different accounting periods.

The private sector has long manipulated accounting data to improve balance sheets and income statements. However, in recent decades, the scope and magnitude of such private sector manipulation has been limited increasingly through mandatory, professional accounting standards. In my private member's bill referred to above, I required that the government follow these same private-sector accounting principles, and that Canada's auditor general be made responsible for assuring compliance. If this requirement were placed into the proposed property rights clause of the Charter, it would ensure that accounting manipulation problems would be minimized.

Enforcement provisions

A final objection to the enshrinement of property rights in the Charter involves the question of enforceability. What if a government or central bank simply decides to disregard the Charter's imposed limits and merrily engages in deficit spending and inflationary policies? The government might believe that it has the right to do so on ideological grounds, or simply because its members of Parliament have convinced themselves that they represent the people and that the people are always right.

Of course, the same questions arise in the context of the enforcement of human rights. To the best of my knowledge, no Canadian government has ever deliberately disregarded human rights provisions or refused to accept the decisions on the contentious interpretation of these rights by the Supreme Court. On the contrary, Parliament has always taken such judgements very seriously, and typically has either abandoned or rewritten the offending legislation to make it acceptable to the Court. I believe that Parliament would show similar respect for the provisions in the property rights enshrined in the Charter.

The simple fact is that a government that disregards the Charter and Supreme Court decisions is likely to face a major constitutional crisis. The solicitor general would be caught in the unenviable position of having to enforce the laws of the land while acting against the will of the government and its parliamentary majority.

Let me conclude by suggesting that the proposed property rights clause can include financial incentives to meet the required inflation, fiscal, and other targets. The government of New Zealand has adopted such a system for the managers of its government departments and the central bank. If the targets are met or exceeded, these managers are paid bonuses. If the targets are missed, there are financial penalties.

In my private member's bill, I proposed such financial incentives be established not just for professional managers, but also for ministers of the Crown and government MPs. The few media reports on these provisions and the response of the general audience to my presentation on phone-in radio shows indicated that these financial incentives were very popular. Canadians obviously believe that financial rewards and punishments are useful for getting the best job done in the private and public sectors alike.

Summary and conclusions

The Canadian Charter of Rights and Freedoms limits the power of the people exercised through a properly constituted legislature. The Charter focuses on human rights. My paper argues that the power of the people needs to be limited also through the entrenchment of private property rights. Such an entrenchment would be fair and increase efficiency, as is suggested by the models of public choice and bureaucracy.

Inflation, deficits, restrictions on foreign dealings, and an excessively large government lead to the expropriation of private property directly and through inefficiencies. These property losses are best prevented by a property rights clause in the Charter, which specifies policy targets in each of the areas that the government is required to meet.

In an uncertain world it is not possible to meet targets at all times. Deviations should be allowed as long as they are within specified boundaries and as long as targets are met over certain lengths of time. In the case of serious emergencies, the targets and bands can be violated for a time if this action is approved through a super-majority vote in Parliament.

Limits on the legislature can also be self-imposed or created by international treaties. The latter approach represents an attractive alternative to new clauses in the Charter. It has already been used in the form of NAFTA and the WTO to limit the power of Parliament in international trade. A North American Monetary Union constrained by a proper constitution would prevent inflationary policies by the Bank of Canada.

There are many devils in the details for implementing these limits. My analysis has identified some of them and suggested how they can be dealt with. In the end, my defence of recommendations has unfortunately required me to conclude with the assertion that "in my opinion" certain favorable results would be produced. This assertion of my private judgement leaves me uncomfortable. I wish I could have cited a large body of theoretical and empirical evidence that clinched the case. This state of affairs implies that much more work by social scientists and politicians is needed to make a definitive case for the adoption of property rights in the Canadian constitution. Perhaps a constituent assembly charged primarily with changing governance, as discussed at this conference by other speakers, would be a forum for the discussion of these issues.

In conclusion I also wish to note that the enshrinement of property rights in the Charter and limits on government through international treaties are no panaceas to the ills of democracies. However, they offer enough hope for improvement that they deserve the attention of thinkers and policy makers who are already considering reforms of political institutions designed to make Parliaments more representative of, and responsive to, the will of the people.

References

Chao, Johnny and Herbert Grubel (1998). "Optimal Levels of Spending and Taxation in Canada." In Grubel, ed. (1998), pp. 53-68.

Grubel, Herbert (1999). *The Case for the Amero: The Economics and Politics of a North American Monetary Union.* Critical Issues Bulletin. Vancouver, BC: The Fraser Institute.

_____ ed. (1998). *How to use the Fiscal Surplus: What is the Optimal Size of Government?* Vancouver, BC: The Fraser Institute.

Grubel, Herbert, Douglas Purvis, and William Scarth (1992). *Limits to Government: Controlling Deficits and Debt in Canada.* Toronto, Ont.: CD Howe Institute.

House of Commons of Canada, Second Session, Thirty-fifth Parliament, 45 Elizabeth II, 1996. Bill C-213, *The Constitution Act, 1996* (balanced budget and spending limit). Introduced by Mr. Grubel.

Uhler, Lewis (1989). *Setting Limits: Constitutional Control of Government.* Washington, DC: Regnery Gateway.

CHAPTER 13
Transparency, Accountability, and Access to Information

Discussion by John Reid

I am intimately acquainted with both politics and politicians, having been a member of Parliament and a Cabinet member. Now, as an officer of Parliament, I still deal with politics and politicians on a daily basis, but from a totally non-partisan perspective. My new perspective leads me to the theme of my remarks: transparency, accountability and access to information.

It has been a humbling realization for me to discover that what Parliament has asked me to do, as information commissioner, is to keep our democracy healthy by enforcing the "right to know." Yes, I know full well how important a step we took 18 years ago in this country when Parliament passed the *Access to Information Act*. As an MP, I worked with Walter Baker, Ged Baldwin, and others to craft an enduring, powerful tool which would radically shift power from the state to the individual. But I did not fully comprehend what a central place this law would come to occupy in our democracy. Three years after its passage, the House Justice Committee reviewed the law; in its unanimous report it asserted that the *Access to Information Act* is of "similar significance" to the Canadian Charter of Rights and Freedoms. The Supreme Court of Canada recently referred to the Access law as being "quasi-constitutional."

Members of Parliament, the judiciary, members of the media, academics, business people, and the public at large now recognize that the *Access to Information Act* is one of the cornerstones of our democratic process and one of the best tools available to provide accountable and transparent government. I am told that the principal tool used by members of Parliament (in all parties) to gain information about government activities and decisions is the *Access to Information Act*.

Responsible decisions regarding voting and daily interaction with the government can only be made if adequate and accurate information is available. While informal methods of information dissemination provide much of what is necessary, the more formal and independently reviewable method provided by the *Access to Information Act* is essential for the free flow of information and for good, responsible government.

Let me open a parenthesis here to underline the distinction between "government" and "governance." In the years to come, we will want to extend the right of access to a large number of quasi-governmental and private sector firms, which wield increasing power over our lives. To close the parenthesis, and return to our topic, I want to give some historical perspective on access to information.

While Canada has had a federal *Access to Information Act* for 18 years, since 1983, we are relative latecomers to the process. The United States passed its Freedom of Information law in 1966, Denmark and Norway passed their laws in 1970, and Holland and France passed theirs in 1978. Australia and New Zealand got their acts in 1982. Then, aside from Canada, there was a hiatus until 1992 when Hungary passed its law. Since then, there has been, if not a flood, then certainly an increasing stream of countries enacting, or considering enacting, access to, or freedom of, information laws.

Currently, almost 40 countries have such legislation and more are on the horizon. This includes such unlikely, at least until recently, countries as Argentina, Belize, Bosnia and Herzegovina, Bulgaria, South Korea, Nepal, Pakistan, and the Russian Federation. Who could have predicted this list when Canada passed its law in 1983?

I've left mentioning one country to the last—Sweden—because it is unique. Sweden has had access to information legislation since 1766! Sweden's long-standing and firm commitment to access to information was one of the stumbling blocks to it joining the European Union in 1995, and has been a constant source of friction between Sweden and the other member countries since it did join.

Access laws are remarkable achievements. It takes courage and self-confidence for a government to subject itself and its bureaucracy to such transparency. Yet even governments cannot ignore the reality that access laws have become an essential cornerstone to a vibrant and healthy democracy. The benefits of such laws are tangible and profound and they are transforming the way in which public business is done. There is greater care, frugality, integrity, and honesty in government because of access laws.

Unfortunately, while more and more countries are opening up to their citizens, there are still well over 100 countries with no freedom of information laws and, worse still, some governments, including our own, are attempting to close the doors and windows that have already been opened. For example, last year, seemingly verifying Sweden's fears, the European Union proposed new rules to limit access to official EU documents. These rules are still being fought over. The most recent example, in Canada, is the anti-terrorism legislation passed following the events of September 11, 2001 in the United States, more of which later.

Thus, at the same time that access to information laws are blossoming, there is still a climate of hostility towards them by the bureaucracies and governments sworn to foster and uphold them. At the federal level in this country, after 18 years under the act—and of governing in what may seem to them to be a fishbowl—the government and the bureaucracy are still not comfortable with the regime of access to information. Perhaps no government ever will be. The noble principles and the flush of enthusiasm that reigned when the act was put into force in 1983 rapidly gave way to the forces of expediency, secrecy, and, from time to time, all-out hostility against the information commissioner and the act.

In his 1996-97 *Annual Report*, my predecessor, John Grace, in what now seems like a flash of prescience, referred to a pessimistic and provocative book by Jean-François Revel titled, *The Flight from Truth: the Reign of Deceit in the Information Age.* Revel wrote that "the withholding of truth, which is falsehood in its elementary form" is directed "first of all against public opinion" (p. 161). Why? Because, as Simon Bolivar observed, "The first and foremost of all forces is public opinion" (Revel, p. 161).

This comment was reaffirmed more than a century later by Thabo Mbeki, now President of South Africa, in a panel discussion in *Time* magazine in 1997 on the impact of information technology on the art and practice of government. He acknowledged that access to information changes the way leaders deal with their people. He said, "Before you had the politician as a professional, an expert who mediated understanding of events" (*Time*, February 17, 1997). Now, instant access, unfiltered through either government or press, "reduces the mystique that surrounds a politician." He went on to conclude that it is easier to govern "if the population is ignorant." During the same discussion, United Nations Secretary-General Kofi Annan went even further by commenting about access to information: "if you are into control, it's frightening. This thing cannot stop."

It should not be a surprise that some of those who wield power also recoil from the accountability that transparency brings. Over and over again, we learn the lesson, even in the most vibrant democracies, that a few public officials seek private advantage from their positions of trust. Almost without fail, selfish motives masquerade in the garments of "public interest."

Ethical conduct cannot be enforced; conduct can only be scrutinized. Any society aspiring to be free, just, and civil must depend upon and nurture a wide array of methods for exposing, and imposing sanctions on, ethical failures. Thus the need for a free and skeptical press, irksome and even irresponsible as it can be; thus the need for a fiercely independent judiciary and legal profession; a professional public service; a freely elected legislature; and an informed, engaged citizenry.

In one way or another, all the checks and balances designed to limit abuses of government power are dependent upon there being access by outsiders to governments' insider information. Perhaps it is wrong to refer to it as "governments' insider information," for the information doesn't belong to government, nor to the bureaucracies, the managers, or the public servants who create it. Indeed, it belongs to all of us who live in this country, who pay the salaries of those who create and then jealously guard that information from our prying eyes. A government, and a public service, which holds tight to a culture of secrecy is a government and public service ripe for abuse. Too many of our senior public servants still subscribe to the views of Sir Humphrey in *Yes, Minister*, when he tells his prime minister, "You can have good government, or you can have open government. But, prime minister, you can't have both."

There is one shining exception to this culture, at the provincial level. Alberta is one of the very few jurisdictions in Canada where the leader of the government is a vocal supporter of the public's right to know. Premier Klein was premier when the *Alberta Freedom of Information and Privacy Act* was passed. By his own admission, he has been "FOIPed" more than anyone else in the province, yet he is proud to say that the passage of this act is one of his most important accomplishments. When the Alberta act was passed, Premier Klein appeared in a video, looked directly into the camera, and told public servants to embrace openness, obey the new law, and get on with it. No Canadian prime minister has urged his ministers and officials to make the federal access law work.

Since few government insiders are fans of the public's right to know, I was troubled when the federal minister of justice chose to entrust a reform of the *Access to Information Act* to bureaucrats. I fear that the temptation will be great for them to address their own agenda for relief from what they see as "onerous" obligations, and to do so in the guise of reform. Our *Access to Information Act* is too important, with the basics too well crafted, for us to tolerate a wolf-in-sheep's-clothing package of reforms. A legitimate fear, then, is that a reform proposal, cobbled together by government insiders without the benefit of a full, public, parliamentary review, will address the concerns of the bureaucracy at the expense of the concerns of the public. If this should happen, then no reform would be, by far, the better option. Stay tuned. *[Author's note: The Task Force Report came out in June 2002 and all of our fears proved to have been justified. For further details, see* **Response to the Report of the Access to Information Review Task Force—A Special Report to Parliament,** *September 2002, by the Office of the Information Commissioner of Canada.]*

To further complicate the reform process, the events of September 11, 2001, in the US have occasioned Bill C-36, popularly referred to at the *Anti-Terrorism Act.* This statute amends many other acts of Parliament, including the *Access to Information Act,* in an attempt to combat terrorism. The proposal to amend the *Access to Information Act* represents an entirely unexpected, and yet to be explained, weakening of the access law. This bill proposes that the attorney general of Canada be given the power to issue a certificate, the effect of which would be to exclude any information from the act for the purpose of protecting international relations, national defence, or security. The certificate would prevent the information commissioner and the courts from reviewing the documents to see if, indeed, secrecy is justifiable. Under the proposal, there is no need to demonstrate injury from disclosure and there is no end to the period of secrecy.

Thus, there will be no meaningful, independent review of government decisions to refuse disclosure of any records that it considers fit into these categories, just as there is currently no meaningful recourse if the government certifies a record to be a Cabinet confidence. With no independent review, there is every likelihood that this new exclusion will be applied to a broader range of records than intended by Parliament. That, after all, is the experience with the Cabinet confidence exclusion. Worse still, no one but the bureaucrats applying the exclusions may ever know the truth. While Cabinet confidences receive protection for 20 years, information covered by an attorney general certificate could remain secret forever.

Let me give you a stellar example of why I feel it is reasonable to expect that the certificate proposed in Bill C-36 is likely to be abused. The example is drawn from the provision already in the act, allowing the clerk of the privy council to certify that records are Cabinet confidences and, hence, excluded from the right of access.

On April 2, 2001, the Federal Court, Trial Division issued its decision in *Information Commissioner of Canada v. Minister of Environment Canada and Ethyl Canada Inc. (T-1125-99) Trial Division*. That case arose after Ethyl Canada Inc. made a request under the *Access to Information Act* for access to the background, analysis, and options material presented to Cabinet when Cabinet decided to ban the fuel additive known as "MMT." Cabinet confidences are excluded from the right of access except in the circumstances described in subsection 69(3) of the act, which are:

> a) 20 years have elapsed since the confidences came into existence, or
> b) if the confidences are discussion papers presenting background explanations, analysis of problems and policy options to Cabinet and if
>> i) the decision to which such confidences relate have been made public, or
>> ii) otherwise, if four years have elapsed since the related decision.

Ethyl Canada Inc. believed that the conditions set out in paragraph 69(3)(b) of the act were satisfied since the government's decision to ban MMT had been made public when a bill for that purpose was introduced in Parliament and eventually passed.

The Minister of Environment Canada, to whom the request was made, acknowledged that she had documents relevant to the access request but refused to disclose any portions of the records, on the basis of advice from the Privy Council Office (PCO). Environment Canada based its refusal on the ground that discussion papers no longer exist and on the ground that the documents found relevant to the request were not stand-alone records bearing the appellation: "discussion papers." The records were withheld from access as being memoranda to Cabinet and records used to brief ministers of the Crown in relation to matters before the privy council.

My office investigated the matter and concluded that the former content of discussion papers (which Parliament said should be disclosed) had been moved within days of the passage of the *Access to Information Act*, primarily into the analysis section of the "Memorandum to Cabinet." I concluded that the PCO had attempted to extinguish a substantive right merely by changing the name of a record, and brought an "Application for Review" in the federal court seeking an order for disclosure of this information.

In his finding, Mr. Justice Blanchard agreed with the information commissioner's position and stated: "Being the master of its own economy, Cabinet is free to use whatever Cabinet Paper System it chooses and is equally at liberty to modify its paper system at will to fit the practical reality of the day. But such liberty cannot extend to a paper system that, in my view, results in a circumvention of the intent of Parliament, namely the elimination of 'discussion papers' as a document only to include similar background information in another part of the Memorandum to Cabinet and thereby prevent its release as required by law and in accordance with paragraph 69(3)(b) of the *Access to Information Act* or paragraph 39(4)(b) of the *Canada Evidence Act*."

The Court saw through the subterfuge that had been used by the most senior officials of government to subvert the will of Parliament. The court recognized that Parliament had decided that the people of Canada should have access to these important records (which where then called "discussion papers") and the court also recognized that officials, by fiat, had endeavoured to unilaterally remove such records from access by renaming them. Despite this decision, the government continued to refuse to disclose the requested records and appealed the decision. On appeal, the Federal Court of Appeal forcefully upheld the decision of the Trial Division and stated that whenever there is "...a *corpus* of words the purpose of which is to present background explanations, analyses of problems or policy options to Council for consideration by Council in making decision, that can be reasonably severed from the documents..." such *corpus* of words must be severed and released (2003 FCA 68 at p. 76).

In his final report to the House of Commons entitled *Reflections on a Decade of Serving Parliament*, Canada's Auditor General, Denis Desautels, also recognized this growing culture of secrecy when he said:

> Other countries are rapidly strengthening accountability, and Canada is in danger of being left behind. Part of the problem is the nature of Canadian politics. There is a reluctance to let Parliament and the public know how government programs are working, because if things are going badly you may be giving your opponents the stick to beat you with. And even when a Minister is not personally concerned with this, senior public servants assume this fear on the Minister's behalf. The people who write government performance reports seem to try to say as little as possible that would expose their department to criticism. (p. 86)

All of what I have been saying comes down to this: a strong right of access to government-held records is vital to a healthy democracy. Yet, no matter how well-crafted a freedom of information law may be, it will not be effective unless the leader of the government and the head of the public service insist that openness becomes part of the culture of governance. Without an insistence on openness from the top, the culture of secrecy will thrive. If employees feel that compliance with the *Access to Information Act* is not a priority for the leaders, you will see delays, inflated fees, antagonism towards requesters, inadequate searches, and an increasing numbers of complaints. When the leaders decide not to keep minutes of meetings, when they tell others not to write things down, when they perpetuate the myths about abusive requesters, when they tolerate giving the minister's needs priority over legal rights, when they do not foster a culture of openness in general—their employees get the message loud and clear.

So often I hear senior officials say: "I don't have to like this law; I only have to obey it!"—and that grudging attitude is infectious in destructive ways at lower levels. No matter how well crafted an access law may be, it will only be a good law if public officials make it work.

I believe that the courts, the public, members of Parliament, the media, almost every group in society, believe strongly in the right of access. They support a strengthening of these laws and are convinced that openness makes our governance better, our democracy stronger. I am not so sure that those groups are paying enough attention to the challenges that this access right now faces.

Consequently, I make this plea: in these difficult times of international conflict and domestic terrorism, be as vigilant in protecting the rights of a free society as you are in protecting property and loved ones. I am grateful to you for allowing me to reflect upon the importance to a free society of the right to know.

References cited

Desautels, Denis (2001). *Reflections on a Decade of Serving Parliament.* Government of Canada: Office of the Auditor General (February). Available digitally at *http://www.oag-bvg.gc.ca/domino/reports.nsf/html/01cap_e.html*

Reid, The Honourable John M. (2002). *Response to the Report of the Access to Information Review Task Force: A Special Report to Parliament.* Government of Canada: Office of the Information Commissioner of Canada (September). Available digitally at *http://infocom.gc.ca/reports/2002special-e.asp*

Revel, Jean-François (1991 [1988]). *The Flight from Truth: the Reign of Deceit in the Information Age.* New York: Random House.

CHAPTER 14
Q&A for Panel 4:
Constitutional Constraints

Question: Mr. Reid, this summer I was very interested to follow the deliberations of John Bryden's committee dealing with access to information. It was interesting that the prime minister forbade bureaucrats to give evidence for that committee, if I read the reports correctly. But your predecessor, Mr. Grace, spoke. One of the things he addressed was the creative tension between the Privacy Act and the Access to Information Act. Two independent individuals who report to Parliament are responsible for these acts. I believe he proposed that the two acts be amalgamated and one person administer them both. I'd be interested in your comments on that creative tension and whether or not you subscribe to your predecessor's point of view.

John Reid: First, I have to say that I think the PM was operating correctly when he said that his bureaucrats could not appear before Mr. Bryden's committee. The reason for that is that the PM has 25 cases outstanding against me as information commissioner. He and his lawyers were quite concerned that they might say something that could be used against him in the legal proceedings, so I have some sympathy for the position that was taken. I was in the same position as the PM, because I was asked to appear, and we had to consider the fate of these 25 cases. So it was an unfortunate set of occurrences because we were both caught up in the same kind of problem.

Now, let me turn to the creative tension between access and privacy. The worldwide pattern is that these offices are united, so wherever you see access and privacy, they tend to be in one office.

In all provinces in Canada, one office does the two jobs. So the pattern has been to unite the two. At the federal level, the decision to separate the two was taken back in 1983 when the *Access to Information Act* and the *Privacy Act* were passed at the same time. It was felt that it would be better at the beginning to have them on separate tracks because the acts are interconnected.

For example, I enforce the *Privacy Act* in all those questions that are referred to the access of information commissioner. (And, by the way, privacy is the largest exemption that is used within the government of Canada when it issues information.) Second, at the present time, the federal *Privacy Act* has been extended through the *Personal Information Protection and Electronic Documents Act* to deal with information on individuals held by the private sector. It was felt at the time that a separate administration was necessary to handle that new act, which comes into full effect on January 1, 2004. I would have no objection to the two departments joining in the future, perhaps when this second piece of legislation is mature. If you want to join the two offices, there is a provision in the *Access to Information Act* that allows the access to information commissioner to become the privacy commissioner.

John Richards: I disagree with Herb. First, though, I want to pay homage to Herb. In the last ten years, Herb has done more than perhaps any other economist to wake Canadians up to the number of ways whereby fiscal matters actually work in government. He deserves congratulations for having, as an elected politician, said a lot of painful truths to voters that they would rather not hear. Now comes the disagreement.

What Herb has given us in the last half hour is an intelligent discussion about the role of interest groups, and the ability of governments to bugger up the numbers and hide what they're up to. All of which is part and parcel of an intelligent discussion about public policy. My disagreement is with his faith that you can constitutionalize and entrench the kind of sophisticated wisdom that Herb and other Canadians have brought to these kinds of discussions. To my left wing colleagues I say: don't try and entrench the welfare state. Many social provisions are good. Universal education is good. A single-payer health system (and I say it with deference to where I am) is overall a good thing. These are not the kinds of things that lawyers can adjudicate and you render us stupid as a collectivity and community if you try to reduce these complexities to entrenched items. The free market is important. A government that balances its books and is reasonably efficient is another institution of civilized society that is immensely important. Do not delude yourself, Herb, that you can reduce these intelligent notions to something that can be entrenched by the Charter and which goddamned lawyers will debate.

Herb Grubel: You love to talk from principle. But I think it won't get you very far. We will never reach an agreement. I appeal to you with the empirical fact that deficit limitations work in many US states and they have produced superior results. The European monetary union has succeeded in lowering the interest rates in Italy from a premium of 6 percent over Germany to zero. They have had no inflation. Their currency is stable. In many ways, the question always is what is the empirical evidence? I think if we had enough time I could adduce lots of empirical evidence that the kinds of restraints I'm talking about are working.

Ted White: Herb, the day that we get citizens initiatives in Canada, I'll help you take one to get property rights—and we will get it for you, because, frankly, you have more chance of getting it through a citizens initiative than you'd ever have trying to convince governments to do it for you.

You provoked me right at the beginning of your speech, so I had to get up and defend myself. I think you've misunderstood me. I never said the people are always right, but I do think the people have the right to be wrong. That's what I have argued about from the beginning. An example from my own riding is the gun control bill. I provided as much information as I could in 1994 to convince my constituents that it was a silly bill. In the end, they decided that they wanted me to vote for it, which I did, but I made it clear that I thought they were wrong. Over time they have been proven to be wrong. I defend their right to be wrong. As their representative, it is important for me to take that view to Ottawa. So in terms of citizens initiatives, I think when you criticize them you must give some examples to support your arguments. When you say they don't protect minority rights, I want you to show me an example from California, or Oregon, or Washington of any initiative that ever passed that was against minority rights. Yet I can show you many examples that support the things you want including Proposition 13. Many, many conservative decisions come out of referendums. In fact, they support the conservative agenda, so thanks, Herb, but you need to get with the program.

Herb Grubel: Now you all know what I was up against for four years.

Question: I'm concerned that the legislation put in front of our provincial and national assemblies is so complex and so long that there are just not enough hours for the members to deal with it, nor—no discredit to them—do they have the brain cells to absorb the sheer mass and complexity of what's put in front of them. Do you feel as I do that we're getting inadequate laws and an overabundance of confusing regulations because of this situation?

John Reid: It's not too complex for the human mind. When you look at any piece of legislation you see four or five principles operating. If you want to see a committee tearing apart a piece of legislation very effectively, look at the justice committee [or various] senate committee[s]. They put in the hours and they put in the time. The dilemma for most members of Parliament is that doing committee work is a waste of their time. It's a waste of their time because the press doesn't cover it. There's no reward for being a hard-working MP doing legislation. You get no publicity, and when you go back home, nobody's interested in what you've done on committees. So the way the system works, it's a waste of time for a member of Parliament to be knowledgeable. Fortunately, the system operates so that members do take a big interest in legislation, and do work very hard at it. But if you're in opposition, it's awfully difficult for you to keep up, because the government has more manpower, and by the end of the session members of the opposition are exhausted. It's very gruelling in Ottawa, and members from the West Coast carry the heaviest burden of all because they've got the longest distances to fly back to keep in touch with their constituencies. So they work very hard at it, and if you go to a member who is sitting on any committee that has to do with a piece of legislation, you'll find that that member knows what's in the legislation, and has worked hard to understand it.

Question: While I admire the work that committees do, and I think that the committee on C-36 has done good work when it comes to votes in the House, and we all vote on most pieces of legislation, the fact is that most

MPs do not read the legislation that they vote on. We could do a quick poll on the members present now. How many of us have read from front to back, say, one bill in ten out of all the bills we voted on? I can say that I have not, and I know that I've put more time into this sort of thing than most MPs do. Of course there's a good rational reason for that. While the Alliance MPs are an exception, throughout their careers most MPs will always vote along party lines, and if they don't, they will be punished for that.

However, I really want to address Herb's excellent proposal. Since we are now going from the federal level to the provincial level, and are discussing what the BC government should do, I suggest some of the following observations with regard to Herb's proposals. First, section 43 of the constitution allows for amendments to the Canadian constitution, which effectively become part of the constitution of a province. So, for example, there was an amendment to the constitution that imposed duties upon the New Brunswick government to provide French language services. Similarly, there was one with regard to educational reform in Newfoundland. I think that would be an appropriate thing to do in BC. I would like to suggest the BC government could do as those provinces did, pass the law, then go to Ottawa and say we would like you to pass the resolution entrenching this constitutionally. The super-majority override you suggested has some validity at the federal level because of the breakdown of seats. It's rare for a party to get 66 or 75 percent of the seats in Parliament. That, unfortunately, is not true in provincial legislatures. In Alberta, normally, the governing party always has that kind of majority. It's true in BC right now, and could be a pattern that replicates itself in such a way as to make it possible for some governments to override any super-majority requirement simply by saying: "this is a confidence motion; you will vote as follows."

I have a last point with regard to property rights and entrenching them so that some form of super-majority is necessary to override them. I would just observe that the only thing, in my view, that should be overrideable should be compensation being prompt. That is to say that it may be necessary to put off compensation, but I think on principle that in times of crisis, we have a tendency to be willing to confiscate property from those who are a threatening, or an ostensibly threatening, minority. I'm thinking of the Japanese in 1942, for example, or potentially of Muslim Canadians today. I think we have to be very concerned.

The Process for Getting There

Introduction

While it is complex enough to identify and design the appropriate elements of democratic reform, history teaches us that the most difficult thing of all seems to be *making it happen*.

If leaders want reform, though, they can make it happen with relative ease, and we have had concrete examples of that in Canada with the Charter (Pierre Trudeau), and fixed election dates (Gordon Campbell). But these instances are rare, since few leaders voluntarily choose to constrain their own power.

The main impetus for reform will normally come from the citizens—but how to organize such inchoate thought? To that issue we now turn, looking at two sorts of devices, one tried and proven, the other quite new.

CHAPTER 15:
Constituent Assemblies as Vehicles for Change

Casey G. Vander Ploeg

I have lived in southern Alberta all my life. Southern Albertans are well known across the country for several things: common sense, no nonsense, and above all, populism. But that might be a myth, and the myth quickly explodes when an Albertan finds himself in Vancouver to attend a conference on electoral and parliamentary reform.

British Columbia is the one province in Canada where populism not only forms part of the political culture, but where the ideas of direct democracy have managed to gain a toe-hold in the governing apparatus. Since 1990, at least three private member's bills—some coming from the government caucus—have found their way to the floor of the Alberta legislature, where they were quickly slain by an unholy alliance of both government and opposition members representing every political party in the House. Alberta seems to be all talk and no action. But perception is reality, so I suppose the myth will continue.

The Canada West Foundation has a long-standing interest in the notion of direct democracy and parliamentary reform, and is one of the few research institutes in Canada that has dedicated significant resources to the study of the constituent assembly as a means of achieving such reform. This interest comes from the mission of the Canada West Foundation itself, part of which is to provide opportunities for citizen engagement in the public policy process.

So what is a constituent assembly? Why are they held? What are the advantages of the approach? What are the disadvantages? How are they constructed and how do they work? Most important, does the process fit with pursuing electoral and direct democracy reform in British Columbia?

What is a constituent assembly?

A constituent assembly is an *ad hoc* and temporary addition to the current structures of government. It is an extra-governmental body that exists alongside current political institutions. It consists of people selected and delegated to address a specific issue of extreme importance, typically constitutional matters. A constituent assembly has no sovereignty in the sense that it can render a final decision; its authority is restricted to the mandate for which it has been created, and makes proposals only. However, a constituent assembly is more than a consultative body. It is a group designed to take action, but any proposals emerging from a constituent assembly need a separate ratification process.

Why are constituent assemblies convened? Typically, there are four reasons.

- A nation might be emerging from a major crisis, such as Germany was at the end of WWII, or as South Africa was when apartheid came to an end.
- There may be a threat of significant political upheaval that needs to be contained. Such was the case in India in 1946 when independence from Britain was followed by the threat of civil war with Pakistan.
- There may be an absence of functioning political institutions. Such was the case in Spain after the death of Franco.
- Existing institutions may be proving incapable of arriving at a solution to a pressing problem. Such was the case in 1787 when the United States Constitution was drafted.

In the Canadian context, the call for a constituent assembly has been pursued because of this fourth reason. Many see a constituent assembly as the best method to achieve a constitutional peace and avoid the break-up of the country. The current process of executive federalism and power brokering among first ministers is largely bankrupt in the eyes of the Canadian public. Over the last 30 years, the traditional process has been unable to achieve a constitutional settlement.

Advantages

What are the advantages of the constituent assembly? Why select a specific group of people aside from the regular political actors to settle an issue? There are many reasons.

- The constituent assembly provides a broadly-based vehicle for change by creating an opportunity for extensive citizen involvement. This in turn, helps create a deep and popular commitment to the principles driving the change, and the details of the change. As such, a constituent assembly responds to the priorities of citizens, not just governments or special interests. Depending on how the assembly is constructed, it offers the potential to dramatically reduce the impact of partisanship and envisions a broader agenda than that contemplated by political actors alone. It encourages fresh perspectives.
- Unlike governments, which deal with many issues at one time, the constituent assembly has a clear mandate and singleness of purpose. It is working full time on the issue and thus is a much more deliberative body. It creates intense pressures to succeed.
- The process recognizes the inherent limitations of government in deciding huge issues such as constitutional reform or the restructuring of the electoral system. In many ways, government mandates just cannot be stretched far enough to include reform because governments are the ones that stand to gain or lose the most from any rearranging of the political furniture. It makes no sense for government, as only one actor in the political game, to decide on the rules of the game. The constituent assembly injects legitimacy and credibility into the

decision-making process, because ultimately, citizens are the ones who own the constitution and the political process.

- Constituent assemblies are highly independent. They can bypass entrenched positions and excessive partisanship, both of which resist reform. The process sidesteps old political and institutional baggage and can renew a stale debate. Constituent assemblies have no institutional vested interests or turf to protect. They stand apart from governments and parties. Successful assemblies can work alongside existing institutions, but are neither captured by those institutions, nor do they pre-empt those institutions' current responsibilities and powers.
- The real advantage of constituent assemblies is that they build consensus in the community before any changes get final approval. Constituent assemblies help "bullet-proof" reforms by ensuring support from a diverse set of interests. They build substantial momentum and popular acceptance of change. A constituent assembly is an innovative process—a rare political event—that captures the public's imagination.

One of my first assignments at Canada West was to review the experiences of Australia, Switzerland, and California with constitutional referendums. At that time, we were anticipating a referendum on the Charlottetown Accord. Our research showed that referendums that failed to build consensus prior to the vote usually suffered dramatic defeats. Would the Charlottetown Accord have been such a spectacular flop if the agreement had been vetted and smoothed by a directly-elected constituent assembly? I think the outcome could well have been different.

World experience suggests that constituent assemblies rarely fail. A diverse group of people in sufficiently large numbers that can act freely with access to good advice from experts and an opportunity to debate and negotiate over an extended period, typically meets the challenge. Constituent assemblies create the conditions where agreement becomes possible, particularly when there is enormous general interest in the issue, but a multitude of special interests that stand in the way. They have been held the world over and on every continent. If any generalization can be extracted, it is that constituent assemblies demonstrate a remarkable track record of success. The bigger the job, the more successful they seem to be.

Possible disadvantages

If those are the upsides, what is the downside?

- The biggest threat is that an elected assembly, possessing both a high level of legitimacy and credibility, runs wild, changing the fabric of a constitution or the political process in ways no one anticipated. No one can predict the direction in which a constituent assembly's interest might turn, or the range and scope of its recommendations. At the same time, a constituent assembly can only propose—not impose. While a runaway assembly is a possibility, our research indicates that this has not been overly problematic in other jurisdictions.
- The process takes time. A constituent assembly is not a weekend conference or a one-day meeting. The time it takes depends on how the assembly is constructed, particularly whether it is elected or appointed. But the assembly must also select a chair, appoint an executive, establish voting procedures, and create committees. In many ways, it has to start from scratch, and will likely re-invent at least some of the wheels before it begins designing the carriage. The shortest constituent assembly with relevance to Canada took four months in Switzerland. The longest took 12 years in Australia. South Africa's assembly took two years, and India's three years. The average runs 8 months to just over a year. So these are not short events. But time also works to the constituent assembly's advantage. Sufficient time is necessary for them to do their jobs well. A key failure of traditional consultation methods—conferences, summits, and the like—is that they take too little time for meaningful participation to occur.
- It is possible for a constituent assembly to reproduce, in a new forum, the existing disagreements and stalemates—putting old wine in a new bottle. But this is not inevitable, and highly unlikely if governments resist the temptation to dominate the process by forming the majority in the assembly or appointing to it individuals who reflect prevailing sentiments and positions.

Some have argued that constituent assemblies may be inappropriate for dealing with complex issues. But most assemblies have available expert advisors and a competent research staff. If its proposals are also phased in, complexity becomes less of a problem as solutions are phased in. In 1996, Canada West held a modified constituent assembly composed entirely of randomly selected young people from across Canada to discuss and formulate options on national unity, economic development, and direct democracy. The group was diverse—a microcosm of Canadian youth. The group arrived at recommendations that were very similar to ones emerging from conferences and forums that had only experts in attendance. *[Editor's note: The next chapter describes this process.]*

- A constituent assembly is often seen as a last ditch effort. What if it fails? Failure creates the real danger of removing any hope for meaningful change. The possibility of failure cannot be discounted, and failure would surely discredit a return to a more modest process of reform.

Creating a constituent assembly carries some risk, but so does walking across the street. The question is whether this risk offsets all of the advantages.

Constituent assemblies are rare. Why? An assembly needs the support of the very politicians it is pushing to the sidelines, which is compounded by the fact that its recommendations will shape politicians' future powers and limitations. As such, the constituent assembly process should not totally discount political leaders. Many constituent assemblies have had at least some politicians represented; politicians have even dominated some, although this is clearly self-defeating. The optimum situation is one in which political leaders stay active and engaged in the process. They can do this by setting the terms of reference for the assembly, meeting with delegates, making and responding to suggestions, giving testimony at assembly committees, and commenting in the media.

A frequent argument against the constituent assembly is that the process is new and untried. This is a red herring. It is neither. Nor is the process "un-Canadian" as some would have us believe. The best example in the world of a pure constituent assembly—one of the few that were directly elected—comes from Canada in 1946, in what is now the province of Newfoundland. Newfoundland joined Canada following a referendum, but the proposals on the ballot were drafted and decided by a constituent assembly.

Practical matters

How are constituent assemblies constructed? How do they work?

Constituent assemblies come in a variety of forms. We can distinguish among four types based on how their members are selected. If all members are directly elected, the body is properly labeled a "constituent assembly." Such assemblies are very rare, and Newfoundland represents the only example with relevance to Canada. The assembly can be indirectly elected by parliaments and legislatures. In this instance, the assembly becomes a "constitutional convention." Such was the type of assembly in the US in 1787, and in India, Germany, and Australia in 1973. A third type is the "constitutional council" whose delegates are appointed by the government of the day. Such was the case in Switzerland in 1848. Finally, the "hybrid constituent assembly" employs a blended selection process. This was used in Spain in 1977, Australia in 1897, and South Africa in 1996.

Deciding how members are selected is the most critical decision that has to be made because it directly affects the assembly's levels of legitimacy and credibility. Clearly, a directly elected assembly will be more independent than one that is indirectly elected or appointed. Each election method has its advantages and disadvantages, which is one reason for the hybrid assembly.

However its members are selected, it is critical that the assembly is, and is perceived to be, broadly representative of the diverse range of interests in society. An assembly stacked in favour of one group or another, or one that excludes a significant voice in society, or one that includes individuals who have always had entrenched positions, will not meet expectations.

In our thinking, if an assembly is to be elected, the election system used should be the single transferable vote (STV). This system enables voters to select delegates based on a broad range of crite-

ria, such as the strength of individual candidates, how environ-
mentally sensitive they are, whether or not they are women or
aboriginal candidates, or whatever. The STV system is most likely
to produce a diverse group reflective of society. This system also
avoids the tricky problem of having to hand pick people, or arbi-
trarily set quotas.

Of course, the selection system is not limited to these forms
alone. An assembly can be as innovative and creative as the people
who are convening it. In 1991, former Supreme Court Justice
Estey proposed an assembly that would be comprised of citizens,
experts, and articulate spokespersons for specific communities
who had been nominated by individual legislators and then chosen at random. The random selection of "ordinary" Canadians has
been used in Canada West conferences, and by the Alberta government at one of its economic summits. For the 1992 "Renewal
of Canada" conferences, "ordinary" Canadians were invited to
apply as delegates by writing an essay on constitutional reform. A
committee then judged these essays, and those that were deemed
thoughtful and articulate joined a pool, from which a group was
randomly selected.

At the other end of the process is the whole question of ratification. In most assemblies around the world, the referendum has
been used to popularly ratify the proposals. This is followed by
formal approval of the government or governments of the day
through legislative resolutions. Only in India did the constituent
assembly ratify its own proposals. While South Africa followed a
similar approach, there was provision for a referendum if the proposals did not secure a ⅔ majority in the assembly.

Between the selection of delegates and final ratification is the
assembly process itself. Aside from setting the general parameters
and the broad mandate, the assembly can be left to decide for itself
how it will reach consensus. The degree to which this has taken
place depends largely on the control sought by the convening
authorities. Clearly, there is a balance that must be struck
between allowing the assembly to proceed, and frustrating its
members with a set of tight rules and restrictions.

Creating a constituent assembly

So what are the steps to be taken? The quickest, easiest, and most legitimate way to create an assembly is through an act of Parliament or a legislature calling for the creation of an assembly. This act would lay out the composition of the body, stipulate how members are to be selected, identify in broad terms the mandate and purpose of the assembly, and provide for final ratification of the proposals that emerge. The selection process then works itself out and the members meet to establish the procedures of the assembly. Work then begins on hammering out agreement on the specific reforms. Once proposals have been developed, the legislature and the public can then review them. The proposals might then go back to the assembly for revision. Once a final proposal is in place, the process can move to referendum. If that is successful, formal ratification by the legislature can take place.

How an assembly would work in BC

How does this process fit with reforming politics in British Columbia? First, the issues are obviously significant enough to warrant an extra-parliamentary process that provides for broad citizen representation and for bypassing entrenched interests opposed to altering the status quo. Second, if the assembly were to be elected, it would provide a good way to test alternative election systems, and would surely attract attention in the province, across the country, and even around the world. Third, if a referendum were to be held on the changes, the constituent assembly approach would help ensure a successful outcome. In many ways, there seems to be a fit.

However, I also sense a mismatch. First, you don't casually unleash constituent assemblies, and in some ways, this process seems too elaborate for the envisioned reforms. A key question is whether the power of the constituent assembly that is struck is commensurate with the reforms or changes that are envisioned. In many ways, the constituent assembly is a constitutional howitzer that is hauled out when governments have a significant problem with legitimacy.

Second, the government in BC is in a unique position. It possesses both a fresh mandate and a strong mandate. While one can certainly argue for the constituent assembly approach because the issue of political reform is very much one of "re-writing" the rules of the political game, the optics of a full blown directly-elected assembly may not register well. Voters will likely ask why the government's mandate, recently secured, is not enough to do whatever they want to do, including system reform, and that is no small hurdle.

In Canada, the push for a constituent assembly process is grounded in addressing the constitutional issue within a federal context where we have 14 governments of various partisan stripes with long-standing entrenched positions on certain issues, in addition to other interests such as first nations. The interests are legion, and there is a sense that neither the federal government alone, nor even the provincial and territorial governments, can speak for Canadians on constitutional issues. National institutions face serious limitations, but provincial governments are in a different situation. In that case, there is one government that is better able to speak on an issue, and that voice, for the most part, is uncontested.

On the other hand, the constitutional issue is certainly significant enough to warrant some form of direct and meaningful public participation. There really are two extremes: a full-blown constituent assembly, and government action with no public input whatsoever. Perhaps both have to be avoided. The good news is that governments have been experimenting with a variety of means that look and sound very much like the same thing. The question is, can we pare the constituent assembly idea down and still have it work?

CHAPTER 16:
Deliberative Democracy
and Electoral Reform

David K. Elton

Public consultation is an essential element of democratic societies every bit as much as are elections, the right to petition, and the right to protest. It therefore follows that democratic societies need to continually seek to develop transparent and legitimate consultation processes to encourage citizen engagement. The British Columbia government's commitment to hold a Citizens' Assembly on Electoral Reform provides an excellent opportunity to use a recent development in public consultation often referred to as deliberative democracy.

Over the past century, numerous techniques for consulting citizens have been devised. The most popular mechanisms for consultation include elections, referendums, legislative hearings, Royal Commissions, constituent surveys, public opinion polls, town hall meetings, focus groups, policy conferences, and policy round tables. In the past decade, alternative mechanisms have been developed that seek to build on the strengths of many of the traditional techniques and minimize many of their weaknesses. One of the most innovative and valuable techniques has become known as the deliberative democracy process. Some refer to this consultation mechanism as "citizens' forums."

Deliberative democracy and effective consultation

Deliberative democracy has been designed to employ the strengths of each of the nine traditional mechanisms mentioned above, and to minimize their weaknesses.

One of the best ways to determine the effectiveness of deliberative democracy is to identify a set of measurable criteria and undertake an assessment. For the purposes of this presentation, eight specific criteria that were use in a Canada West Foundation report entitled *Meaningful Consultation* have been used: representation, focusing the debate, access to information, open discussion and debate, consideration of alternative solutions, individual efficacy, achieving closure and cost and effectiveness. While there may be considerable disagreement over whether each of these eight criteria are essential, or whether other criteria should be included in the list, there are good reasons for using each of these eight in measuring an effective consultation process.

Representation

Deliberative democracy provides for representation of all elements in the community by using a random selection process to identify participants. In this regard it is similar to public opinion polling in that it gives every citizen an equal opportunity to participate. Indeed, the actual participants are often selected randomly from people that have previously participated a public opinion study.

Focusing the debate

Deliberative democracy consultations are similar to policy conferences in that they focus on a limited number of predetermined issue areas (e.g., specific economic development issues, specific environmental issues such as clean air, specific governance issues such as electoral reform, recall, or use of referenda).

Access to information

In order to ensure that meaningful deliberations take place, participants are provided with easy-to-read summary overviews of the issues under consideration and given access to a wide range of expert opinion on those topics. This access to information and expert opinion thus employs the best elements of both policy conferences and policy round tables.

Debate and discussion

Deliberative democracy consultations take place in a setting where all participants not only have the opportunity to participate, but are encouraged to do so. Trained facilitators lead small group discussions to ensure that a few outspoken persons do not dominate the discussions and debate, and where individuals have the opportunity to challenge one another's assertions. These small group discussions are one of the strengths of policy round tables and focus group processes.

Alternative solutions

Participants are encouraged to not only examine a range of viable alternatives to a particular issue, but also to search for additional options, as is the case in policy round table and focus group consultations.

Individual efficacy

Participants are given the opportunity to exchange their points of view with decision makers (e.g., elected officials and senior policy makers) and their conclusions are recorded and reported to these decision makers. The involvement of symbolically important people and assurances that decision makers will carefully consider conclusions reached by the group are essential given the high level of cynicism about consultation processes within both the public and the media regarding government processes.

Achieving closure

> Appropriate decision-making rules are put in place to ensure that the group has a means of reaching a consensus and that individuals can register their dissent.

Cost and logistics

> The consultations often take place over several days or over one or more weekends. Costs related to travel, lodging, and meals are provided. This makes deliberative democracy consultations considerably more time consuming and expensive than most of the traditional consultation mechanisms such as focus groups, constituent surveys, or even policy conferences. However, they are considerably less expensive than elections, referendums, and even public opinion polling.

Experiences with deliberative democracy consultations

> Several versions of deliberative democracy consultation have been held over the past decade in the United States, Australia, and Great Britain. One of the first attempts to integrate several aspects of this process into consultations in Canada was undertaken a decade ago when the federal government sponsored a series of conferences on constitutional change called the "Renewal of Canada Conferences." These conferences were set up following the embarrassing collapse of parliamentary hearings on constitutional reform in Manitoba when no citizens showed up to participate.

> The key to the success of the Renewal of Canada Conferences was the decision to encourage all Canadians to write to the organizers of the conferences (four research institutes) indicating their interest in participating in the conferences, and the subsequent random selection of a group of "ordinary citizens" as participants in the conferences. These ordinary citizens not only took an active role in discussions and debates, but they were also found to be

both willing and capable of making the necessary tradeoffs and compromises necessary to reach workable solutions. Equally important, their participation added significantly to the transparency and credibility that both the public and the media accorded the conference deliberations.

In 1996, the Canada West Foundation, the Council for Canadian Unity, and the Atlantic Provinces Economic Council sponsored "Assembly '96" at the Terry Fox Centre in Ottawa. This particular consultation was based on the random selection of 96 young Canadians under 30 years old from across Canada. The results of the assembly and an assessment of the consultation process are available on the Canada West Foundation web site (*www.cwf.ca*). The Public Policy Forum held a third consultation, entitled "The British Columbia Regional Citizen's Forum on Clean Air," in Vancouver in the summer of 2001. The results of this consultation process are available on the Public Policy Forum's website (*www.ppforum.com*).

As with any consultation process, not all participants were completely satisfied with the results, but there was a strong consensus among both participants and sponsors that this consultation experience and process provided for more meaningful discussion, and for increases in awareness, knowledge, and understanding.

Assessing the usefulness of deliberative democracy consultations

In 1997, the Canada West Foundation published a report entitled *Meaningful Consultation: A Contradiction in Terms?* This report compared and contrasted the ten consultation mechanisms mentioned at the outset of this report on the basis of the eight criteria discussed above. The three authors of the report then evaluated each of these consultation mechanisms as excellent (4 points), good (3 points), fair (2 points), and poor (1 point) and gave them a letter grade based upon the total score obtained. As figure 1 shows, deliberative democracy was determined to be a superior method of consultation compared to the others when all eight criteria were used. This conclusion may, of course, be due to the preconceived notions of the authors, but their assessment warrants careful consideration given the all-important role that meaningful consultation plays in shaping public policy. Further, it invites others to use the above-mentioned consultation assessment criteria, or variations thereto, in assessing the merits of any specific consultation processes that may be contemplated in the future.

Citizens' Assembly on Electoral Reform

Electoral reform is something that has been talked about in England, the United States, and Canada for well over a century, but nothing much has been done about it. In fact, on occasion, governments have created oxymorons to avoid meaningful discussion of electoral reform, such as the "Government of Canada's Royal Commission on Electoral Reform" in the 1980s that explicitly forbade the commission to call for any changes to the voting system! The British Columbia government's decision to not only examine alternate voting systems, but to place the responsibility for developing alternatives that will be voted on in a future referendum in the hands of the province's citizens is a bold public policy initiative of historic proportions.

The deliberative democracy consultation mechanism described above is tailor-made for the British Columbia government's Citizens' Assembly on Electoral Reform. It provides not only a mechanism for the selection of assembly members through a random selection screening process, but also a blueprint for managing the deliberations of the assembly. The additional responsibilities of the assembly to identify alternative electoral models, undertake public consultations, and prepare an appropriate referendum question will add yet another dimension to the assembly's responsibilities that will reinforce the role of citizens in decision making.

Conclusion

There is no one best way to provide for the representation of citizens' opinions. Consulting the electorate of a democratic society

Figure 1: Matrix of Effectiveness

	Represen-tation	Agenda Setting	Access to Informa-tion	Discus-sions	Creating Options	Individual Participa-tion	Cost	Closure	Grade
Elections	Excellent	Poor	Fair	Good	Fair	Poor	Poor	Fair	50%
Referendums	Excellent	Excellent	Good	Good	Poor	Poor	Poor	Excellent	66%
Legislative Hearings	Poor	Excellent	Excellent	Fair	Fair	Excellent	Good	Good	72%
Royal Commissions	Fair	Excellent	Excellent	Fair	Excellent	Fair	Poor	Fair	66%
Constituent Surveys	Poor	Excellent	Fair	Poor	Fair	Fair	Excellent	Poor	53%
Town Hall Meetings	Fair	Good	Good	Fair	Fair	Fair	Good	Poor	56%
Polls	Excellent	Excellent	Poor	Poor	Fair	Fair	Fair	Poor	53%
Focus Groups	Fair	Excellent	Fair	Fair	Good	Excellent	Excellent	Poor	69%
Conferences	Fair	Excellent	Excellent	Fair	Fair	Fair	Good	Fair	66%
Round tables	Poor	Excellent	Excellent	Excellent	Good	Excellent	Good	Good	81%
Deliberative Democracy	Excellent	Excellent	Excellent	Excellent	Good	Excellent	Fair	Good	88%

is probably the best way a democratic system has of ensuring that the opinions of all of its citizens are represented. But even electoral consultations have their problems, since many people (sometimes an extraordinary majority in the case of civic elections) do not exercise their right to vote. Because consulting the electorate is extremely time consuming, expensive, and if used too frequently, causes voter fatigue, it is not a process that can or should be used too often.

Deliberative democracy consultations seek to use the strengths of traditional consultation mechanisms while minimizing their weaknesses. The use of a random probability selection process not only gives every citizen the opportunity to become a participant in the process, but also makes the selection process transparently unbiased and provides a symbolic link to citizens who can identify with the participants. The fact that the consultation is structured in such a way as to provide for access to a wide range of information and expert opinion not only increases participants' ability to reach reasoned decisions, but it also provides stakeholders with an opportunity to articulate their various points of view. Finally, the openness of the debate and the need for people to confront differences of opinion and make the compromises necessary to generate viable policy options increases the likelihood that whatever conclusions are reached will resonate with the public as a whole.

CHAPTER 17
Q&A FOR PANEL 5:
THE PROCESS FOR GETTING THERE

Question: We now have the opportunity, because of technology, to get input from all of us immediately, thanks to telephones, computers, televisions, and social security numbers. We have the technological means to count the white rocks and the black rocks used by the Greeks thousands of years ago to give everybody a vote. Is anybody doing anything using technology for direct democracy? I don't have time to sit on committees, but I do have the time to go to a web site or watch a television station and log in my vote when the pros and the cons are presented.

David Elton: At the Canada West Foundation we've looked at using technology as a means of providing effective citizen engagement. We found, in our experience, that it's important to get whatever group you have together. This belief comes from the deliberative democracy experiment back in 1996. Face-to-face communication, living together for that one week, getting to actually know your fellow colleagues at the assembly, is absolutely essential, and it seems that that dynamic can't be bridged entirely with technology.

Question: If you choose an assembly randomly, the three of you would not be in it, because of the very, very small chance of you being picked, like a lottery ticket. So we've missed you three as the experts by such a process.

David Elton: That's right. But what you would have gained in the trade-off is that every British Columbian would the opportunity to be in that assembly. And, at the end of the day, the optics of that are important as long as you include in that process adequate background information, and access to experts, to resource people. That's a critical part of the mix. I didn't get into it because it's in the paper I distributed. You need to have those components of it.

Question: My point is that what I see happening in our political forum is that it is always the shrill minority interest getting represented. If you had a random selection, you'd have a much broader consensus of the general electorate, and thus a much more balanced representation on a lot of these issues. What's happening right now is only the shrill interests are getting their voice out there, and they are driving the agenda while the majority is being left behind.

David Elton: The key part to that is you also don't get people who are so fixed in their positions that they refuse to move because they're articulating the position of a group of people and are always aware of the fact they're being judged by that group. When you bring a group of citizens together, we have found that their ability to make the necessary compromises to develop a viable alternative into a practical opportunity is much greater.

Gordon Gibson: This has been a wonderful day. We've had an incredible smorgasbord of ideas. Long as the day was, though, there was one subject that was implied in the words of many speakers, but not directly covered, as specifically pointed out to me by John Reid. We did not get into the question of internal party democracy, which has so much to do with how the system operates. But this conference, I'm sure you'll agree, was a good starting place.

A Concluding Note

As this book goes to press in May of 2003 there have been several developments that bode well for the progress of democratic reform in Canada.

Most notably, the British Columbia government has finally constituted the long-promised and awaited "Citizens' Assembly on Electoral Reform." This will be a "deliberative democracy" approach of the sort described in David Elton's chapter, made up of randomly chosen citizens (subject to some self-screening). The experiment will be significant, and if it works will undoubtedly point the way to other assemblies of this sort on varied topics.

As a second extraordinary experiment in democratic reform, the BC government has provided that the assembly will report, not to the government or the legislature, but directly to the people. If the assembly proposes a new electoral system, the idea will be put directly in a referendum at the time of the next scheduled election on May 17, 2005. Putting such trust in direct democratic machinery without any provision for government intervention or modification of the result is truly extraordinary.

Related events are under way elsewhere in the country.

In Prince Edward Island, the legislature has commissioned and received a report on electoral reform. The government has since appointed a commissioner to hold hearings and report. The P.E.I. first-past-the-post system routinely delivers lopsided legislatures, so the history of the province has become sensitive to the need for electoral reform.

Quebec held a major "Estates General" in February 2003. This 1,000-person meeting canvassed the entire spectrum of democratic reform ideas, from a change to a republican system, to a provincial Upper House, significant devolution to regions, and changes in the voting age, as well as the more usual questions of direct democracy and of electoral and parliamentary reform. Now that a new government has just been elected in that province we shall have to wait and see if this impetus is maintained.

In Ontario, where an election is expected soon, the Official (Liberal) Opposition has made democratic reform a centrepiece in its platform. Concepts include fixed-term elections, sweeping campaign finance changes, a referendum on electoral reform, empowerment of the ordinary MPP, and the routine use of deliberative democracy to make recommendations to government on major issues.

Even at the federal level, where democratic reform is arguably most required, small stirrings are visible. The Alliance, the Tories and the NDP all have some elements of reform in their platforms, though not usually at the forefront. This may change as the front-runner in the Liberal leadership campaign (and therefore the next prime minister, at least *pro tem*), Paul Martin, has himself identified democratic reform as a priority, though with few specifics as yet.

In short, matters are moving as they have not done since Confederation. If much of this talk turns to reality, we will see a very different politics in our land.

Appendix

Introduction

The following report was released in early 2001 by press release, a few hard copies, and electronic printing. It was also distributed at The Fraser Institute conference where earlier forms of many of the other papers in this book were also presented. However, this is the first proper publication of the document, which comments on most aspects of the democratic reform agenda in British Columbia.

APPENDIX 1
A Report on the Need for Certain Constitutional Change in British Columbia, and a Mechanism for Developing Specific Proposals

Gordon Gibson, Gary Lauk,
Nick Loenen, and Rafe Mair

Introduction

Why this report? Why consider the suitability of the basic rules governing our elected representatives? After all, British Columbia is a reasonably peaceful and prosperous province. While many people have strong political views of a partisan nature, no one is marching in the streets to demand changes in the *system.*

In the past 50 years, this province has grown from just 1.8 million souls constituting just over 8 percent of Canada to a population of over 4 million and over 13 percent of the Canadian whole, and our growth continues. Those satisfied with the current state of affairs might say, "If it ain't broke, don't fix it."

On the other hand, various indicators show that we are performing far below potential in important areas. While we are traditionally thought of as a rich province, and until recently were among the Canadian leaders in economic growth, our GDP per capita has now fallen below the Canadian average—to about 95 percent. Our position in the "new economy" of technology is weak compared to both our neighbours and our potential. Serious battles continue to rage on the environmental and aboriginal fronts.

While some governments with strong leaders have made a real difference to this province (for better or for worse, and often some of each from the same leader), the *legislature*—our elected representatives—has over the years had virtually no effect other than, by the counting of partisan noses, to decide who will be premier from time to time. Few academic or journalistic observers would differ with this statement.

Many people today see government more as part of the problem than the solution. Few people believe that they personally can make any difference, or that the system is responsive to ordinary people (except in the grossest sense of who wins in this or that constituency every few years).

This matters, because government matters. While government is no longer growing in terms of absolute size or the date of "Tax Freedom Day," it has stabilized at a very high level as an influence on our lives. Moreover, regulatory directives also affect the lives of more people on an ongoing basis. All of the above, but particularly our perception of citizen frustration, leads us to conclude that our governance machinery *does* need fixing.

Sovereign governments in Canada are found at two levels: federal and provincial. From British Columbia, there is little we can do directly about the federal government under the current system. In any event, the provincial government's decisions are more important to most of us, in such things as health care, education, social services, municipal law, resource administration, policing and so on. In British Columbia we have a jurisdiction of a sufficiently manageable size that there is a prospect of real change.

The authors of this report believe that most of the problems identified by the citizenry today come back to the control structure of government, which is supposed in theory to be a democracy run by our elected representatives.

Winston Churchill famously said that democracy was the worst imaginable way to run a country—except for all of the other systems that had been tried. Today, that is accepted wisdom, but there are many components to "democracy" beyond the simple holding of elections. In particular, those elected must then be enabled to actively represent us.

In what follows we will analyze certain failures in the system, outline possibilities for productive change, and suggest a mechanism through which the people of British Columbia can work together to decide upon and institute agreed change.

The committee

Why this committee?

No one asked us to produce this report. We decided to get together and do it, believing there was a problem to which we might make a contribution based on experience.

While none of us have any continuing partisan connections, each of us has sat in the legislature as an MLA for one of the three main parties in British Columbia in recent years, namely (in alphabetical order), Liberal, NDP, and Social Credit. Two of us today are commentators on public policy, one is a lawyer, and one a political scientist.[40]

We represent no one but ourselves. We do not embody the diversity of BC society that would have to make final judgements on the questions we raise. We are but technicians. If our ideas are of any value, it is only because of content, not provenance.

In that spirit we submit the following.

---

40   Gordon Gibson is a former MLA and leader of the BC Liberal Party, Gary Lauk is a former minister in the NDP government of Dave Barrett, Nick Loenen is a former MLA, and Rafe Mair is a former minister in the Social Credit government of Bill Bennett. Full authors' biographies can be found at the front of this book.

Perspective

For the common good, we need some government. Exactly how much is a never-ending debate, but we need some.

The plainest definition of government describes it as that institution in a society that effectively maintains a monopoly on the use of force or coercion. That harsh description cannot be repeated too often. Governments are based on coercion, be it as subtle as quietly extracting taxes, or as forcible as a police action.

Government activity is always said to be for the common good. It ain't necessarily so. The danger is that governments will use their monopoly on force for their own ends, or those of its friends. Such tremendous power must be used only when justified, and controlled with care.

To this end, democracy is a concept that governments should be controlled by the governed. Unfortunately, this idea does not, in itself, carry any sense of limit. Indeed, many people today believe that democracy means that whatever desire we vote for by a majority should be satisfied by the coercive power of government. Many politicians have based their careers on telling the public it can have whatever it wants. But this is not what democracy means.

In fact, government (including the courts), is but one of the two main decision making systems in our society. The other is the body politic, including the private market, where millions of private actors, including the owners of capital, labour, and consumers, deal with each other on a voluntary (rather than coercive) basis. Private dealings may involve individuals or families or firms or non-profit agencies or whatever, but the distinction is that the relationship between them is voluntary, not coercive.

The choice between which of these two decision making systems (private markets, and government, or the "political market," if you like) to use with respect to managing any given area of life may be based on pragmatism, tradition, or ideology, but the fact that one system is "democratic" does not argue for its preference. Indeed, a general lesson of the twentieth century has been that markets work better than governments for the management of most things.

It is only when we collectively decide that government must become involved in this or that area that we come to the issue of control systems. Democracy, to underline again, is that class of system that provides for *control of governments by the governed,* rather than by monarchs, or a priesthood, or elites of other kinds.

Of course, democracy is not the only foundation of our civil order. Indeed the Supreme Court of Canada (in its decision on *Reference re Quebec Secession*) found democracy to be one of the four pillars of our society. In the court's view, the others are federalism, the rule of law, and respect for minority rights.

Some might think even this listing incomplete. For example, the concept of the sovereignty of the individual (which sees all governmental legitimacy as residing in individuals and being only loaned or delegated upwards to governments) is even more fundamental. This principle also allows for the possibility (and actual fact) that most individuals choose to achieve most ends through non-governmental machinery, and even when they resort to government as their chosen instrument, the choice is for smaller government rather than larger, where possible. (This is made explicit in the concept of *subsidiarity,* one principle of the European Union honoured as often there in the breach as in the application.)

Our system in Canada evolved from a different theory than that of individual sovereignty. In our tradition, sovereignty has resided in the state, and more particularly in the person of the monarch who literally owned the state in early English times. The idea of the individual sovereignty of the people (the founding doctrine of the United States) has increasingly taken hold in Canada, reflected in such documents as the Charter of Rights and Freedoms. Indeed, most Canadians think that individual sovereignty is our basis, but in truth the old reality lingers. The monarch-like powers of our first ministers give an important and unfortunate example.

It is worth noting that at the federal level the prime minister appoints the head of state (the governor general), the heads of the military and national police, the heads and deputy heads of all government departments, all members of the upper House (Senate), the judges of the Supreme Court and all other important judges, all significant boards and commissions, writes or approves all legislation, writes or approves the budget, approves or controls chairs of committees and office space, promotion and foreign travels of MPs, controls all important House of Commons business, approves candidacies at election time, and unilaterally calls elections at his or her pleasure.

A premier has a comparable degree of power in provincial jurisdictions less glamorous but more important than the federal level. (Provincial governments have far more real world impact on individuals and businesses than does Ottawa.)

As this list of prime ministerial or premierial power makes clear, between elections neither the public nor the representatives of the public run the show. Whatever else this system used in Canada may be, it is not what most people think of as democracy. It is, in effect, a four year elected dictatorship.

In practice, the rule of law (long ago assented to by monarchs as being demonstrably in their own interest) and the traditional role of state sovereignty as exemplified by the executive branch (the premier and his or her Cabinet) have been far greater influences in Canadian and British Columbia history than has democracy. The codification required by the rule of law gives stability and consistency over time, without which a society cannot prosper. The broad reach and sweeping powers of the executive branch, subject only to generally ineffective and uninformed questioning by the opposition and the media, have brought policy coordination across governments and over time. That none of this has been particularly *democratic* (except, as noted before, in the grossest sense of the word) has not seemed to matter much. We have developed and prospered.

And yet... to more and more people something increasingly seems to be missing. This committee believes that that "something" is democracy in a genuine sense of the word. When, as is the case today, our elected representatives, MLAs, and MPs, have no real power to act on our behalf, when governments tell their back-benchers exactly what to do and always prevail in a majority situation, then that, we say again, is not a true democracy. A true democracy exists only when the public, either occasionally acting directly (by referenda, say), or more usually through their direct representatives, can actual control the course of policy on a day-to-day and issue-by-issue sense.

To recap, there are two states of evolution of the civil order. The first consists of *constraints* on power. There has been great progress to this end over the years, achieved by the acceptance of the rule of law and independent courts, and a growing respect for minority rights. But within these minimal constraints, power has been wielded by our political masters subject only to a verdict of "in" or "out" every four years or so. This is not a sensitive control mechanism.

The second, higher level adds actual and effective *governance* of the power exercised by the executive branch through the machinery of democracy. We have only begun this second stage in Canada. That is the current challenge for British Columbia, if we wish to pursue it.

The elements of democratic governance

There are three stages of increasingly sensitive democratic control.

Stage 1. Voters choose the people (MPs or MLAs) who choose the boss, who thereafter makes the laws, levies the taxes, controls expenditures, and generally runs the show for a given time. This is our current system. It is known in Canada as one version of *responsible government*. [41]

Stage 2. Voters choose representatives who themselves, as free actors, make the laws, levy taxes, and control expenditures. There is still a chief executive officer, but he or she is closely controlled by those elected. This is known as *representative government*. One version can be seen in the United States, but the concept can also be wedded to our parliamentary structure.

Stage 3. Voters themselves make direct decisions on public policy via the ballot box and such machinery as initiatives or referenda. This is known as *direct democracy*. The most notable example of a country making considerable use of this technique is Switzerland, but even there the overwhelming majority of the nation's business is done by the indirect democracy method—in the case of Switzerland, closer to the "representative" than the "responsible" model.

The only regular use of direct democracy in our system is the direct vote afforded each elector on choosing a constituency representative once every few years. Other opportunities, such as occasional referenda, are quite rare.[42]

No one seriously proposes that much of the business of government can be guided by direct democracy, even in this age of instant and widespread information and communications. Except at a high level of abstraction, good decisions on public policy typically require both expertise and an ability to reconcile tradeoffs and priorities and linkages with other public policy issues that the average citizen cannot practically take the time to acquire, even were there an interest in so doing. Therefore, as a practical matter, we hire full-time experts in the public service to manage this work, and elect full-time representatives to manage the managers.

There is a case for an expanded use of direct democracy and we will comment in that regard, but our greatest focus as a province

---

41   There is much confusion about this label. The government is not of course necessarily "responsible" in its behaviour, but rather is responsible *to* someone. What is not generally understood is that in this theory the "responsibility" is to Parliament, not to the people. But if the executive branch effects a reverse takeover of Parliament, as was done in England centuries ago on the grounds that the weighty matters of state such as empire and war could not be left to transient and erratic amateurs, then most of the democratic control imagined in the original theory of responsible government disappears. We have inherited that British system and made it significantly more rigid.

42   However, when they are available they may be treasured, as in the referendum on the Charlottetown Accord, a watershed moment in Canadian history and seen as such by the participants.

should be on moving to stage 2, true representative democracy, which has to do with the *legislative branch*.[43]

There are two broad categories of questions to be considered in respect of legislative branch reform. The first is how do we choose who our representatives are to be. This is the question of *electoral reform*. The second is, once representatives are chosen, what will be the rules of their relationship to the machinery of government that best enable them to do their work. This is the question of *parliamentary reform*.

There are two categories that we will not discuss. One has to do with *executive branch reform*. This deals with such matters a patronage, the selection and promotion of public servants, the structure of boards and commissions and Crown corporations, and the like. While not wishing to downplay the importance of these questions, we have not dealt with them in this report. Equally, we have not dealt with *judicial reform*. The justice and adjudication system (which includes other tribunals such as Human Rights, Labour Code and other such panels) is of tremendous importance, and parts of it are enmeshed in both change and controversy. We do not tackle these questions.

To keep this report manageable, we have restricted its scope to that portion of governance dealing with representative and direct democracy. If those areas are functioning well, they provide the means for the reform of other areas of importance.

The selection of representatives

The selection process has three essential components: *machinery, timing, and electoral systems*.

---

43   The traditional division of governance analysis deals with the legislative, executive, and judicial branches. The legislative branch does much more than legislate. It is also the priority-setting body for raising and spending public revenue, and the oversight agency that monitors the work of government as a whole.

The *machinery*, which ensures honesty and efficiency in the electoral process, is of course of fundamental importance. We are fortunate that this area is reasonably well under control in Canada, though the growing use of electronic voting will bring new security problems.

One unresolved machinery question relates to appropriate restrictions—if any—on election spending by political parties or others, partisan contributions, and public disclosure of such, advertising and polling, and public funding of political parties. While many of these issues may seem arcane, especially to those who (correctly, we think) have faith in the common sense and shrewd assessment capacity of the public, we note that these same arcane issues have major implications for the balance of power between small parties and large parties, rich ones and poor ones, parties and their own candidates, partisan candidates and independents, and political parties *vis à vis* other organized interests in society. For example, is it right—as the current federal government believes—that political parties should have a virtual monopoly on issue advertising during elections?

Important as these questions are, we believe the answers to be the proper subject of election law, to be amended from time to time on the basis of experience and circumstance, rather than a part of the constitution of the province. Accordingly we did not consider them further.

There are three main choices on the issue of elections *timing*. One is for discretionary timing within an overall maximum period, as at present. One is for fixed dates except in the case of the defeat of a government on a vote of confidence in the legislature. The third is an election date fixed under all circumstances—as with municipalities in Canada, for example, and all governments in the United States.

The timing issue is central. The current system gives an enormous tactical advantage to the government in power in terms of choosing the most favourable moment to call an election. It also gives enormous disciplinary power to the premier, who is able to say to his followers that a lack of support on any given issue will lead to an election. However, much as politicians in power speak well of democracy, they detest elections even more than business people detest competition, and are therefore much persuaded by the threat of this power of the premier. They invariably fall into line.

Discretionary election dates are sometimes justified as giving a way to "consult the people" on this or that issue. This is nonsense, of course. A simple referendum would give a far more precise consultation without the requirement for an election.

Fixed election dates remove a certain tactical advantage and the disciplinary power from the premier, and provide certainty. They also ensure that the *de facto* election campaign is much longer than it would be if we had flexible election dates, which many would regard as a disadvantage.

The mixed option of a fixed date except in case of loss of a confidence vote by the government is a way of marrying the idea of "responsible" government requiring "confidence" votes, to what would in effect be mostly a fixed date system. The matter of timing is thereby inextricably linked to the type of parliamentary system—i.e. "confidence" or not. We believe that the matter of election timing is sufficiently fundamental as to be a matter for the constitution of the province.

The *electoral system* debate encompasses such questions as the size of constituencies (and therefore the size of the legislature), single or multi-member ridings, the manner of selection of candidates, and the system by which voters indicate their preferences and how those preferences are counted and weighed to choose representatives.

As our system has come to work, the role of parties is central. The nomination of candidates amounts in most cases to a "pre-screening," and restriction of the *de facto* choice of the electorate.

In Canada, with one important exception, to be noted below, candidate selection by parties is not a matter of election law. If the people of a given constituency in a partisan way want to vote, say, NDP, but would really prefer Sally Brown to Joe Black, both party members, it matters not. If the party nominates Joe, that's that.

Other countries deal with this differently. In the United States, primary elections give many more electors a voice in this decision. In some states, all Democrats get to vote for the choice of Democratic candidate. In other states all *electors* who so wish get to make that choice.

In other countries, there is balloting on a "list" system, under which each party submits a list of, say, 100 candidates for the 100 positions open, and is entitled to elect one candidate for each 1 percent of the vote. With this system, the order of the "list" might be done by the party bosses (in which case they in effect get to say who the winners from their party are) or by the voters, who therefore in effect control not only the winners, but the nominations as well. In other words, electoral law can have an immense impact on internal party democracy.

In Canada and British Columbia, our practice is to not only leave partisan nominations up to each party, but—incredibly, in the view of this committee—to give a veto to the party leader. A premier is thereby given another immense disciplinary power over individual party members. If they do not toe the line, they cannot be candidates—enforced by the law.

The rationale for this is that a leader must be able to guarantee to the public a team that will carry out the party's promises. The real world result is that the role of the representative to represent the views of his or her electors is seriously weakened if those views are inconvenient to those of the leader, and the already powerful position of the leader tremendously strengthened.

Thus, the first question arising from a consideration of electoral law is, do we wish to privilege the position of the party (and its leader), or of the local people in selecting candidates? If the latter, do we wish to privilege party members only, or give influence to the general electorate?

The next question deals with how representative the legislature is. Do we wish to use a system that attempts to reflect the views of the population in the membership of the legislature as faithfully as possible? Or, on the other hand, do we seek other objectives, such as deliberately constraining minorities that might otherwise use delicate legislative balances to exert power far beyond the number of voters they represent (as in the Israeli Knesset)? Alternatively, do we want to achieve strong majority governments—even if the public has no majority view—that are, therefore, based on a minority opinion, as in almost every election in Canada and BC within living memory? (As at this writing *[Editor's note: February 2001]*, BC has a majority government elected by only 39 percent of the voters, and Canada has a majority government elected by only 41 percent of the voters. Both governments, in effect, exercise 100 percent of the power of their legislatures.)

Our current system is called "first past the post" for obscure historical reasons. It is really a *single member plurality* (SMP)—whoever gets the most votes wins, whether that amounts to 51 percent in a two-person contest or 26 percent in a four-person contest. Election of members and governments by much less than 50 percent is not unusual. This system tends to produce majority governments, even from badly split electorates.

Another option is the *run-off election* or the *alternate vote* (AV). These systems, either on a single preferential ballot or a second run-off election, drop minor candidates until the winner has a clear 50 percent plus one.

Then there are the many versions of *proportional representation* (PR). Broadly, these systems attempt to more faithfully reflect the diverse views of the electorate in the legislature. The precise rules are very important, and can be fine-tuned to add or screen out very small parties.

SMP and AV elections are normally based on quite small geographical constituencies. PR constituencies may be larger, or may even use national lists. The ranking of candidates on the "list"—i.e. who is closer to the top and therefore has a good chance of winning—may be by the parties or by individual voters. Some systems, such as the *single transferrable vote* (STV), provide for quite small constituencies and citizen ranking of the lists.

Finally, some countries have mixtures of more than one system. For example, both Germany and New Zealand elect half their members by SMP and half by national list PR. France has a modified run-off system. Hardly any countries except Britain and Canada rely exclusively on the SMP (the United States primary system effectively converts that country's SMP into a run-off system), and Britain has moved to PR for the European Parliament and is seriously looking at electoral reform for the House of Commons (see Parliament of the United Kingdom, 1998, "The Jenkins Commission Report").

As a committee, we recommend that the constitutional reform assembly that we will be proposing review British Columbia's electoral system. If agreement is reached on a new system and then approved by citizen referendum, that new electoral system should become a part of the constitution of the province. The new system would not be immune to change, but would require citizen consent to change, unlike at present where the electoral law may be changed at will by the party in power, as was done in 1952.[44]

We take no joint position on which electoral system would be best.

The effectiveness of representatives

However well we select those who are to represent us, it matters not if those representatives are hobbled in the performance of their jobs, as is the case at the moment. This is the subject matter of *parliamentary reform*.

In an earlier section we noted the extreme concentration of power in the office of the premier. The way our system has evolved, gov-

---

44   The 1952 British Columbia election was held under a new system of "preferential ballot" imposed as a dying act of the Liberal-Conservative "Coalition" to keep out the socialists, then running under the banner of the CCF. The new system, to everyone's surprise, elected the Social Credit. After a second election in 1953 gave the Socreds under W.A.C. Bennett a majority, he immediately changed the law again to return to the old system. This, he calculated (correctly) would re-polarize the province and keep the Socreds in power for many years.

ernment MLAs do what the premier tells them to do. Therefore, they cannot represent their electors faithfully. Opposition MLAs normally do what their leader tells them to do as well, though that leader has far less in the way of sanctions to enforce his or her will. Since the rules of the game say that the government of the day has to be destroyed in order for the opposition of the day to do its good work of saving the province, opposition members work together to that end. In our system, it is considered a sign of weakness if there are public differences within the opposition.

So the tradition of "bossism" is maintained. No other country in the developed world has anything like this degree of executive branch control of the legislature. To say it again: Canada has become what amounts to a four-year elected dictatorship.

There is a whole web of interlocking factors that maintain the system, which, of course, could theoretically be blown apart on any given day by a majority of MLAs deciding to change the rules that give the premier such power. Chief among these rules are:

- The premier may call an election at any time, thereby putting his members' jobs at risk
- At election time, the premier may stop any given member from being nominated (to represent his own party)
- In the legislature, any bill that proposes the spending of money must be introduced by a minister
- Any government legislation must be approved by the premier
- Failure of any government measure to obtain passage is considered a matter of *confidence*. By convention, failure of a confidence motion forces an election. Government MLAs, therefore, support all government measures, whatever they think of them
- The premier has very broad powers of appointment to the Cabinet or lesser government jobs, plus extensive favours (paid for by the taxpayer) which he can confer in terms of public works, special regulations or grants to assist this or that union or business, and so on
- The premier controls the agenda and majority membership of the standing committees of the legislature.

There are some checks on premierial power. The courts enforce the law (but the premier passes or can change most of the laws). The few and normally cautious officers of Parliament responsible for oversight, chief among them the auditor general and the conflict commissioner, have their place. Competition with other levels of government, especially Ottawa (because the municipalities cannot afford to fight Victoria, which controls them) brings some discipline. The media turns up some problems, but many issues of public policy are too complex or boring to ever see even the back pages. And, of course, we do get to vote for that one representative on an all-or-nothing basis every four years or so.

However, if premiers follow correct procedure and keep the books correctly, they can do just about anything they want between elections, including pass laws, spend money, and dole out jobs, despite whatever the legislature would say if its members were free. For of course, when our representatives are not free, we can never know what they really believe.

Premiers and leaders often say there is really no problem, because members speak freely in caucus. This is nonsense. First we do not *know* what they say. Second, as they say, justice must be *seen* to be done. Third, the premier can, in any event, ignore whatever is said with impunity. (We know of no effective caucus revolt in the history of Canada with the exception of the downfall of Premier VanderZalm in 1991. To take two recent examples of highly unpopular first ministers, Brian Mulroney left voluntarily with a still-adoring caucus, and BC premier Glen Clark was forced out by his legal problems.)

We have set out this lengthy description of political reality in order to provide the foundation for our major recommendation in this section. We believe that for a democracy to function properly:

Elected representatives must genuinely be able to represent their constituencies.

At the moment their freedom is seriously compromised. To remedy this, we say:

The concentration of political power in the office of the premier is unhealthy and needs to be broken.

The point is not to end the premier's power. He or she speaks for the government, which is a repository of a great deal of expertise as well as being the body charged with actually carrying out the fine ideas of legislators. This point of view is valuable, and must be protected and involved. Our reforms should not seek to change that. However, protecting the power of governments has never been the problem in Canada. The problem has not been the voice of the government, but rather the voice of the people, which, to reiterate, can only flow through elected representatives or, in rare cases, direct democracy.

The basic quest is for a redress in the balance of power between the executive and legislative branches.

There are two main channels to follow to achieve this balance of power. The first is to attempt to empower the ordinary MLA in his or her representative capacity within our traditional parliamentary system. In this context, one must look at the powers of the premier listed above and consider which of them might usefully be transferred to (or more likely, shared with) a free legislature. In addition, the whole notion of "confidence" must be reviewed, for this is the central control mechanism by which the premier prevents the legislature from varying his or her proposed laws and budget.

The other channel is more radical. It would involve moving from a more or less "responsible" form of government to an avowedly "representative" form, or what one of us calls a "republican" system. Our committee was of mixed views on this option.

Apart from the above-noted firm belief that the key to parliamentary reform is the empowerment of the elected representative *vis à vis* the executive branch, we take no joint position on the details.[45] We believe, however, that these questions are central to the functioning of democracy, and therefore central to the work of any body constituted to consider revisions to the constitution of British Columbia.

Other matters

There are four other matters that we think should usefully be considered by any body mandated to study the constitution of the province.

The first is *direct democracy*. Some matters are so fundamental that they require direct democracy techniques.[46] However, the control of government and the balancing of the many demands from the public is an enormous task, and most citizens have neither the time, the interest nor the expertise for anything more than a casual involvement in most matters of public policy. Thus, almost all governmental decision making must be done on a delegated basis, and modern communications and the internet do not change this.

That said, there are exceptions. The obvious and universal exception is the selection of one's representative at election time. However, there are others. One such area, which we in BC have agreed should be subject to a direct citizen vote, is any proposed change to Canada's constitution. If BC adopts a "constitution" in a similar sense of the word, the same rules should apply.

We have also approved as voters in a referendum in 1991 of the concepts of *initiative* and *recall*. There is considerable criticism of the mechanics of these procedures as implemented by the NDP government in 1995. They are thought by many to be effectively impossible to activate.

The underlying theme must be balance and proportion. The tools of direct democracy are the tools of the *majority*, and a majority must be able to trigger them. However, a wise democracy will

45   For a recent review of many of the possibilities as they relate directly to the BC Legislature, we commend to the reader Jay Schlosar's *Towards Greater Efficacy for the Private Member: Possibilities for the Reform of the British Columbia Legislature*, August 2000, commissioned by Jack Weisgerber, MLA.

46   The usual list of techniques includes the referendum, the initiative, and the recall, which is activated by the public. Of course, the right to vote for a candidate in elections is also an example of direct democracy.

exercise restraint in imposing the will of the majority in controversial cases if there is any voluntary or negotiated (by way of delegated democracy) method for addressing the given question.

In our view, certain tools of direct democracy—the initiative, the
referendum, and the recall—must be available to the public on the
expression of sufficient public will to activate them, but they
should not be simple to invoke. The exception is constitutional
change, where citizen approval should be an automatic requirement. The availability of, and restrictions on, tools of direct democracy should be set out in a constitution for British Columbia.

As a second subject in this section we propose the matter of
supermajorities. (A "supermajority" is something larger than 50
percent plus one.) A supermajority requirement should be considered on questions where it can be argued that the consequences of
change are so significant that a greater-than-ordinary level of support is required. This is quite a usual rule around the world in
respect of the amendment of constitutions. It might also be considered for such questions as deficit financing, over-riding the Charter
(by the "notwithstanding" clause), changing election legislation,
changing the standing orders of the legislature, and so on.

The quantum required for a supermajority can be of two kinds.
One sort is a hurdle based on numbers—60 percent of those actually voting, say, or 50 percent of all of those eligible to vote. The
other sort, which can take sectional interests into account,
requires that a given measure obtain the votes of MLAs *representing a majority of votes cast in the previous election*. The charm of this
system is that it goes some distance to redress the failure of a
given electoral system to faithfully reflect the views of the electorate. For example, with such a rule in place, neither in BC nor in
Ottawa could the current government caucus acting alone pass
any legislation which fell under the supermajority requirement, or
change the standing orders to further oppress the opposition.
Cooperation with at least some of the opposition would be
required.

We believe that *transparency* is absolutely fundamental to the
proper functioning of the democratic process. With very few

exceptions, government information should also be public information. This principle is obviously to be modified by the usual
protections required for individual and commercial privacy. However, it should *not* be modified as at present by alleged blanket
requirements for "Cabinet confidences," official secrets, secrecy
in dealings with other governments, and the like. The public has a
timely right to know the results of ongoing monitoring of depart-
mental performance, the options available on questions of public
policy, the arguments on each side, and the decisions taken. Nothing less will do.

Each of us has been inside governments. Each of us believes that
almost all government "secrets" are maintained for the comfort of
the government rather than for the good of the public. Ninety-five
percent of all Cabinet documents could be published in the daily
papers. Not only would the public interest not suffer from such
disclosure, but the public dialogue would be much enhanced.

Municipalities approach this standard of disclosure and work perfectly well. The provincial and federal levels of government
remain disgraceful counter-examples, notwithstanding the fact
that BC's *Freedom of Information Act* is progressive by comparison.
But compare these governments with corporations required to
give "full, true, and plain disclosure" when raising money from
the public. By this standard the federal and provincial governments would be in jail for non-compliance.

We recommend, therefore, that:

*A muscular freedom of information provision should be a corner-
stone of a new constitution for British Columbia.*

A final matter in this section is that of *constitutional constraints*. The
body of constraints with which we are most familiar is the Charter
of Rights and Freedoms. It is a very popular part of the constitution. Constraints—things that governments are not allowed to
do—can be very useful to the public, and even to governments
thereby saved from temptation.

The most discussed addition of this sort in recent times has been *balanced budget legislation*.

Getting from here to there

This section contains our core recommendation.

We begin it with a caution. The Law of Unintended Consequences is awesome in its scope, and nowhere is it to be more feared than in matters constitutional. The results of the Canadian experience of 1982 give testimony. Proceeding by way of great principle rather than the small steps of incremental wisdom and pragmatism opens the way for errors as great in themselves as the principles intended to be served. This caution argues for advancing in small steps, and accords well with the innate caution of Canadians.

But there is another argument, which we think on balance persuasive in this case. Experience shows that any entrenched system must be changed sufficiently to permanently alter the old power balances, for another law that often confounds reformers is the Law of Equal and Opposite Reaction. If you try to change certain behaviours in a minimalist way (simply by reforming the legislative committee system, say) the old elites will find a way to restore the status quo. Change must be sufficient to deliver a new equilibrium. Sometimes mere tinkering will not do.

Such change requires a powerful mandate, of a sort that can come only from the electorate. Change always harms powerful interests and always brings unexpected problems. To stay the course, change must have great support.

If there is a general view that the constitution[47] of British Columbia requires review and reform, an instrument must be found to undertake that task. It goes without saying that the legislature—a highly partisan body with special interest in the status quo—is not the appropriate instrument for doing so. (However, the legislature has a special role in creating that instrument, and in reviewing its work.)

We believe that the constitution is the people's business, and that a body democratically selected by the people is the correct instrument for constitutional review. Accordingly, we here propose a "citizens' assembly."

History provides many examples of successful citizens' assemblies. They were used to fashion the constitutions of the United States (1787), France (1791), Switzerland (1848), Australia (1898), Germany (1949), India (1949), Spain (1978) and South Africa (1996). In the United States, some of the states have constitutional conventions (i.e., citizens' assemblies) at regular intervals.

Citizens' assemblies, or constitutional conventions, are special bodies existing alongside regular government institutions. They exist for a special limited mandate, for a limited time, and dissolve when their mandate is completed. Such bodies normally have no authority other than to recommend proposals that are then placed before either a legislature or a referendum of the citizens for either ratification or rejection.

We discuss four features in turn: creation, membership, mandate, and ratification.

Creation

The best and simplest way to constitute a citizens' assembly is by an act of the legislature. Because the usefulness of an assembly depends crucially on legitimacy, it is to be hoped that such legisla-

---

47   Technically, many of the subjects we have discussed are not written down in any constitutional document. Some of them exist as conventions, or practices of the legislature. Some of them are embodied in legislation such as the *Constitution Act* or the *Elections Act*. Indeed, some aspects of BC procedure are governed by the Constitution of Canada, and thus are not susceptible to unilateral change by British Columbians. All of the rules and practices we have proposed for review are, however, under the jurisdiction of the BC Legislature. The only possible exception to this statement of jurisdiction would be any proposal for a republican form of government, which arguably would contravene the requirement of the Constitution of Canada that all Canadian governments be similar in form to that of Britain.

tion would have multi-party support. If that does not seem to be easily available, a government believing in a citizens' assembly process might wish to obtain a mandate from the public by way of referendum. Unless the legitimacy of the assembly enjoys general and acknowledged support, it cannot be effective in dealing with fundamental questions.

Membership

It is this committee's strong view that the assembly should be elected. This turns again on the necessity of legitimacy, which flows in a democracy from election. Unless citizens have specifically selected an assembly for its important work, it will not be taken seriously.

The work to be done here is not the work of a jury selected at random. A simple "guilty" or "not guilty" won't do. Rather, the work requires making multiple, complex, and inter-related choices about rules of governance that will affect our children and grandchildren. That work requires dedication and suitability, both characteristics to be sought by the electorate from among those offering themselves for the job.

We believe that an extraordinary group of British Columbians will offer their services—far more than could possibly be chosen. We recommend that the usual machinery supervise the elections, with expenditure limits. In order that candidates not proliferate beyond reason, we recommend that any candidate must secure the signature support of at least 100 voters in the riding. We recommend that political parties and special interests refrain from proposing candidates, and believe that voters will consider this to be a necessarily non-partisan vote and act accordingly.

We recommend that the citizens' assembly be composed of 100 members, 79 of whom would be elected directly from each of the constituencies of the province. After much internal debate, we recommend that the election procedure for the constituency representatives should be the SMP (first-past-the-post) system commonly used in British Columbia. Though some of us think other electoral systems would give more representative results, use of such a new system might seem to "pre-judge" one of the main tasks of the assembly.

In addition, there should be a further 21 members of the assembly chosen by the constituency members. We recommend that this group of 21 should be made up of 7 persons from each of the province's three regions: the coast, the interior, and the Lower Mainland. The 21 should be chosen at the discretion of the elected members to supply such additional experience, expertise, or representation of interests as the assembly might think useful.

The chair of the citizen's assembly should be the commissioner of reform, a new officer of the legislative assembly described below.

We recommend that members be paid reasonable expenses and a salary commensurate with that of MLAs, prorated for the lifetime of the assembly.

Mandate

The assembly's task should be to hear British Columbians, including such experts as they may choose to engage, and to determine which ideas and proposals for improvement in the machinery of provincial governance should go to referendum, and in what format. The assembly should examine and offer recommendations upon any and all questions that it deems appropriate. Without limiting the generality of that mandate, the assembly should consider:

- elements of responsible and representative government
- parliamentary reforms
- electoral reforms
- direct democracy
- the balance of power between the executive and legislative branches
- the role and powers of the MLA
- transparency and freedom of information

- special constraints, such as balanced budget laws
- ways and means for special legal protection for a new BC constitution; and
- an amending formula

The assembly should determine its own procedures. It should obtain submissions and hear evidence sufficient to inform its deliberations and provide an opportunity for all interested British Columbians to make contributions to its work. The assembly should report within one year to the legislature and dissolve immediately thereafter. Its report should include proposed referendum questions to be placed before the people.

The referendum questions should be as clear and concise as possible, and should indicate where elements are severable (i.e., not linked to other elements), and where they are necessarily linked.

Referendum questions may be sequential and conditional, but each should be capable of being answered with a "Yes" or "No."

Ratification

The citizens' assembly legislation should provide that the legislature may debate the recommendations of the assembly and attach its views to the report. Thereafter and within six months of the report, the referendum questions as proposed by the assembly shall be put to the people for a vote. The recommendations affirmed by the vote should be deemed to be the constitution of British Columbia.

Commissioner of reform

Both for the purposes of the citizens' assembly and to follow up its work, the legislative assembly should establish an office of the commissioner of reform. The commissioner should be appointed in the same manner (i.e., unanimous recommendation of an all-party committee) and with similar compensation and independence as that of the auditor general.

The commissioner should chair the citizens' assembly, and thereafter report to the legislature on an annual basis making observations and recommendations on the subject matter dealt with by the citizens' assembly and other matters of governance as may be referred from time to time by the legislature or examined by the commissioner on his own initiative. The commissioner should have the power to hold hearings. The office should end after 10 years unless extended by the legislature.

Conclusion

After a careful examination of the issues, the main question to be answered is whether the public is sufficiently concerned with the functioning of our government to mandate a fundamental examination of the system. We believe that to be the case.

If such a review is required, we believe it can be done in an orderly, timely, and productive fashion through the approach set out above.

References cited

Parliament of the United Kingdom (1998). *The Report of the Independent Commission on the Voting System* (October). Known also as "The Jenkins Commission Report."

Schlosar, Jay (2000). *Towards Greater Efficacy for the Private Member: Possibilities for the Reform of the British Columbia Legislative Assembly.* Paper commissioned by Jack Weisgerber, MLA, Peace River South (August). Available digitally at *www.pris.bc.ca/mla-prs/ParliamentaryReform.pdf.*